Bunch of Five

Frank Kitson

❄

Bunch of Five

FABER & FABER

London

First published in 1977
by Faber and Faber Limited
3 Queen Square London WC1
Printed in Great Britain by
Latimer Trend & Company Ltd, Plymouth

ISBN 0 571 11050 9

Contents

Part IV—Cyprus

Part V—Studying Experience

Illustrations

---- ✿ ----

Introduction

In its simplest form a bunch of five is a clenched fist; four fingers and
a thumb. There is an aura of menace about the expression, not so
much because of its connection with Communism, as for the fact
that a fist is the basic ingredient of violence. But it was not for this
reason that I chose the expression as the title for this book, although
violence inevitably plays some part in the narrative. Here the four
fingers cover an account of my doings in four separate operational
theatres: Kenya, Malaya, Oman and Cyprus. The fifth part of the
book, or the thumb, covers my assessment of the way in which such
operations should be handled.

It could be argued that my views on this subject are already available in a book which I wrote some years ago called *Low Intensity
Operations*. This is partly true but since writing it I have given a lot of
thought to these matters and my views have developed to some extent. Furthermore, in *Low Intensity Operations* I recounted only the
conclusions which I had arrived at over the years. It has subsequently been suggested to me that a description of the events
through which I lived, and from which I drew those conclusions,
might be of more interest than the conclusions themselves.

The aim of this book therefore is to describe the events which led
me to specific conclusions regarding the way in which counter-
insurgency and peace-keeping operations should be conducted. I
have tried to exclude all extraneous material. The result is a chron-
icle of events which took place over a period of fifteen years and
which is inevitably highly selective. It is necessary to stress that the
process of working out my ideas over such a long time was not an
academic exercise conducted in isolation from the squalor, fear and
suffering of the people amongst whom I was living. Insurgency is
rooted in squalor, and fear and suffering are its flowers. I should
also point out that I did not spend fifteen years working on this sub-

ject and doing nothing else. My ideas came to me gradually over that time, as I, together with hundreds of other people, grappled with our day-to-day problems. All this I have tried to bring out in the narrative so as to give flesh and blood to the bare bones of my theories. If on reaching the end of the book some readers find difficulty in accepting or even understanding these theories it is of little consequence providing that they have a better understanding of the problems which face soldiers, policemen and administrators in dealing with insurgency.

I would like to stress from the start – and ask my readers to bear constantly in mind as they read this book – what I mean by those misused words *insurgency* and *subversion*. My definition is a narrow, not a loose one; *insurgency* is a rising in active revolt against the constitutional authority of a country; and the aim of *subversion* is the overthrow and destruction of constitutional authority. The essential common element is the unconstitutional and unlawful nature of the acts. The army can only intervene when constitutionally called upon by its legitimate political masters to support the civil authorities, and when those authorities are unable by themselves adequately to contain the unlawful and unconstitutional acts of the insurgents and subversives.

The army should never – and in my view in this country can never – act in support of the civil authorities against insurgency and subversion in any other than a lawful and constitutional way. Such an assertion, which I regard as fundamental and to be understood as it were on every page of this book, can surely not be a matter of political controversy in Parliament or among law-abiding citizens. I would like to add that in my opinion the nature of British democracy is such that reforms can always be effected by legitimate political means without the need for violence, and this has been demonstrated many times over the years. Reforms introduced in this way naturally reflect a genuine consensus of the nation which is certainly not the case when they are brought about as a result of illegal action. Another point which needs some explanation is the extent to which violence intrudes upon the narrative. It will be found that my story runs red with gore in places and I may be accused of revelling in it. In fact, having been for more than six years of my service involved in peace-keeping duties or in countering insurgency, I have been more thoroughly sickened by bloodshed than most. Some people try to gloss over the fact that insurgents rely on violence and that insurgency inevitably provokes a violent response. Unfortunately there is no such thing as insurgency without violence because without it, opposition would not amount to insurgency. Bloodshed affects the emotions and judgements of those taking part on both sides and of those who are trying to remain uncommitted. In real life it cannot be ignored, and in writing about the subject its impact should not be diminished.

From the aim of the book as stated above it must be clear that I have not in any sense tried to write a history of the various disturbances in which I have been involved. Each section of the book starts with a brief account of the situation prevailing in the area concerned, but after that I have limited myself to describing those of my personal recollections which are relevant to the purpose. Such recollections are of course no substitute for history but they may none the less be of help to historians in so far as they reproduce the background of frustration, uncertainty, discomfort, and fatigue against which most operational decisions are made in practice.

I should like to feel that my stories will give pleasure to some people who have no desire to make a serious study of either insurgency or history. There must be scores of people scattered around the British Isles and beyond who spent a year or two of their youth pushing through the forests of Kenya or sweating in the Malayan jungle. Others may have memories of the tawny wastes of Arabia or of the milder but varied beauties of Cyprus. There is, I hope, something in this book to remind them of the places which they visited while serving in the forces. Above all I hope that it will in some measure bring back the feeling of comradeship which plays such an important part in the life of those on active service.

Finally, I would like to stress that it is Part V of this book which covers my considered opinion of the way in which insurgency and subversion should be handled. The earlier parts show how I came to these conclusions but the measures described and discussed in them naturally refer to the particular country concerned. I do ask therefore that those people who are interested in my views in a particular aspect of the business should where possible take them from Part V rather than try and deduce them from the events described in Parts I to IV.

Part I

Kenya

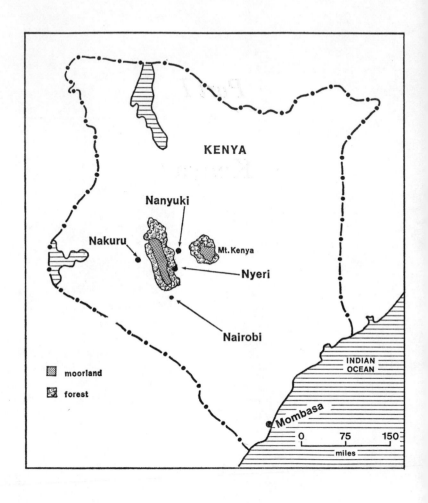

KENYA

Nanyuki

Nakuru

Mt.Kenya

Nyeri

Nairobi

▨ moorland

▨ forest

INDIAN
OCEAN

Mombasa

0   75   150

miles

❀

Chapter 1

The Mau Mau Emergency

Many people regard Kenya as being one of the most beautiful lands in the world, and they are probably right. It is not a large country, being roughly six hundred miles long by five hundred wide, but within its borders is a variation of altitude which provides an ever changing pattern of scenery and climate. The equator passes through Mount Kenya itself which, rising to over 17,000 feet, has snow on its peaks throughout the year. Within a few hundred miles lies a coast-line with the Indian Ocean. In between are areas of tropical rain forest, fertile pasture, and arid scrubland, some of which is inhabited by massive concentrations of game animals. Each of these main divisions merges into the next in dozens of subtly different ways so that the traveller is constantly confronted by unexpected contrasts. The views, the vegetation and the wildlife have fascinated white men since they first started pushing into the interior of the continent from the Arab coastal settlements in the 1880s.

Unfortunately, although Kenya was not at that time a country in the European sense of the word, it was inhabited by peoples who were deeply attached to their surroundings. There were in fact twenty-seven major tribes, some of whom lived nomadic lives as pastoralists in the less fertile areas, and some of whom lived as farmers where the land lent itself to agriculture. No one knows how many Africans lived in Kenya at the turn of the century but by 1950 the number was about eight and a quarter millions. By this time they had been joined by 40,000 Europeans and 150,000 Asians.

Settlement by European farmers and missionaries started seriously during the first decade of the present century by which time Britain had taken over the country as a Protectorate. It later became a

Colony. The Government encouraged settlers because it thought that they would bring stability and wealth to the area. Settlement mainly took place at the expense of the pastoral tribes, often on the fertile edge of their country where it joined land occupied by agricultural tribes, but some settlement took place on land formerly owned by agriculturalists. The pastoral tribes were compensated in ways which left them with no sense of grievance, but a constant tug-of-war developed beween certain elements of the agricultural tribes, notably the Kikuyu, and the settlers who farmed the land which had formerly belonged to them.

The Kikuyu, together with their close relations the Embu and the Meru, formed the largest single tribal group in Kenya numbering slightly over one and a half million in 1950. Their tribal area prior to 1900 consisted of a belt of land about twenty miles wide running down the east side of the Aberdare Mountain forest and round the southern and western side of the Mount Kenya forest. This, together with the two mountain ranges themselves, and the nearby European settled areas, formed the geographical region affected by the Mau Mau revolt. Altogether the area concerned was about one hundred miles from north to south and rather less from east to west.

Before the arrival of the British the Kikuyu consisted of a number of groups and clans divided in the main by the ridges and valleys which gave their land its characteristic form. There was no central government and groups looked after themselves in each location on a system which amounted to rule by custom interpreted by committees of elders. As was to be expected, local witch doctors or prophets exercised great influence, combining the role of physician with that of interpreter for the spirits. Although their ministrations were intended to be benign, their activities produced a backdrop of superstitious terror which all members of the tribe regarded as being a natural part of life. The British when they arrived selected certain influential men in each area mainly from existing committees of elders, to become Chiefs and Headmen and to help administer the country, but these posts had no foundation in tribal custom.

The only towns in Kenya before the arrival of the British were Arab coastal settlements such as Mombasa. Nairobi started as a collection of tents and tin huts on the railway and was little more than that when it became the centre of the Administration in 1906. Other towns sprang up in a similar fashion although none of them ever reached such a size. Nairobi played a central role in the Mau

Mau Emergency and it is worth stressing that it was built originally for Europeans and Indians working on the railway. Nearby, camps for African labourers were established and were occupied by groups from different parts of the tribal area such as Nyeri or Fort Hall or Embu or Meru. Such groups stuck together and by the 1950s, when the population had reached 110,000, Nairobi consisted of a European and Asian city surrounded by a series of squalid shanty towns occupied by people who regarded themselves as men of this or that part of the tribal area living in Nairobi, rather than as Nairobeans.

There was virtually no political activity in Kenya before the end of the First World War. The Government was largely concerned with mapping and administering the land, and with attracting European farmers. Influential Africans joined the Administration as Chiefs and Headmen in order to secure power and riches for themselves and their people. They concerned themselves mainly with trying to arrange for some system of land tenure which would ensure their rights for the future, and they also tried to see that men of their tribe who went to work for European farmers or on the railways got reasonable wages. For the most part Africans appeared to be accepting the colonial system. There were after all many advantages to it, and in any case there was not much opportunity for effective resistance because the way in which the tribes were organized rendered collective action impossible.

The first stirrings of political consciousness manifested themselves in Nairobi immediately after the First War when a group of Africans formed an association to agitate about wages. The importance of this group lay in the fact that their underlying attitude was one of opposition to the colonial system. A second association formed soon afterwards which was designed initially to protect African rights in the country areas, but although critical of certain Government measures the members of it aimed to work within the colonial system rather than against it: a number of Chiefs and Headmen joined this association. Inevitably the two associations came into conflict because they were vying with each other for influence. Naturally the Government supported the association which was prepared to work within the system and which seemed to be the more responsible. By the middle of the 1920s the Government set up Local Native Councils which brought its Administrative Officers in the field together with influential Africans many of whom were members of this second association. Meanwhile the first Nairobi-based association had collapsed only to be replaced a few years later by the Kikuyu Central Association in which opposition to the colonial system was combined with the idea of an ancient Kikuyu culture. These two ideas coloured the way in which its members handled the various issues with which they concerned themselves, e.g. wages and land tenure.

There is no need to follow in detail the fortunes of the various African political groups which developed over the period between the end of the First War and the start of the Emergency in 1952. The cleavage between the two sides was apparent from the start. On the one hand there were those who sought their advancement in co-operation with the Government inside the colonial system; on the other were those who sought it by promoting opposition to the Government, the system, and all that it represented. In this split it might be imagined that all the advantages lay with those who wished to work in co-operation with the Government. From 1923 the Government was formally committed to the paramountcy of African interest which meant that where the interests of the Africans conflicted with those of the immigrant races the former should prevail. The Government naturally saw the African interest as being something which could best be served by gradually turning the tribesmen towards a way of life based on Western civilization and this was not always popular when it involved opposition to old customs, hence the insistence on the ancient culture put forward by the other side. But the Government's practical activities in terms of teaching Africans the rudiments of hygiene, medicine, and improved methods of farming were so obviously good that they earned a large measure of support. In fact there is little doubt that the Government would have been able to retain the support of the vast majority of the population despite the activities of those hostile to it, but for one factor: the influence of the European settlers.

The power of the settlers was considerable for two reasons. In the first place they had come to Kenya at the suggestion of the British Government. They had sunk their capital in the country, and they had devoted their life's work to it. Furthermore many of them were influential in Britain and their cause was one which could win or lose votes in British political terms. The Government therefore felt constrained to support them up to a point. In the second place the financial position of the Colony was largely dependent on the produce of the settlers' farms, and schemes for the development of the

Colony including development in African areas, were therefore dependent on the settlers. This constituted a further reason for Government support. Prior to the outbreak of the Emergency there was little direct confrontation between the Kikuyu and the settlers who usually worked harmoniously together when they came into contact. For the most part European farmers who employed African labour looked after their men with care and affection, but none of this altered the fact that deep-down the interests of the two races were opposed. The most obvious difference arose over a relatively small area of European settled land – about 60,000 acres – which the Kikuyu claimed belonged to the tribe, and over this as over many other issues the influence which the settlers had with the Government prevented the sort of agreement being reached which would have enabled the Government to retain its influence with the Africans. It was this interplay of interest during the 1930s and 1940s which gradually enabled those Kikuyu who were opposed to the colonial system to build up enough support to launch the revolt.

At this point it is necessary to pause and take note of a particular aspect of the struggle as it developed. It has been shown that broadly speaking the aims of the two African groups were the same, that is to say both wanted better systems of land tenure, better wages and, as time went on, more political influence. Both parties passionately desired the return of the 60,000 acres of so-called stolen land. The difference between the groups concerned the way in which they wanted to pursue their aims. With the exception of the leaders, people did not regard themselves as belonging to one side or another. Few could read and in any case there was very little to read. At the mass meetings held around the tribal areas leaders of both groups would often appear together, and even seem to be putting forward the same ideas because most of the talk would be about aims rather than methods. Even the leaders themselves sometimes changed sides in accordance with their understanding of the way the Government's plans were progressing. For example a leading light of the Kikuyu Central Association in the 1920s had become a Chief and one of the principal supporters of the Government by the time the Emergency broke out, whereas the original leader of the first pro-Government Association, a founder member of the Local Native Councils and a senior Chief of the Kikuyu tribe, changed sides after the Second World War because he felt that no more could be achieved in co-operation with the Government owing to the strength of influence wielded by the settlers. Not only did many Kikuyu continue to change sides during the course of the fighting in accordance with their understanding of the way in which the situation was developing, but some genuinely supported both sides at the same time because they were confused as to who stood for what. It is worth trying to understand this fact.

Before describing how the fighting broke out it is necessary to look at one more thing: oathing. The taking of oaths was a traditional method of doing business amongst the Kikuyu. If two parties disputed a problem the veracity of one side's contention could be tested by asking him to repeat it on oath. Providing that the oath was administered in such a way that the person taking it felt that he would suffer from supernatural power if he lied, he would either tell the truth or keep silent. The oath therefore consisted of two parts. First there were the various magic actions designed to convince the person that he was invoking a supernatural power which would take action against any violation of the oath, and then there was the actual undertaking itself. For example the person might be swearing that he did not steal something or alternatively that he would do some particular thing. By tribal custom certain specific acts were used to summon the supernatural force but certain other acts were taboo, the use of these being regarded as pushing both oath administrator and the person taking the oath outside the orbit of the tribe. Despite the fact that some Christian influence had been disseminated in the half-century preceding the outbreak of the Emergency, nearly all the Kikuyu believed in the power of oaths in the same way as mediaeval Englishmen believed in witchcraft. As far back as the 1920s the Kikuyu Central Association, rooted as it claimed to be in ancient Kikuyu culture, had occasionally used oaths to unite their followers in a particular area. In other words, having summoned a supernatural power the people taking the oath would swear to unite together in their efforts to promote their cause. In the late 1940s and early 1950s the Kenya African Union which was a successor organization to the Kikuyu Central Association used oaths on a wider scale for the same purpose. To start with these oaths were regularly administered and designed to attract political adherents, but later they were used to commit people to violence. As time went on increasingly bestial methods were used to summon the power of the oaths including methods which were taboo to the tribe and which were deliberately intended to push the initiates outside the influence of the tribal elders, who for the most part were trying to rally the Kikuyu to reject the violence advocated by the extremists in the Kenya African Union.

It is still difficult to trace exactly how the situation deteriorated during the last few months before the onset of the Emergency in October 1952. It would seem that within the Kenya African Union two separate, clandestine committees existed. The first was a policy-forming body which operated from the countryside just outside Nairobi and it was probably responsible for organizing widespread oathing throughout the Kikuyu areas using local branches of the Kenya African Union. It also organized a series of mammoth rallies at which it put forward its policies, and it urged non-co-operation with the Government. There is little firm evidence that it intended to use organized violence for the purpose of forcing its policies onto the Government although local branches certainly used intimidation as a means of compelling support. The second committee, known as the Central Committee, was formed within the Kenya African Union branches in Nairobi and consisted of representatives of each of the main Kikuyu groups in Nairobi. It was far more extreme than the country-based committee and undoubtedly advocated the use of violence. During the last few months before the Emergency the Central Committee wrested control of the Kenya African Union branches throughout the Kikuyu tribal areas away from the country-based committee, and playing on the mounting hysteria which went along with the oathing and the rallies, organized groups for militant action. Inevitably some of these people became impatient and instead of waiting for instructions started a campaign of assassination against their political and personal enemies. Some even strayed into nearby European farmland to kill and loot. These incidents brought about the formal declaration of a State of Emergency which was accompanied by the arrest of most of the leadership of the Kenya African Union including that of Jomo Kenyatta. Altogether about one hundred men were taken in the first lift and this left numerous groups of dissidents scattered around the country without any central direction.

Over a period the Mau Mau, which was the name by which the dissidents were known, shook themselves out into what can best be described as two main fighting organizations and a support organization. The two fighting organizations were based in the Aberdare Forest and the Mount Kenya Forest respectively. They had little contact with each other. Each consisted of a Headquarters and a number of gangs which were approximately two hundred strong. These gangs were mostly formed of men who came from that part of the tribal territory nearest to their forest base, and they were supported by committees which had been built up from inside their tribal territory. In theory these committees not only collected food and money but were also responsible for directing the gangs' activities. In other words the gang was supposed to be the committee's weapon for uniting all the people in a particular area behind the movement, for which purpose it would attack the forces of the Government and those who supported them. In practice the gang leaders decided on their own course of action which was mainly concerned with survival. The third organization which operated in Nairobi and the tribal land nearby known as the District of Kiambu, concerned itself with collecting supplies and recruits for the forest gangs. There was a large reservoir of unemployed Kikuyu in Nairobi which was being swelled at this time by men discharged from employment on European-owned farms. The supporting organization was run by the Central Committee, which, using a network of subordinate committees and small gangs, parcelled off the recruits and supplies and despatched them to the appropriate forest gang. Although most of the original members of the Central Committee had been arrested in October 1952 they were immediately replaced. The new Committee not only carried out the function described but also considered itself responsible for the policy formulation of the whole Mau Mau organization. But in this respect they did not carry much weight with the leaders of the two forest organizations who merely paid sufficient lip-service to the Central Committee to ensure a steady flow of recruits and supplies.

Opposition to the Mau Mau was rooted in that part of the tribe which still considered that achievement of their aspirations could best be reached in co-operation with the Government, and the campaign was organized by the Government through the normal machinery of the Administration. In each District the chain of control ran from the District Commissioner through the District Officer to the Chief who was the leader in what was known as a Location, a territorial division which incidentally often served as the basis for the Mau Mau organization as well. Early in 1953 the decision was taken to build up a force of local people working under the direction of the District Officers and based on defended posts throughout the Location, known as the Kikuyu Guard. This body became the principal embodiment of the loyalist movement, bore the brunt of the fighting, and suffered most of the casualties inflicted by the Mau Mau. It is difficult to get accurate figures of the strength of the Kikuyu Guard but an estimate of 30,000 would not be far wrong.

Various other Government forces assisted the Kikuyu loyalists in their fight. The Kenya Police was officered by UK nationals and manned by Africans drawn from tribes throughout the Colony, not necessarily Kikuyu. Although mainly operating in the towns and settled areas it had always maintained a few posts within tribal territory. The Kenya Police expanded rapidly during the Emergency and established a number of extra posts which provided, amongst other things, the main communications network for operations. The police also raised a mobile and well-armed field force for use when required. A part-time force called the Kenya Police Reserve was also raised from Europeans and Asians to reinforce the regular police and relieve them of various routine and defensive tasks such as security patrols in the settled areas. The total strength of the Kenya Police together with its reserve force was about 20,000.

Three types of army unit operated in Kenya during the Emergency. The Kings African Rifles, manned by Africans drawn from all the East African territories and officered by Europeans, consisted of six battalions, a varying number of which were in Kenya at any one time. A few normal UK battalions were also used but never more than five at a time. Finally there was a Territorial Army battalion formed from Europeans living in Kenya which was embodied for the Emergency, but although it operated as a battalion initially, it was soon split up so that its members, with their invaluable knowledge of the country and the language, could reinforce the police and the Kikuyu Guard. Altogether the total number of soldiers being used at any one time was just short of 10,000, slightly over half of whom were Africans.

At the height of the Emergency it has been estimated that there were about 15,000 Mau Mau in the gangs, backed by a larger number of supporters in the various committees which existed. Opposed to them were about 60,000 in the Kikuyu Guard, Kenya Police and army, nearly all of whom were African and most of whom were Kikuyu. Over a period of four years it is thought that about 11,500 Mau Mau and 2,500 loyalists were killed, but accurate figures are impossible to obtain. Recently some ill-informed or ill-intentioned writers have offset the 11,500 Mau Mau dead against the 100-odd Europeans killed, making no mention of the 2,400 African casualties. This has been done in order to suggest that the whole revolt constituted a campaign of black versus white in which brutal colonialist oppressors butchered large numbers of black freedom fighters at negligible cost to themselves. Although it is true to say for reasons already explained that the interests of the settlers over a period of decades was one of the causes of the trouble, this is totally different from saying that the campaign itself, when it came, took the form of a battle between black men and white men. Such a suggestion does scant justice to the majority of the Kikuyu, Embu and Meru who rejected the violence of the extremists and who made immense sacrifices for the sake of the future of their tribe and country. It also does scant justice to the work of Europeans, Asians and Africans alike in their efforts to root out the horror which Mau Mau brought in its train.

In concluding this brief introduction to the Mau Mau revolt it is necessary to point out that neither the settlers nor the soldiers nor the members of the Administration nor the Africans themselves saw the situation at all clearly at the time. Indeed many years of research, stretching into the period after the Emergency was over and into the years of Kenyan independence, were necessary before anything like a true understanding of the situation emerged. At the time the Kikuyu were confused and frightened.

Members of forest gangs were mostly very young and their motives for joining varied greatly. Some had joined because they had been thrown out of work in the general exodus of Kikuyu labour from European farms, some had joined because of the prospect of adventure, and some because they were criminals on the run. Some had been members of strong-arm groups attached to the old Kenya African Union committees or oath administrators and had made their way into the forest when the Security Forces started to make arrests at the beginning of the Emergency. Members of the Mau Mau committees in Nairobi and in the tribal areas tended to be older and more politically sophisticated. Many of them were prepared to look on things in a different light as circumstances changed and, as mentioned earlier, many were active on both sides before coming down firmly on one side or the other. The same sort of confusion was felt by many of the loyalists who opposed the Mau Mau because they disapproved of the oathing, disliked being coerced into providing money or other forms of support, but who none the less agreed with the aims of the movement. In considering the attitude of the Kikuyu it is necessary to bear in mind all the time how close they were to their past. A man in his forties would have been brought up before any form of European influence had made itself felt. Even the wheel was unknown before the arrival of the white man.

If the Kikuyu were confused the same can hardly be said of the settlers. They had little sympathy with Kikuyu aims and felt that the interest of the African could best be achieved by the building up of a rich and civilized community administered mainly by themselves, but run for the benefit of all its members. They considered with some justification that Kenya owed its existence to them because they had created its wealth, and they felt that their lifelong daily contact with Africans had taught them to understand the Africans far better than either the British Government or the colonial Government understood them. The settlers were furious about the Emergency which they considered to be the fault of the colonial Government for playing around with those African politicians whom they regarded as being disloyal. The members of the Administration on the other hand probably knew more than either the Africans or the settlers and certainly took a more balanced view because they had, over the years, been involved in trying to reconcile the conflicting interests of the other two groups. Although they were often intensely frustrated by the obduracy of the settlers they were none the less totally hostile to the Mau Mau for upsetting the precarious balance which had been achieved and for plunging a prosperous and happy country into the horrors of civil war.

In passing it is probably just worth noticing how the situation presented itself to the British army. In 1952 the army was engaged in operations in Korea and Malaya as well as Kenya and had recently been involved in Palestine as well. Anyone with more than seven years' service had been in the Second World War and this meant all the company commanders, commanding officers and senior officers. Against this background the Mau Mau uprising was looked on as a sideshow amongst sideshows. From the soldiers' point of view operations were uncomfortable because of the extremes of temperature but they enjoyed the adventurous aspects of the business. Most of them saw evidence of revolting Mau Mau brutality from time to time, and probably regarded the finding and disposing of the gang members in the same way as they would regard the hunting of a dangerous wild animal. Although regimental officers would have taken a more sophisticated view of the situation there were no books to inform them about the events of the previous fifty years. Very senior officers had a better understanding of the position but basically the army's view was of an outlandish campaign left over from the Victorian era and one which had little to do with warfare or the modern world.

Africans, administrators, settlers and soldiers; these were the people who were locked in combat with the Mau Mau when my story begins. I arrived in Kenya nine months after the Emergency was declared to find the struggle at its height. I had absolutely no idea what it was all about when warned for duty in Kenya and had only managed to glean a little understanding of it by the time I arrived one month later. I had been sent out as one of seven or eight officers who were to reinforce the intelligence branch of the Kenya Police. Having had no training in intelligence work and having no knowledge or experience of anywhere beyond the confines of Europe I was doubtless considered to be well suited for the task. At any rate it was my turn for the outback.

❈

Chapter 2

The Taste of Insurgency

A gust of wind parted the clouds and a shaft of moonlight rested for a moment on the form of an African squatting beside the remains of a wood fire. His head was nodding forward on his chest as he dozed. A black-and-white terrier slept by his side. Behind them were three round huts and a long low building typical of the sort of house built by the early British settlers in Kenya. A high wire fence encircled the compound. Outside the wire a group of eighteen Africans lay under some coffee bushes. Their clothes were in tatters and their long hair hung in plaits to their shoulders. They clutched a variety of weapons: one had a light automatic, four or five had service rifles and the rest were armed with home-made guns put together from wood, old bits of pipe, door bolts and elastic bands. One also had a can of petrol.

Soon another cloud obscured the moon and the man with the petrol edged forward. He unscrewed the cap of his can and started to climb the wire opposite the hut which he had selected as his target. Very slowly and quietly he reached the top and lowered himself inside the compound. His heart hammered against his ribs as the moon again appeared for a moment but he was not seen by the sleeping sentry. During the next dark spell he reached the hut and started to pour out the petrol. He felt in his pocket for a match but at that moment something disturbed the dog which started to bark. The sentry looked up to curse the dog and saw the intruder. With a yell of alarm he fired his shotgun into the air and ran behind another hut. At the same moment the terrorists outside the wire started firing their weapons at random into the compound whilst their comrade dropped his can and bolted for safety. During the next few seconds the silence of the night was torn apart by the firing of guns, the shouts of men and the incessant barking of the dog. A window shattered and a child in one of the huts began to cry. A moment later a tall fair youth streaked naked out of the house and fired one or two bursts from a sub-machine gun into the coffee bushes. This proved too much for the gang which decided to withdraw. Having lost the advantage of surprise they judged it futile to try and storm the post. Gradually other men came tumbling out of their beds and stood peering into the bushes. They carried shotguns or rifles and wore heavy blue overcoats over not much else.

The clouds parted and the moon once more lit up the scene. Suddenly everyone started talking. The sentry who had reappeared was telling his friends how he had watched the gang assemble and had kept quiet hoping to get in one or two shots at close range. He explained how the dog had spoilt his plan by barking and how he had immediately charged forward after raising the alarm. A hail of fire had met him and a fierce struggle ensued. Only the timely arrival of the Bwana with his Stirling gun had tipped the scales and saved the post. Meanwhile the Bwana had taken advantage of the discussion to slip back into the house for his clothes. He now reappeared to sort out the situation. The first thing to catch his eye was the can of petrol lying up against one of the huts, a good ten paces from the fence. This was not the first occasion on which the post had been attacked and the Bwana fully realized that the dog was more likely to give the alarm than anyone else. All the same the sentry had obviously been less alert than usual in this case and such gross negligence was unacceptable even in the somewhat haphazard organization to which they all belonged. He therefore broke into the sentry's graphic account of the action with a few well-chosen words and sent him packing. The man disappeared into one of the huts to the accompaniment of laughter from his comrades.

One or two other jobs had to be done. The local operations centre was informed by telephone and in due course a police patrol arrived which was briefed and set on the tracks of the gang. The broken window was boarded up against the imminent probability of a downpour. More logs were thrown on the fire and a new sentry posted. Gradually the men drifted back to their beds and the busy chatter sunk into muffled grunts within the huts. Far away near the edge of the forest a red Verey light rose into the sky and one or two shots were fired. Then all was silence.

When the gangsters ran away, they had at first hidden in some bushes on the bank of a river not far from the post. From there they watched the arrival of the police patrol, but soon afterwards left their position and started to wade downstream in order to avoid leaving tracks. After a few hundred yards they doubled back along a path through the coffee bushes which took them to within a short distance of the post. By this time the police were hunting around the river so the gang walked onto the main road and went about two hundred yards along it before cutting across country for a further three miles. They moved at a sharp pace and met up with the rest of their group in a disused quarry soon after midnight.

Since arriving in the area five days earlier the gang had been using a dilapidated shed as a headquarters. It was made of old petrol cans, a few sheets of corrugated iron and some bits of sacking. Here the gang leader decided to hold a council of war to discuss the raid. The raiding party had been led by the gang leader in person although only a small part of his command had been involved. Altogether he had nearly a hundred men, and six of his officers plus the witch doctor were members of the council. All eight of them squatted on the floor smoking cigarettes round a paraffin lamp.

As soon as they were settled the gang leader launched forth in an account of the incident, talking in a fast and compelling manner. He told of an engagement which had lasted for over an hour, of a fierce hand-to-hand struggle with overwhelming odds. He estimated that the enemy had sustained heavy casualties, but had to admit that his party had been driven off before they could finally burn down the post. From time to time another member of the council who had been on the raid interrupted to corroborate the story or to make flattering remarks about the magnificent way in which the leader had commanded the operation. Outside the hut similar tales of heroism and fantasy were being told by the raiders to those of their friends who had not been involved.

After a time the leader came to the end of his story. All the members of the council had formerly taken part in similar operations and well understood the way in which the report had been presented. They knew that the speaker was not one to sacrifice dramatic effect for the mere sake of truth and in any case that formed no part of their tribal heritage. Even so they were puzzled to know why the attack had been such a failure, as their leader was undoubtedly a good tactician with a record of success equalled by few other Mau

Mau generals. How had it happened that the raiding party had not achieved surprise?

One of the reasons why the witch doctor was kept was to answer questions such as this. His opinion was now sought in the certainty that he would solve the puzzle and it only remained for the council to wait patiently while he went through the rigmarole of his profession. First of all he produced a little bag out of his pocket and emptied the contents on the mud floor in front of the lamp. There were twenty beans whose polished skins and contrasting colours gave back the light like so many precious stones; the witch doctor studied the pattern they made on the ground before returning them to his pocket. Next he produced a small mirror from somewhere and some powder from a horn at his belt. He sprinkled the powder on the mirror and then rubbed part of the surface clear with his sleeve. He gazed into it as though through a window and started mumbling.

The men were familiar with the proceedings but were none the less awed by them. By the time the witch doctor started to talk they had all drawn back into the shadows and had to strain to hear his words. Gradually the sense of his remarks became apparent. He was telling them that the plan for the attack had been betrayed by one of the gang's supporters. Inevitably the news was welcomed because it removed the burden of failure from their own shoulders. The next problem was to discover the identity of the informer and after a lot more looking into the mirror and mumbling this too was disclosed. The witch doctor named an African who worked on a coffee estate about half way between the quarry and the post which they had attacked. The gang leader looked at the watch which he had recently taken from a dying policeman. The time was 1.30 a.m.

An hour later six of the terrorists crouched outside the labourer's hut, and a seventh knocked on the door. After a time the door was opened a fraction and two wide, frightened eyes were pressed against the crack. The caller identified himself and the owner of the hut opened the door, relieved to find that he was not being visited by the police. But his relief was short-lived because at that moment he was grabbed by six pairs of strong hands and dragged outside. For a moment he could not understand what was happening. These were his friends; why were they in such a hurry to tear him away from his wife and child? Before the truth could sink in he was lying on his back and a handful of grass and mud was pushed into his mouth. The weight of several men pressed down on him. He looked up and started to struggle but at that moment a knife was thrust into his eye. The sudden pain was atrocious, but it was soon swallowed up in an ever mounting agony as a razor blade cut into the lower half of his body. A few more moments went by which seemed longer than the whole of his life. Then a panga sank into his arm and others started hacking their way into his legs and body. Five minutes later the gangsters slunk off into the night taking with them some grisly souvenirs for use in subsequent oathing ceremonies. A blood-soaked heap of flesh and rags was left behind for the benefit of the next of kin.

The post which had been attacked was the one which I had established soon after arriving in Kenya. The unfortunate African murdered by the gang was not as it happened a person with whom we had had contacts, but in any case the Mau Mau often acted without much evidence to back their suspicions and many Kikuyu had perished in this way. Sudden attacks and the murder of innocent people form the backcloth to insurgency. They provide an element of terror designed to gain the support of people who will not give it voluntarily. Only the very brave will support the forces of the government unless they can be afforded adequate protection.

Like most of our Colonies, Kenya was divided into Provinces and Districts for the purposes of administration, and when it became necessary to operate against the Mau Mau the Government organized its forces within this administrative framework. Operations were directed by a committee consisting of the senior government official, the senior police officer and the officer commanding any soldiers who might be stationed in the area at the time. At District level such a committee would consist of the District Commissioner, the Superintendent of Police and probably an army lieutenant colonel. When army officers such as myself were sent to Kenya to reinforce the police Special Branch, the idea had been that one should be provided for each District but there had not been enough to go round. Although my primary responsibility was to the District of Kiambu, I was told that I should also have to keep an eye on the neighbouring District of Thika. I therefore rented a house in the village of Kamiti on the borders of these two Districts. I fortified it and used it as a base for my activities.

Kiambu and Thika Districts were each about thirty-five miles

B

from north to south and thirty miles from east to west. Thika fitted
onto the eastern edge of Kiambu so that the two Districts together
formed a block sixty miles across. Along the western edge of Kiambu
District ran the southern end of the Aberdare range running up to a
height of 10,000 feet. This range was densely clad in bamboo forest

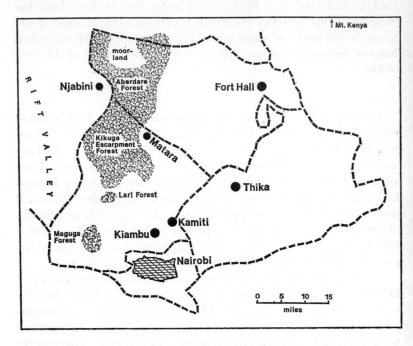

and from it a series of ridges and valleys pushed out towards the east.
As the streams which ran along the valleys travelled towards the
Indian Ocean they combined so that the ridges became broader
and the valleys less steep. As the altitude decreased the vegetation
changed. Below the bamboo-clad ridge was a belt of rain forest:
huge trees with a dense undergrowth of fern, thorn and creeper.
There was perhaps five miles of this before the forest cleared and the
country took on the appearance of a patchwork quilt. There was
open grass, fields of maize and beans, wattle plantations and
bananas. This was the native reserve of the Kikuyu tribe, roughly a
third of which lived in Kiambu District, excluding those who had
left their land to seek a livelihood in Nairobi or on European farms.
Twenty miles to the east came the edge of the reserve and the next

belt was owned by European coffee farmers, whose regular lines of
coffee bushes stretching for mile after mile were in sharp contrast to
the variation found in the reserve. Even so, round the African labour
lines the small holdings and banana plantations survived. There
were also swamps of reed and rush in the river valleys. The border
of reserve and settled area ran roughly along the boundary between
the two Districts. Further to the east again the country became too
dry for coffee and its place was taken by huge sisal estates, some
owned by individuals but many by European companies. In the extreme east of Thika where the altitude was down to 4,000 feet it
became useless to try and grow anything. Farmland gave way to
arid scrub.

The pattern described was more complicated in the south than in
the north. Reserve and settled area ran round each other in a be-
wildering way, lapping the ever growing capital Nairobi, soon to be
proclaimed a city. From Nairobi north to Thika ran one of the few
metalled roads in the two Districts. Apart from this, communication
was by murram tracks which ran east and west along the ridges and
which were joined by laterals where gradients permitted. These
roads were treacherous mud for half the year, and for the rest of the
time were inches deep in red dust which rose like a cloud round anything that moved. To the west of the Aberdares the country dropped
5,000 feet vertically into the Rift Valley in what must be one of the
most spectacular escarpments in the world.

The general idea of putting army officers into Special Branch detachments was to relieve police officers of the task of getting information about the operational aspects of Mau Mau, thus leaving them
free to concentrate on the political problems of subversion. The
dividing line was pretty thin especially in an area such as Kiambu
District which, as explained earlier, formed with Nairobi the main
support and policy base for the Mau Mau movement. At the time
when I arrived, the Mau Mau were deliberately trying to keep the
area quiet so that the business of collecting money and recruits could
go ahead without interference from Government forces. Such activity as came to our notice took the form of assassinations, the
movement of gangs of recruits which were usually no more than a
hundred strong, and the occasional foray by a large gang into the
north-west corner of the District. At the time no one had worked out
why Kiambu was less active than other Districts: it was optimistic-
ally assumed that Kiambu men were less warlike than their neigh-

bours further north, but this was found to be wrong as time went by.

It is hardly surprising that the true situation was unknown to the authorities. Before I arrived the intelligence resources of Kiambu District consisted of one European Inspector and two or three African police constables. Thika District also had one European Inspector but he was helped by only one African constable. To help me I had one sergeant of the Kenya Regiment and one member of the Kenya Police Reserve for the whole area: they were known as Field Intelligence Assistants. Being unhampered by preconceived ideas as to how one should collect intelligence, and having no money or resources of any sort I was at least able to evolve a system suited to the prevailing conditions. To start with I used to drive around my area collecting gossip from anyone who would give it to me, such as District Officers, policemen, soldiers, Chiefs, settlers or other casual acquaintances. By bringing it all back to Kiambu and writing it down I was able to get some sort of insight into events, although it was a poor substitute for the authoritative information about enemy intentions which commanders naturally prefer. But the operational committees in Kiambu and Thika Districts had become so accustomed to getting nothing at all that they were grateful for the scanty fare which I was able to offer.

As time went on I was able to get hold of some more helpers in the form of young settlers called up for service in the Kenya Regiment. The two original Field Intelligence Assistants left soon after I arrived, but by Christmas 1953 I had collected three for Kiambu District and two for Thika. A sixth man called Eric Holyoak had come to me, but he was only just eighteen and was supposedly too young to be sent out to a remote corner of the District by himself. He therefore stayed with me and lived in the post which I had set up at Kamiti.

On the morning after our post had been attacked I had to go into Kiambu to give a briefing. The situation in the District was beginning to change because some of the more militant terrorists were getting impatient with their unspectacular role and wanted to form larger gangs and take more offensive action against the Security Forces. Such a one was the man who had led the attack the previous night. Whilst my briefing was going on, news arrived that a large gang about two hundred strong had come out of the forest in the extreme north of Kiambu District, burnt down a post belonging to the Kikuyu Guard, and was rampaging through the countryside terrorizing the local loyalists. It was urgently necessary for us to discover what gang it was and what its intentions were so that it could be destroyed without delay. For the next three days I was very busy and did not return home. I spent most of the time visiting police or Kikuyu Guard posts in the battle area or talking to the Field Intelligence Assistants who had become involved in the chase. From them I tried to build up a picture of what was going on. I spent the second night sitting in on the interrogation of a prisoner, and I made two flying visits to Nairobi to brief senior military and police commanders. Altogether I enjoyed the helter-skelter pursuit of information, never knowing where the next meal was coming from, or which of my new friends would turn up next. I slept for odd moments in the Landrover to avoid wasting time in bed and drove when not sleeping in order to give the driver a break. On these occasions I developed the habit of singing to keep myself awake.

Once I managed to get involved in the fighting. I was driving along a ridge when firing broke out from across the valley. Through my binoculars I could see that the fire was coming from some soldiers, who had obviously just arrived by truck, on top of the ridge directly opposite us. They were firing into some thick cover which lay between us, but at first I could not see what they were shooting at. Then the terrorists appeared from a wattle plantation which was growing along the banks of the stream: it was an exhilarating and impressive sight seeing so many of them all together. They had not adopted any known military formation and were walking fast, but without any sign of alarm. Every now and then one or two of them would stop for long enough to fire a shot in the direction of the soldiers. They mostly wore old mackintoshes over ragged trousers and carried a blanket slung bandolier fashion over one shoulder and a haversack over the other. At this time they must have been about five hundred yards away from the soldiers who were shooting at them and perhaps a little further from us. Looking through my binoculars I could easily see what sort of weapons they had and could pick out those who from their gestures and behaviour seemed to be men of authority. I wondered whose gang it was. It could easily have been the one formerly led by Matenjagua, a very well-known Fort Hall gang leader, but perhaps these terrorists had come from the other side of the mountain and were led by Muraya Mbuthia or from the north of Fort Hall in which case I might be looking at Njuguna Kirunyu. I knew the names and background of all the principal leaders in all the gangs throughout the Aberdares and it was intensely exciting watching and wondering. It made the battle seem so personal.

It soon became evident that the gang intended to climb the slope on our side of the valley so as to cross the road on which we were stationed. They could do this on foot far more quickly than the soldiers could follow them in their vehicles because there was no track joining the two ridges for at least five miles. In the hopes of delaying them, my driver and escort each fired a few rounds but the range was too great. All the same we did cause the gang to change their direction slightly to avoid us. Some of the terrorists returned our fire but the bullets all passed over our heads. Evidently an officer decided that the chances of hitting us did not warrant the expenditure of ammunition involved because the shooting soon stopped. As soon as we saw that the gang had changed direction, we moved along the ridge hoping to get another shot at closer range. Unfortunately the gang ran into the fire of some Kikuyu Guard who were manning a stop. This caused the terrorists to turn further away from us and although we stayed around for some hours our luck was out and we never saw them again. Later on we found the body of a terrorist which we loaded into the Landrover and dropped off at a police post. It would probably be identified from fingerprints which might help to provide background information about the Mau Mau unit involved.

The gang turned out to be one of those normally resident in the forest to the north of Kiambu District. It had probably been called in to frighten our Kikuyu Guard because the Kiambu Mau Mau had no gangs strong enough to do the job, and this one certainly succeeded in causing some casualties in the course of their foray. They also lost a number of men in the skirmishes before getting back to the shelter of the forest.

One afternoon a day or two later I was visiting a police post in the area near where the battle had taken place, in search of any odd bits of information which we might have missed, when I got a telephone call to say that a large scale action was in progress in Thika District. Saying goodbye to the police station commander I drove rapidly to the scene and found an imposing array of soldiers and policemen surrounding an area of swamp. Although there was no sign of the enemy there was plenty of activity. Machine guns and mortars were firing into the rushes to pin the Mau Mau down while reinforcements were sent for to establish a really tight cordon round the area.

By the time the cordon was strong enough the light had begun to fade so it was decided to contain the enemy during the hours of darkness and deal with them in the morning.

As it got dark I found myself sitting on the ground with a Field Intelligence Assistant from Thika, two of his interrogators and a prisoner who had been captured earlier in the day. All around us men were moving. Some were fixing up spotlights and others were strengthening the cordon. Here and there command posts were being set up and then the supply echelons moved in disgorging company colour sergeants with their cooks and storemen. Near to where we were sitting three soldiers and a sergeant were pitching a tent which would act as the Regimental Aid Post should there be any casualties. Gradually the men and vehicles became blurred and melted into the darkness. The firing died away except for the occasional flare sent up by a mortar to illuminate the scene, and the soldiers settled down to their vigil, determined to prevent a break-out during the night.

We did not seem to be making much progress with the interrogation of our prisoner. Although most of the talking was done in Kikuyu I was kept informed by occasional summaries issued in English. After a time we decided that it was pointless to go on providing free food for the mosquitoes so we moved back to my post. Later in the night we were joined by Eric Holyoak who had been out on some business of his own. With his help we succeeded in getting some information out of the prisoner. We learnt that the gang consisted of a small number of terrorists from the forest together with eighty-odd recruits gathered during the past ten days from Nairobi. Having discovered the area from which the gang originated we were able to alert the Security Forces along likely return routes in case any of them managed to break out of the cordon. We returned to the scene of the operation arriving just before dawn and gave our news to the officer in command there. We then settled down near his headquarters to await developments. As it started to get light the mortars again fired into the swamp. The mortars themselves were sited well back. When they fired we first saw the flashes and then heard the whine of the bombs as they passed through the air. This was followed by further flashes and bangs as they exploded in the swamp and finally there was the sound of mud and water, flung into the air by the explosions, falling back into the reeds. After ten minutes of mortar fire there was a lull and a van drove along the edge of the swamp broadcasting an appeal to the gangsters to come out and surrender. There were no results.

By now it was fully light and Eric and I were wondering whether the terrorists had managed to slip away during the hours of darkness. But at that moment firing broke out two or three hundred yards away. We immediately got into a Landrover with some of our men and drove to the scene. We arrived at a point where the swamp was about one hundred yards wide. On our side the cordon consisted of Home Guard armed for the most part with spears and simis, although there were a fair number with shot-guns and a few with rifles. One or two old herdsmen had bows and arrows. British soldiers manned the cordon on the opposite side of the swamp.

The loudspeaker van had been the cause of the firing. A terrorist seeing such a large target trundling along in front of him had been unable to resist the temptation of firing at it. He had been joined by one or two others and they all turned their attention towards the Kikuyu Guard once the van had moved away. Although the reeds successfully concealed the terrorists, the soldiers returned the fire hoping at least to disturb the gangsters' aim. This was the situation which prevailed when we arrived. Bullets were throwing up spurts of mud all the way across the swamp and others were even landing in the scrub on our side. After a time the soldiers stopped firing and almost at once a terrorist fired several shots at the cordon. I half expected that the soldiers would plunge in, but they were not allowed to do so. The overall plan was for a sweeping force to advance down the length of the swamp while the cordon gave covering fire and stopped the gang from escaping. No purpose would be served by letting odd sections or platoons chase little groups of terrorists round the rushes.

The main operation soon started, but it was some time before the sweeping party reached us. While they moved forward the odd shot continued to come from the swamp and every now and then there would be a disturbance in the rushes which showed that a terrorist was moving down the line of cover away from the beaters. It was rather like watching the movement of rabbits in a cornfield which is being cut, except that guns round a cornfield wait for the rabbits to bolt before wasting ammunition whereas in this case every movement drew fire from a dozen weapons.

While all this was going on I saw an African herdsman armed with a bow and arrow stalk and kill a terrorist. The circumstances

were so unusual that they are probably worth recording. The herdsman, who was part of the cordon on our side of the swamp, must
have been watching very carefully because he had managed to spot
a gangster who was lying in the mud with only his head above water
and that was well concealed in the reeds. He had probably seen him
take up the position after moving from another part of the swamp.
The herdsman, being too far away to use his weapon, crawled very
slowly up to the edge of the swamp thus reducing the range to about
thirty yards. He did this without being observed. Slowly and with
great care he raised his bow and fired. The arrow passed through
the air with much less force than I had expected and I wondered
whether it would do any damage on arrival. In fact it caught the
gangster in the neck and cut through the jugular vein. He staggered
to his feet clutching his throat from which blood poured forth in a
dark crimson torrent painting the rushes round about so that they
looked like the decorations some people keep in their house when
flowers are out of season. There was no denying the effectiveness of
the weapon and the incident made me think how lucky we were that
the Mau Mau never used them. They greatly preferred home-made
guns which were mainly dangerous to those who tried to fire them.

Eventually the sweep ran its course accounting for two enemy
killed and ten or twelve captured. Many more must have escaped
detection by lying in the mud. Some submerged themselves totally
and breathed through hollow reeds. Following the sweep there was
a further appeal on the loudspeaker van and then another sweep.
This went on all day and by the late afternoon over fifty Mau Mau
had been killed or captured. It subsequently transpired that some
had eluded the cordon during the previous night, but most of these
were accounted for by patrols who were scouring the area. The
whole operation was remarkably successful from the army's point
of view.

So far as the Mau Mau was concerned the operation had been a
considerable set-back. The Central Committee and its agents had
spent several weeks collecting the recruits together and a group of
forest men had come all the way south from Mount Kenya to collect
them. The recruits had been sent out of Nairobi in groups of ten or
twenty to a rendezvous just outside the town and had only gone a
few miles before being spotted and engaged by the army. In fact in
this case they had been intercepted by sheer bad luck from their
point of view because there had been no intelligence tip-off about

their move: they had been seen by a routine police patrol. The intelligence organization, in the form of my people, may have been of minor assistance in handling the prisoners, but the operation would have taken place in much the same way had we never existed. The same could be said for the earlier operation when the gang came out of the forest in Kiambu District. We were marginally useful: no more than that.

Chapter 3

Birth of an Idea

The British army in the 1950s normally conducted its counter-insurgency campaigns along the lines indicated in the last chapter. Units expected whatever intelligence organization existed to provide pinpoint information regarding the whereabouts and future intentions of enemy groups so that soldiers could be put into contact with them. The intelligence organizations were seldom capable of doing this regularly, so the army did two things. Firstly it complained about the inefficiency of the intelligence organization and secondly it set about looking for the enemy by conducting large-scale operations in likely areas on a hit-or-miss basis. Because its staff procedures were effective it was well suited to exploiting such success as it may have had when carrying out random searches for the enemy. For example, if a patrol bumped into a gang the army could concentrate large numbers in the area quickly. But if it was unlucky with its random operations nothing happened. The army was not able to exploit the sort of background information which the intelligence organization was often able to produce even when it could not provide pinpoint contact information. In other words we, in the Special Branch, thought that the lists of gang members, the details of weapons and the accounts of gang policies and long-term plans which we got from our interrogations and contacts would be of great value, but military commanders expressed little interest in such material or in the people who were producing it.

By the spring of 1954 my organization really was beginning to produce a great deal of this stuff which the army did not want. My parish had been extended by the addition of Nairobi District, so I now had three Districts to look after instead of two, but I had been

given two extra Field Intelligence Assistants for Nairobi together
with three officers, one for each of my Districts. For some weeks the
Field Intelligence Assistants had been employing Africans to run
informers so that a covert information gathering network was becoming established throughout the area for which I was responsible.
To start with we had no funds with which to pay these people so we
were obliged to finance our activities with money captured from
gangsters supplemented occasionally from my private resources. But
this was irregular and laid us open to the charge of looting, so as soon
as it was apparent that our methods were paying off we were given
a proper budget. By the summer of 1954 I had over two hundred
men working for me, but that is to anticipate events by several
months. At the time of which I am speaking my chief concern was
for the fact that although we were becoming efficient at collecting
intelligence, no one knew how to exploit it because it was not
exactly what was wanted. Since we were meant to be providing a
service, it seemed that the fault must lie with us, although in years to
come I was to change my views in this respect. Meanwhile I determined that somehow we would discover a way of turning the
vast quantity of background information which we were collecting
into the detailed contact information which the soldiers wanted.

But this major matter of policy was not our only source of worry
at that time. There was a day in April 1954 when I found myself
sitting on a bench in the main passage of the Nairobi Supreme Court,
waiting to give evidence. Two Field Intelligence Assistants were
with me. The accused had been captured in a battle and had passed
through our hands on the way to prison. Formal evidence to this
effect was required from all of us. At half past twelve the judge adjourned the court for luncheon and we were told to be back by 2 p.m.
I had arranged to meet an African at 2.30 p.m. and could not
afford to put him off. Had I done so he would have swum away and
we would have missed an unusual opportunity for collecting information and one that would not recur. I explained as much of the
situation as possible to the officer in charge of the court and asked to
be excused until 4 p.m. He appeared deeply shocked and warned me
that there would be a fine for contempt of court were I to be absent
when required. I returned at 4 p.m. to find that my turn had not
yet come. Ten minutes later the court was adjourned until the
following day.

Next morning we were again on our bench in the passage by 10 a.m. Neither of the Field Intelligence Assistants had been to bed because they had spent the night making up for the lost time of the day before. One of them started telling the other of the occasion on which Eric had come to court as a witness. He had engaged a gang of four, killing two and capturing two others. One of these prisoners was charged with being an armed terrorist, but the other one had thrown away his weapon before capture and could only be charged with consorting. Both charges carried the death penalty. When the case was tried the armed man persuaded the court that he was a prisoner of the gang and that he had been made to carry a weapon so that he would be compromised in the eyes of the law. He was accordingly acquitted. The other terrorist was also acquitted of consorting on the grounds that the man he was consorting with had been proved innocent. I had often heard the story from Eric but could not help laughing again. At about midday, taking the law into my own hands, I told the other two to go about their business and undertook to pay any fines for contempt of court out of intelligence funds. A clerk from my office was left behind to contact us when it seemed that our appearance was imminent and then I departed also. When the court adjourned for the weekend our turn had not come up.

On the Saturday evening a message reached me from a police station on the forest edge via the operations room in Kiambu. An army patrol had come out of the forest having fought a battle with a large gang. They had killed four terrorists and captured a number of documents. There was little rest for any of us that night. First there was a long drive through the countryside, windscreens lashed by torrential rain and the cab permeated by the smell of mud baking on the exhaust pipe. This was followed by some hours crouched round a paraffin lamp in the Field Intelligence Assistant's hut near Gatundu. It was too cold to open the window so we endured air polluted by dozens of cigarettes. Some fresh air found its way through the door as people came in and out. The Africans brought in sticky red mud on the soles of their feet and left 'Man Friday' footprints all over the floor.

Gradually a picture of the gang emerged as the documents gave up their secrets to the translators. Outside the sky turned grey and it became even colder in the hut. The last of the flying ants flew into the paraffin lamp and collapsed in the squidgy mess at the bottom of it. Soon the lamp was unnecessary but it continued to burn be-

cause no one could be bothered to turn it out. By 11 a.m. the picture was completed and I decided to go to General Headquarters in
Nairobi to pass on the news. We were nearly out of petrol by the
time we reached Kiambu so we went to the military unit there,
which was responsible for replenishing us. An old sergeant was in
charge of the petrol and we found him in the mess. He declined to
supply us on the grounds that it was Sunday! At that moment the
adjutant came in and he supported the sergeant. Black rage welled
up inside me as I walked out intent on getting the colonel to smash
some ginger into his people, but I changed my mind and bought
petrol at the dukka. It was a cardinal rule of mine not to scrap with
our own side because we depended on them for so much. All the
same I was still simmering when I reached Nairobi.

In actual fact the petrol storeman was only behaving in the same
way as dozens of others throughout the base area. The judge with his
interminable adjournments, or workshop crews going away for the
weekend leaving vehicles unrepaired were other examples of the
same thing. There is always a cleavage between the men in the field
and those in the rear areas and Kenya was no exception. Indeed it
often seemed as if the Governor was trying to give the impression
that as the rebellion was only affecting one tribe it was not of major
importance in the context of the Colony as a whole. The inevitable
consequence of this attitude was for the people not actively engaged
to think in terms of 'business as usual'. Such an attitude may have
helped to maintain confidence in the City of London, but it had a
singularly unfortunate effect on the spirits of those in the field. Some
cried out for a Templar or a de Lattre, but most of them would have
been sacked by either of these men within a few days.

Altogether there were plenty of frustrations, but the men in my
organization were young and very fully occupied. Furthermore the
life involved endless activity in the open air, much of which was both
interesting and exciting. It is not very likely that the Field Intelligence Assistants worried overmuch about whether they were producing information in exactly the form which the police and the
army required. They were doing their best and achieving an increasing amount. That was good enough for them and rightly so.
For my own part I was always on the look-out for a breakthrough
but I could not think how to achieve one. Although I did not know
it at the time, I was waiting for something to turn up. Eventually
something did.

One day, towards the end of March 1954, we were interrogating a prisoner called George who had been captured by the Kikuyu Guard in an action with a gang near the forest edge. We were not having much success with the interrogation because George kept telling lies and we did not know when he was doing so. One of the secrets of effective interrogation is of course to know the answer to most of the questions asked so as to trip the prisoner up when he lies. After a time the prisoner becomes resigned to telling the truth because he does not want to be caught out in his lies too frequently and it is then that the interrogator slips in the questions which he particular wants answered truthfully. Unfortunately we did not know enough about George and his former friends to work this system effectively.

Then I remembered that some weeks earlier we had found a book on the body of a gang member killed in the same general area from which George had come and which contained details of men and weapons. Thinking that this book might refer to George's gang, I shouted in English to the clerk who was sitting at the far end of the room to throw it to me and I caught it as it came over George's head. George had not noticed the clerk who had not been in the room when we had started the interrogation, nor had he understood what I had said. All that he knew was that I had said a few incomprehensible words and a book, which he imagined to be in the possession of his gang leader deep in the forest, had suddenly appeared out of thin air and was going to be used to prove him a liar. To his mind this represented strong magic and from that moment on he was my man whose sole aim was to do all possible to help me.

After completing the interrogation we took George out on a patrol and he pointed out several huts near the forest edge where his gang used to go for supplies. He went into one pretending to be still in the gang and the owner gave him some interesting bits of news. Over the next few days we did the same thing in other areas where George's gang was known to work, making up a suitable story each time to account for George's presence. On one occasion a contact made in this way told George that a supply group from his gang was lying up nearby. George went and met them and led them back to where we lay in wait so that we were able to engage them with our weapons. In the subsequent skirmish we killed or captured all the members of this group. We had in fact done something far more important than that: we had at last broken through the great divide and had developed background information, represented by George's knowledge of a supporter's identity, into contact information.

Eric Holyoak was the man chiefly responsible for exploiting this break-through when eventually it came. Because he had been considered too young to be a Field Intelligence Assistant he had been designated as the interrogator for my area. In order to fulfil this function efficiently he had collected together eight loyal Kikuyu to act as guards for any prisoners which might be passed to him for interrogation. These were the men who had built the huts around my house and who had fortified the whole complex as a defended post. He had also been involved in taking George out on his early patrols and had been responsible for thinking up the stories which George told to his contacts. Eric soon found that there were grave difficulties in making up convincing stories to account for the presence of one stray gang member wandering around on his own. so George taught our team of loyal Kikuyu to dress and act like Mau Mau. Eric would go with George and some or all of our team and hide up near a known gang supporter. He would then send George and the team, all of whom were acting as Mau Mau, to talk to the supporter who might in turn put them into contact with a group from a real gang. The team would then talk to the gang before returning to Eric who could direct a military or police patrol onto them, or just note down the information for future use if that seemed more satisfactory.

Soon after we had started doing this our team fell in with a real gang before Eric had broken away and taken cover, but in the dark the real gang failed to notice his presence. Realizing that he would soon be discovered he ordered his team to attack the real gang, which being taken by surprise was easily overcome. From this incident we reckoned that if we disguised ourselves with face blacking and wigs and if we put some yellow dye in our eyes, we could pass as Africans in the dark and accompany our team. This would be advantageous from the point of view of getting good first-hand information. Thus was born the pseudo-gang system which we enlarged over the coming months, recruiting additional ex-terrorists like George as we went along. Sometimes I accompanied Eric on these operations in order to get first-hand experience, but I was rather a liability because of my uncertain grasp of the language and he never exactly welcomed the help which I so anxiously proferred.

One morning a few months after George's arrival I was having breakfast with Eric Holyoak on the verandah of our house. It had been a wet night but the clouds had now passed and shafts of brilliant sunlight shone through the raindrops on the roses so that they sparkled like diamonds. The air was intensely clear: trees, huts and rocks several miles away looked like finely modelled ornaments in a cabinet, an illusion which can only be understood properly by people who have lived in East Africa. In front of us on the lawn a small blue bird was pecking at the grass. A few hundred yards away three or four kites circled hopefully over the dukka where an African was skinning a goat. The sharpness of the air and the beauty of the scene would have stimulated the appetite of an invalid let alone two active men enjoying in retrospect the excitement of previous events.

We had been discussing ways of making our camp more secure from attack which was a common topic of conversation between us. As usual we got nowhere for the simple reason that we did not have enough men to post sentries in pairs and when we posted them singly they always went to sleep. After a while we changed the subject and talked about an operation in Thika District which the local Field Intelligence Assistant was engaged in, helped by Eric. The object of this operation was to destroy a small, but exceptionally nasty gang of fifteen which had been terrorizing the labour on the coffee farms bordering the native reserve. Since Easter they had killed nearly seventy loyalists. On several occasions we had provided information to the army, but on each occasion something had gone wrong. As a result the army were losing faith in Thika Special Branch and we in turn were becoming convinced that the soldiers always mucked up information collected at the expense of much effort and risk. We therefore decided to release no more information about this gang until we could get them into such a position that the army could not possibly make a mess of it.

The main reason for the survival of these terrorists was that we had been unable to make contact with our pseudo-gang. We knew who the terrorists' supporters were and we sent various members of our team to meet them pretending to be visitors from Nairobi or emissaries from the forest. Whatever the story the local Mau Mau committee received them courteously and promised to arrange a meeting with the gang. But a meeting never took place. Eventually the Military Intelligence Officer for Thika devised a long-term plan.

Near to the area in which the gang operated were a number of farms which had no Mau Mau committee on them because they had all been arrested some months earlier. He decided to introduce a pseudo-gang who would tell the labourers that they had been forced out of their normal area in Kiambu. Our gang would ask for support and encourage the formation of the normal chain of committees to provide it. Once the system was operating freely he would arrest all the supporters of the real gang from the other group of farms. He hoped that the real gang would be forced into getting supplies from the committees which he had set up to support our pseudo-gang. Our gang would then be well within their rights to demand a meeting with the terrorists in order to co-ordinate operations.

The early stages of the operation went well. Our pseudo-gang found the labourers in the selected area only too willing to provide support and the supporters of the real gang were removed according to plan. We then suffered a set-back because the real gang went to the Fort Hall Reserve instead of moving into the area which we had prepared for them. Luckily they came back after a few days and made contact with the new committees. Ten days later one of our men met three of theirs in the hut of a leading supporter. On this occasion it was arranged that the leader of our group with a bodyguard of three should at last meet the real gang. The matter being discussed between Eric and myself was the composition of the team to go to the meeting, which was due to take place the following night. The leader would have to be George and the Thika Field Intelligence Assistant, suitably dressed up, would be the second member. These two had been part of the pseudo-gang which had built up the committees and were known to the supporters. Eric had agreed to go along to keep the Field Intelligence Assistant company and he had undertaken to provide a good man from our team to make up the number. We ran through the names of our men to see who would be the most suitable but there seemed to be a snag to each one.

We had finished eating and were still undecided when an African came wandering round from behind the house. He was carrying a dustbin lid full of posho which he was scattering on the ground for the chickens. He wore a khaki shirt hanging outside a ragged pair of shorts; he looked under-nourished and his legs, which were swollen, were covered in jungle sores. His hair hung to his shoulders in the plaits of the hard-core terrorist; his nose was flat and wide and he had huge, gentle eyes which were completely out of keeping with his general appearance. His name was Kamau and when he saw us at the table he gave us a nervous, but friendly smile. Kamau had been captured about a week earlier during a battle in the forest and we had kept him on after his interrogation was finished to see whether he would be suitable for use in pseudo-gangs. For the first few days he had been confined, but he was now being allowed to walk around the compound by himself so as to get the feeling that we trusted him. In a week or two he would go out with another member of our team visiting low-grade informers and then when his reliability was proved he would go on his first pseudo-operation. That would have been the normal programme at any rate.

Eric suddenly said that he would take Kamau as the fourth member of the party. He then produced all the reasons for not doing so and shot them down one after another. It was certainly a risk, but Eric had an uncanny knack of knowing about Africans. There was no doubt that Kamau looked the part and had more recent experience of life in the gangs than anyone else in our team. As usual I agreed and a broad grin stretched across Eric's pointed face. He rose from the table and I could not help wondering how he had ever passed himself off as a Kikuyu. He was well over six feet tall and was so slim that he seemed to consist entirely of arms and legs, an illusion that was heightened by the fact that he seldom wore anything but a short pair of khaki shorts and a little check shirt. He had a mass of fair, tousled hair which he brushed about once a week and altogether it would be hard to imagine anyone who looked less like an African. It is remarkable what good disguise can achieve.

After breakfast I had to go away on some business or other and in the event I did not return to our post for three days. It was then that Eric told me how the patrol had turned out. In the morning after I had left for Nairobi Eric had spent an hour or more with Kamau going over every detail of the imaginary background of the pseudo-gang. In the evening he dressed Kamau in the old clothes in which he had been captured and then set about disguising himself. First he blacked his skin with actor's make-up and then put on a black woolly wig. Next came an old pair of trousers and the inevitable mackintosh; he wore brown leather ankle boots made at the Bata shoe factory, a bush-hat with a wide brim and two strings of coloured beads round his neck. A boy scout belt with the buckle upside down completed the outfit. By this time he looked the part of a Mau Mau terrorist to perfection, even if he was a little on the large side for a Kikuyu.

Soon after 8 p.m. they went to Thika and met the Field Intelligence Assistant who was running the operation. A police patrol commanded by a mutual friend of theirs was going to help round up the terrorists because the soldiers who had originally been given the task had been called away to help chase a big gang in the north of Kiambu District. That at any rate was Eric's story and I did not press him on the subject. The police inspector knew where and when the meeting was to take place and intended to surround the hut. With a bit of luck the terrorists would surrender if they saw that they were outnumbered and in a hopeless position. We always made simple plans because experience had shown that anything elaborate could be relied on to miscarry. Also by leaving lots to luck we did not expect events to follow any particular course so we were less alarmed by what actually happened.

Our party drove away from Thika and left their Landrover about three miles away from where the meeting was due to take place. From there they moved off on foot with George leading, followed by the Thika Field Intelligence Assistant, Kamau and Eric, in that order. George had a pistol stuck in his belt and he carried a kiboko. Kamau had a simi and the two Europeans each carried Mau Mau home-made guns. It was a clear, still night with a strong moon and although it had been dark for nearly three hours it was still quite warm. The men walked fast and silently between row after row of coffee bushes. The moon made long shadows of the men and the bushes, giving rise to the illusion that four giants were gliding noiselessly through a forest. Once they left the coffee bushes for about a quarter of a mile and walked through some grass by a bit of swampy land where thousands of crickets and frogs were disturbing the night with their clamour. Soon they were back in the coffee bushes and the silence seemed all the more profound by contrast.

Almost before they realized it they had arrived on the edge of a grass clearing. Thirty yards away a dozen conical huts with thatched roofs were outlined in the moonlight against a background of banana trees. According to recent regulations, African labour lines should have been surrounded by a strong perimeter fence, but on this farm the Bwana had not yet got round to completing the task. Our men sunk down on the grass while George slipped out of the shadows and

walked to the hut on the end of the line. He scratched on the door
and was admitted almost at once.

To the men waiting outside the next twenty minutes seemed like
an hour. Something might have gone wrong and the gang failed to
appear. Alternatively they might be in the hut and be unconvinced
by George in which case they would probably be taking him apart.
All the time the moon shone down and the tension rose, but the men
had to keep still and quiet while the sweat cooled on their backs.
Eventually the door opened and a form slid out into the shadow of
the hut. Thinking it was George, Eric was about to move but stopped
himself just in time. The man passed less than five yards away and
disappeared into the darkness. Nothing more happened.

Then before they realized it George was with them again. It
transpired that only one member of the gang had been in the hut
when George arrived; the rest were waiting a few hundred yards
away. The terrorist had been suspicious but George thought that he
had convinced him. He had now gone to fetch his friends. Meanwhile our team were to go into the hut where two members of the
committee were waiting for them.

So far so good, although the situation was not altogether satisfactory. For one thing the gang might not be convinced, in which
case our men would be hopelessly trapped once they went inside the
hut. Another hazard was that the gang supporters might become
suspicious before the gang arrived. They had seen George often
enough, but they had not met Kamau or Eric before. Finally the
preliminaries had taken longer than had been expected and the
police might arrive before the gang assembled or they might all
arrive at the same time which would give rise to an appalling
shambles. Despite these considerations there was only one thing to
do and the four men went into the hut.

Luckily it was very dark inside. George and the two committee
men sat on stools round the glowing remains of the fire in the centre
of the floor. They did all the talking while the other members of our
party squatted in silence up against the wall as befitted the bodyguard of a gang leader. For the first time since his capture Kamau
seemed to be entirely at ease and enjoying himself.

Five minutes later the gang appeared. No one had heard a
whisper or the snap of a twig. Although momentarily expected,
their arrival produced the effect of an electric shock. These were the
people we had been hunting for so long, but as they crowded in

through the door and squatted down on the floor it was an open question as to who was hunting whom.

Altogether eleven terrorists had turned up. Of the other four, there was a good chance that two or three were away so that only one would have been left outside as a sentry. Of the men in the hut, two had pistols, three had rifles and the rest had home-made guns or simis. The first few minutes were taken up with formal greetings between George and the leader of the real gang but then they got down to business.

Inside the hut, as the talks went on, conditions were quite disgusting. Smoke from a dozen cigarettes and from the fire mingled with the smell of food and of the men themselves. Visibility was down to a few inches. Under these circumstances it was difficult to think clearly and decisive action by anyone, pressed together as they were like sardines in a tin, would be very difficult.

Unlike most settlers Eric knew a bit of Kikuyu as well as Swahili, so he was able to follow the gist of the discussion. He knew that George and the gang leader would go round and round the main purpose of the meeting for a long time before actually grasping the nettle because this is the Kikuyu way of approaching a problem. At the same time he soon became aware that the negotiations were not going well. They had got on to the explosive subject of whether the Mau Mau in Kiambu or Fort Hall were contributing most to the movement. Our pseudo-gang and therefore George represented terrorists from Kiambu whereas the real gang were men of Fort Hall.

At one moment it seemed as though the issue would give rise to a free fight but then a strange thing happened. Kamau had edged his way forward so that he was sitting between George and the gang leader, but slightly behind them. He now took a hand in the conversation and, although he talked quietly and slowly compared with the other two, it soon became clear that he spoke as one having authority. As the minutes ticked by, the tension relaxed and friendship was restored. It seemed as though everyone wanted to be on Kamau's side so there was no longer any point in having an argument. Watching from the wings Eric got the feeling that Kamau had forgotten that he was working for us and was back with the terrorists in spirit as well as in body.

Suddenly this new-found harmony was shattered by two terrific bangs followed by prolonged and piercing screams. Then the door of the hut flew open and the police inspector stood in the opening, sub-machine gun at the ready.

Our own men who had been expecting the interruption were none the less frightened by what had happened. The real gang were naturally terrified. Kamau was the first to collect his wits: he kept shouting out that all was lost and urged surrender. The terrorists would undoubtedly have done so without delay had it not been for their leader who raised his pistol to fire. At the same instant George pitched him forward into the fire and Kamau jumped on his back thrusting his face down into the red-hot embers. His command to fight changed abruptly into a yell of agony.

For the next few moments all hell was let loose. The police inspector was followed into the hut by his askaris who laid about them with their rifle butts, roaring with excitement. All our men received bruises and the unfortunate George was knocked unconscious. Eventually order was restored and the prisoners secured. Outside in the moonlight two policemen bent over an African who was lying on the ground. His shrieks had given way to a persistent low moaning as a pool of blood seeped slowly out of his body into the grass. It was the sentry and he died within a few minutes.

That was the end of Eric's story. There was no doubt that the operation had been an immense success and the credit was due to the Thika Military Intelligence Officer who had planned it and to the Field Intelligence Assistant who had carried it out. Credit was also due to Eric for the part he had played and in particular for his selection of Kamau as back-up for George. This had been a risk, but one which had paid off handsomely. It would have been interesting to know what Kamau thought about the business. As Eric told his story I could see him through the doorway of our house: he was squatting on the ground playing draughts with another member of the team. It did not look as though his conscience was troubling him for the way he had betrayed his former friends. On the contrary he looked relaxed and completely at one with his surroundings. Later I came to know Kamau well. In doing so I formed one of the most rewarding of friendships and I also learned how to use the best in one's enemies to achieve one's military aims, a lesson which I was able to put to good use far beyond the borders of Kenya.

Chapter 4

❋

Kamau

Seven terrified Africans were sitting in a circle on the floor of a hut round a big bowl. Beside it lay a dead goat, a dripping red gash across its throat. Over the bowl was an arch of banana leaves and thorns on which were impaled the goat's eyes. In the centre of the circle stood a hard-core forest terrorist. Round the wall were four more gangsters each holding a naked simi. Lanterns lit the scene.

In turn each of the seven Africans lifted the bowl to his lips seven times. It contained an unspeakably revolting mixture, the least foul ingredient being blood from the goat and a few handfuls of sacred soil, that is to say, earth. As each of the men drank, the terrorist in the centre of the circle intoned these words:

> 'If anyone tells about this oath, he will die like this goat has died.'
> 'If you tell your wife, or anyone who has not taken this oath – you will die.'
> 'If the father of the girl you wish to marry asks you about this oath – you will die.'
> 'You will forsake your friends, if they have not taken this oath.'
> 'At night you will not sleep heavily, but will be ready for a call.'
> 'You will help all those who have taken this oath.'
> 'If you help anyone who has not taken this oath, you will die.'

The sentry, who was looking out through the door of the hut, half saw and half felt the forest-clad mountain which hung over them like a thundercloud. The forest edge was less than half a mile away. He turned to see how the ceremony was getting on and found one of the goat's eyes staring at him from the arch of thorns. I was the sentry, Kamau was administering the oath and the other gangsters were all members of our Special Methods team.

In order to pass ourselves off as gangsters we had to administer the Mau Mau oath from time to time. Most oathing ceremonies started by disembowelling a live goat, castrating a donkey or beating a dog to death with seven heavy blows from a club. I considered such activities inconsistent with my membership of the RSPCA. By careful research we discovered methods of invoking the power of the oath which were effective in the eyes of the Kikuyu, repulsive enough to satisfy the Mau Mau and which did not involve any greater suffering for goats than was inevitable for the provision of raw meat, blood and other necessary parts.

In due course this particular ceremony came to an end and one of our men collected the money. He demanded twenty-seven shillings from each person, but no one had that much on him, so he took what they had and duly entered the amount received and the amount still owing in an exercise book.

Inside the hut the smell of the goat's blood and stomach content mingled with the smell of the men and the heat of their bodies to produce an atmosphere which was most unpleasant. Walking outside was like diving into the icy waters of a Norwegian fjord. We were at an altitude of 8,000 feet and there was little similarity with the balmy air of the Thika coffee farms. We moved off along a track which followed the crest of the ridge and a bitter wind cut through us despite our heavy coats. After a time the track left the crest and wound down the precipitous side of a valley through thick bracken onto the bank of a stream. At this point we entered the forest.

There had been little enough light in the Reserve because, despite a waning moon, the sky was overcast. It was October and it was raining. Once inside the forest it was pitch-dark and I could only stumble forward, my sights on Kamau's back a few inches in front of my nose. We were led by a man who knew the area intimately and who had no difficulty in finding his way around. Early on we ran into great mounds of elephant droppings on the path and we must have passed close to the elephants themselves because we could hear them as they moved around crushing and crumpling half-grown trees in their slow and deliberate way. Some time later we scrambled up a slope and came out onto a broad track. It led from the Tribal Reserve to a saw-mill deep in the forest. We had driven in along it and our Landrover was hidden nearby. I had no idea which way we should turn but our guide knew all right and we soon found the vehicle. We piled in and set off for home.

The journey back to our post took about an hour. To start with the surface of the road was pure mud and we skidded slowly from side to side. As we got further from the forest it became dryer and the clouds above us thinned out. Eventually the sky cleared and the moon came through to light up the hairpin bends and embankments, the streams crossed by primitive log bridges and the clusters of round thatched huts as the road wound its way from ridge to ridge through the fertile Kikuyu farmland. Just before we reached the border of the Reserve and the Settled Area a leopard trotted across the track for all the world like a fox returning from a visit to an English farmyard. Although there were plenty of leopards around it was unusual to see them.

We arrived home at about 1 a.m. to find a dance in progress. Every now and then Eric allowed our men to brew native beer which they made with yeast from either honey or bananas. Friends and acquaintances from round about would foregather and dance out of doors in the compound to the music of a bucket struck by an iron bar, augmented by rattles and tins tied round the legs of the dancers. We parked the car and I went into the house to change, after which I joined the party. I soon found myself sitting next to Kamau on a wattle bench under the avocado pear tree. I asked him whether he was going to dance, but he said that dancing was for the young men. At twenty-four he was considerably older than most of our people and for that matter older than most of the terrorists in the forest.

The assembled company represented a pretty fair cross-section of the sort of Africans with whom we did business. All our own men were there together with a number of workers from the nearby coffee estates. Some of them I recognized as men who occasionally picked up odd bits of information for us, whereas others were definitely Mau Mau supporters. Across the compound Eric was talking to the son of one of the Chiefs and three or four tribal policemen were happily drinking away with the African foreman of a big European farm. This man was a great personality in the area, a pillar of the Christian Church and leader of an enthusiastic band of Kikuyu Guard. Four months later we discovered that he was also a member of the Mau Mau Central Committee, but for the moment he was an honoured guest, held up by the Government as the perfect example of a fearless loyalist and devoted subject of the Queen. Two of the men actually dancing were prisoners, captured in the forest a few days previously. Within a few weeks one of them might easily be a member of our team, sharing in our expeditions and joining in the life of our community.

As so often happened my thoughts turned to the question of what it was that made men change from one side to the other. Our success as an intelligence organization depended on their doing so. I asked Kamau in my primitive Swahili but his answer was not very informative. 'I don't really know,' he said and then after a long pause added, 'everyone who does change must have a reason, but they don't all do it for the same reason.'

I knew Kamau's history well enough. He had been born and had grown up on a European farm in the Rift Valley, but when the Emergency started he and his parents had been sent back to that part of the Reserve from which the family had emigrated years before Kamau was born. They went to live in a seven-acre farm belonging to Kamau's cousin but the farm could barely support the cousin's family let alone any extra. From all the country round about the young men were flocking off to join the gangs in the forest and when Kamau received a summons he went without regret. Whilst still in the Rift Valley Kamau had taken the first Mau Mau oath which was designed to gain the support of all members of the tribe. This was the oath which we had been administering earlier in the evening. He had not been particularly keen to do so but the only person who had refused flatly was murdered, and in any case Kamau did not disapprove of the Mau Mau aim of getting back land stolen from the tribe by Europeans. He had no means of knowing that the land issue was largely bogus and was being exploited by African politicians for their own purposes.

When he joined the gang he took the batuni oath, reserved for the fighters, and was subjected to further propaganda in the form of songs which the terrorists sang, extolling their political leaders and expressing their determination to liberate the sacred soil. The gang lived deep in the forest, received ample support from the Reserve and did very little. Sometimes they debouched from their hide-out, burnt a few huts and murdered any supporters of the Government they could find. It was a good life. Later on as a result of operations by the Security Forces, the gang found that they were getting less support from the Reserve and they were frequently obliged to move their camp. Some of them were killed and others became ill from lack of a suitable diet and from constant exposure to the weather. Long before he was captured Kamau had begun to wonder whether the Mau Mau were ever likely to achieve anything by their actions. When he reached our post and started talking to our team his doubts were confirmed. Whatever else happened the Mau Mau were obviously not going to beat the Kikuyu Guard, backed up by the police and the British army. Kamau decided that the best thing for the Kikuyu was to stop fighting and try and achieve their aspirations in conjunction with the colonial Government. He had nowhere particular to go so he decided to stay with us. He also felt that by making himself useful he might avoid being hanged which was the penalty for being a gang member. He had told me all this before, except for the last bit and I believed him.

'I know why you joined our organization', I said, 'but what about George?'

'George is different', he answered. 'George does not mind about the Mau Mau or the Government and he certainly does not care who wins. George just likes excitement. He wants to walk around with a pistol and get plenty of loot. He changed sides because he could do all this better with you and be more comfortable at the same time.'

'Well then, what about Chege? He would not help us in any way at all, even though you all tried to show him that the Mau Mau could not possibly win. I can't believe he joined the Mau Mau for loot or excitement. Why do you think he was so stubborn? He was not even a prominent member of his gang.'

'Few men are like Chege,' Kamau said. 'When he gets an idea into his head the only way to get it out is by cutting it out with a simi. He was not a gang leader, as it happens, but some of the gang leaders are like him. Also some are like George, for that matter.'

'Are any of the gang leaders like you?' I asked.

'No,' he said smiling slightly. 'All gang leaders are Kali Sana (very fierce). I am not fierce.'

Although Kamau might not regard himself as fierce, he was of course quite happy to take part in raids which would inevitably result in burnings and murders. He was not in the least squeamish about such things and his simi would slash away with the rest. He was in fact a perfectly normal Kikuyu and had been brought up like his father before him to regard such action as the routine business of tribal fighting. To be on the losing side merely meant that death came from an enemy rather than from a charging elephant or some virulent epidemic. Although there was more security under British rule than there had been, the Kikuyu still lived much closer to disaster than we did in England. It is quite pointless to try and judge people against a background which is not their own.

My discussion with Kamau was one of many. I was gradually arriving at a conclusion which I have found to hold good in various different places. Briefly it is that three separate factors have to be brought into play in order to make a man shift his allegiance. In the first place he must be given an incentive which is strong enough to make him want to do so. This is the carrot. Then he must be made to realize that failure will result in something very unpleasant happening to him. This is the stick. Thirdly he must be given a reasonable opportunity of proving both to himself and to his friends that there is nothing fundamentally dishonourable about his action. Some people consider that the carrot and stick provide all that is necessary, but I am sure that many people will refuse the one and face the other, if by doing otherwise they lose their self-respect. On the other hand few people will choose the harder course if they think that both are equally consistent with their ideals.

If these three factors are accepted then the next problem is to discover enough about the person concerned to enable them to be applied in the right proportions. For example, in the case of George the incentive of a happy life with lots of fun and loot might have been accepted without the alternative of a death sentence being suggested. But even George was glad to be able to say that he thought that the good of the Kikuyu lay more in co-operating with the Government than in opposing it. Kamau on the other hand genuinely believed that this was true and this belief actually became part of the incentive for him to change sides. Employment, good company and a steady wage were important additional considerations. Everyone was different and during the last year of my appointment I used to spend a lot of time discussing gang members still in the forest with those already captured so as to weigh up their characters and be ready to get to work on them as soon as they were caught. By this means we were sometimes able to persuade people to change sides within a few hours of capturing them, which could produce spectacular results because the information gained thereby was correspondingly up to date.

It is perhaps unnecessary to add that the system only works when a suitable incentive can be offered, when it can be balanced against a sufficiently horrific alternative and when an honourable reason for changing sides can be displayed. It is part of the Government's job to see that such a situation exists, not only for the benefit of the intelligence service, but also because the whole aim of opposing rebels is to deprive them of the people's support. In Kenya I took such a situation for granted.

At about 3 a.m. I went into the house and read a book for an hour which I had to do in preparation for taking the Staff College entrance exam. I then went to bed. The room in which the captured gang members lived opened out of my bedroom. They slept there to show that we trusted them which was an important aspect of preparing them to join our pseudo-gang teams, but it sometimes made me feel a bit nervous. Luckily I was usually too busy or interested to feel nervous, but it would be foolish to pretend that the life we were leading was entirely free of care because a certain element of risk attached to our activities both in the post and when we were outside it on operations. But most of my people were young enough to take risks without much bother. I had arrived in Kenya when I was twenty-six and was almost the oldest man in my force.

By the late summer of 1954 my job had been further enlarged. I still covered Kiambu, Thika and Nairobi Districts and had certain responsibilities in Fort Hall District as well. These four Districts were collectively known as Central Province South. But by this time it looked probable that the trouble might be spreading into the area to the south of the Kikuyu country so I was told to watch Southern Province as well. Another task which came my way was to set up a Training Centre to which all the Military Intelligence Officers and Field Intelligence Assistants in the Colony would go for short courses. I was by this time a major and I had six captains helping me. There were also about twenty young settlers from the Kenya Regiment like Eric Holyoak, who did the work. Most of the Field Intelligence Assistants had built posts in the area in which they operated and had collected groups of loyalists and ex-terrorists to man them and to form pseudo-gangs of their own. Altogether our part of Special Branch had become quite large.

It is perhaps worth saying a word about the way in which the pseudo-gang idea spread because in one form or another it played an important part in defeating the Mau Mau. There was in fact nothing original about the idea itself, variations of which have been used in countless wars throughout history. It was taken up by Field Intelligence Assistants in many parts of the Emergency area and although there can be little doubt that Eric and his men were first in the field in terms of time, it does not mean that everyone else got the idea from him. They could easily have thought it up for themselves and they certainly did develop it to suit conditions in their own areas as they developed various other ideas for getting information.

In this context there was one important exploitable factor which was that many Africans were only too eager to help us destroy Mau Mau if they could do so without being discovered. An effective method of using such people was to get the police and army to cordon an area where Mau Mau were particularly active and round up every single person. At the same time we would collect together a few of the people who wanted to help us and who had knowledge of the area in which the round-up was taking place, and clothe them from head to foot in huge hoods with holes for the eyes. We then brought them to the cordon and made all those who had been rounded up pass in front of them. When one of our hooded men recognized one of these men as a Mau Mau he told us what he knew about him. If two or three hooded men, who were often not even known to each other, said the same thing, we arrested the person and interrogated him. A big operation of this sort lasting all day might result in our catching fifty or sixty prominent supporters and a handful of forest gangsters who were visiting them. It was in fact another method of turning background information, that is to say our knowledge of once-time Mau Mau supporters who wanted to help us, into contact information.

In the last resort everything depended on the background information which we could collect and on our ability to store it and find it when we wanted it. We were soon aware of the importance of informers and interrogation in providing background information, but it took us some time even to realize that a problem existed in terms of the storage of information. Our Field Intelligence Assistants were all young outdoor men. To start with many of them made no written record of interrogations and informer reports, but relied on remembering what was important when they needed it, rather like I had suddenly remembered when interrogating George, that we had captured a book which might be helpful. But gradually the penny dropped and we started to build up proper records. In fact I spent a lot of time working out exactly what degree of detail should be kept at each level and I even made it mandatory for every Field Intelligence Assistant to carry a skeleton card index and a book record of certain particular things on his person wherever he went. Years later, having introduced a similar sort of system in Belfast I saw it described in a newspaper as 'making war with a filing cabinet' and that is exactly what it is.

By the end of 1954 the Mau Mau were beginning to break up under the pressure exerted on them. The committees of supporters in Nairobi and in the Tribal Reserves were constantly being arrested and consequently the gangs in the forest were becoming weaker. One result of this was that the whole concept of a Mau Mau base encompassing Nairobi and the District of Kiambu collapsed and the various strong-arm groups coalesced and took to the forest instead of carrying out their proper function of coercing people into providing money and organizing the collection and despatch of recruits. Although this represented a significant weakening of the Mau Mau position overall, it did mean that Kiambu District became more disturbed, as relatively large gangs raided into the Kiambu Reserve from the forest in the same way as forest gangs had done in the Districts further north in the preceding year. 1955 was therefore a stormy year in my area.

It could be argued that it took longer to rid Kiambu of its gangs than was strictly necessary and if this is so the reason probably lies in the difficulty which the army found in making use of the background information which was produced for it. If we could develop it for the army by using special methods such as pseudo-gangs all was well, but if not the military mind stuck firmly to the large-scale hit-or-miss type operation. One such operation known as Dante was launched in July 1955.

The plan for this operation provided for four battalions to surround that part of the forest in which it was thought that two large gangs were living. Each battalion would establish a string of ambushes in their own area after which bombs and artillery would pound the region inside the cordon in the hope that the gangs would move outwards and run into the ambushes. After ten days the battalions would advance into the middle to mop up. The only trouble was that there would be about ninety square miles of dense forest inside the cordon.

Early in the morning of July 15th the Kiambu Military Intelligence Officer and I drove to a village called Matara in the extreme north-west corner of the Reserve to watch the first moves of the operation. We established ourselves in the tower of the Kikuyu Guard post there while it was still dark. June is perhaps the coldest time of the year in Kenya and this Friday morning was no exception, but the surprising thing was the light. It had been raining for most of the night, but the sky had cleared a couple of hours earlier and dawn, when it came, flooded the landscape with a hundred shades of blue, purple and red. The huge outline of the South Aberdare peak, known from its shape as the elephant, seemed to rise out of the ground a few hundred yards away, an illusion produced by its size and by the extreme clarity of the air. Stretching away to the north-east of us lay the ridges and valleys of the Fort Hall Reserve and beyond them the plains of Embu. The backcloth of this magnificent scene was its crowning glory: 17,000 feet of Mount Kenya reached up into the crimson sky, its snow-capped peak dominating the whole picture.

For a long time it was impossible to look at, or think about anything else, but eventually the noise of army lorries grinding along the muddy road below our tower caused me to look away. Beyond the fort soldiers were jumping out of trucks and joining a snake-like procession which disappeared into the forest. Close to us other men were erecting an aerial rod and a tent. This was to be the command post of 2/6 Kings African Rifles, one of the four battalions taking part in the operation.

I could only have been looking at the soldiers for ten minutes at the most, but when I turned back the view had gone. The brilliant colours of a moment ago had given place to grey and great banks of cloud were already building up over the forest. Mount Kenya had disappeared completely, although the foot-hills were still faintly visible across fifty miles of dull, damp land. This rapid change was both startling and ominous. A further spell of foul weather seemed certain.

We climbed down from the tower to start a round of visits to the units taking part. We were not expecting to get any information on this occasion because the first day would obviously be taken up by the soldiers moving into position. Our purpose was to ensure that

the various Commanders and their staffs – most of whom were new
to the area – would know how to contact us if they wanted to do so.

Somewhat naturally our first call was to the battalion of the Kings
African Rifles who were setting up their command post in Matara.
We arrived just as the Commanding Officer returned from the
forest edge where he had been watching his men move into position.
He was in great form and was particularly pleased that all the vehicles had managed to get to the debussing point on time despite a
long approach in the dark down muddy tracks and without lights.
It turned out that all four battalions had succeeded in this respect
and credit is due to the staff of the brigade Headquarters for
organizing this part of the operation. The planning and execution of
activities of this sort usually shows the British army at its best.

From Matara we drove along an appalling track through the
forest emerging ultimately on the west side near Njabini. Here we
visited the Gloucestershire Regiment and the brigade Headquarters.
The next leg of our journey ran south down the west side of the forest
to the Kings Shropshire Light Infantry. On the way we passed a
battery of anti-aircraft guns, which for want of rebel aircraft were
going to fire into the centre of the forest as part of the plan. Their
long barrels and lightweight shells seemed to symbolize the hopeless-
ness of our tactics: they could hardly be expected to do much good,
firing blindly into forty or fifty square miles of dense jungle.

The final part of our drive involved passing back through the
forest, this time from west to east, in order to visit the Irish Fusiliers
whose Headquarters had been set up on the edge of the Kiambu
Reserve. We arrived in time to witness the start of the bombard-
ment. This consisted of the anti-aircraft guns firing a few shells into
the trees followed by an attack from the air. As we watched, a flight
of Harvard trainers dived out of the clouds and dropped 250-pound
bombs. Finally a few Lincolns, ancient relics of Hitler's war,
lumbered across the target area dropping 1000-pound bombs and
spraying the forest with cannon fire for good measure. Standing in
the doorway of the Irish Fusiliers' Mess tent with a cup of tea in my
hand, I wondered what the effect of this action was likely to be. The
target area was pretty vast and the dense vegetation and steep slopes
would greatly reduce the effect of the explosions. One way or another
it would be surprising if the enemy were frightened, let alone hurt.

By the time we got home it was dark. The operation lasted for
three weeks during which time one of us or Eric went round the

units daily. When a terrorist was killed we took the body for identification. We also translated documents, traced the history of captured weapons and did what we could to build up a picture of
events. There were no prisoners until two men were captured in the
last few days of the operation. In the end Dante was reckoned to
have accounted for about thirty terrorists, but this figure included
everyone killed within ten miles of the operational area!

On the whole the operation was a colossal and expensive failure
like all other big operations mounted in similar circumstances.
Fortunately it was the last of its kind. In all fairness it is necessary to
add that many more terrorists would have been killed had the
soldiers shot straighter.

Soon after operation Dante an operation of a totally different
sort took place. While Dante was going on we were unable to patrol
into the forest with a pseudo-gang for obvious reasons, but as soon
as it was over Eric and I went in. Although we failed to make
contact with a gang, we found plenty of recent tracks and camp-
sites. We also found a dead letter-box containing a note to the leader
of one of the supply groups which indicated that the gang itself
would be in the area shortly.

A few days later one of the District Officers developed a new sort
of hit-or-miss operation based on the theory that as the troops could
not find gangsters in thick cover he would try removing the cover.
As an experiment he selected a small area of forest where he thought
a gang might be living, surrounded it with Kikuyu Guard and then
set 5,000 local women to work cutting down the undergrowth. By
the evening all the undergrowth had gone and three terrorists who
had been hiding there were literally cut to pieces.

Our patrol and the development of this new method set the scene
for a most unusual operation. The Kiambu District Emergency
Committee decided to try what had become known as a population
sweep in the area where we had found the letter-box, in the hopes
that the gang to whom the letter had been addressed would by now
have arrived there. Arrangements were made to collect a cutting
force of no less than 17,000 women. The operation was scheduled to
take place on August 18th.

Nine a.m. was selected as the time at which the line of cutters was
to move forward. Making my way to the area was like driving to
Epsom on Derby day. While still some miles off I started to pass
little groups of women moving towards the rendezvous: further on

the track became increasingly crowded. Soon there were women to
be seen in all directions: there were young ones, slim and graceful,
and old ones bent from humping heavy loads up and down the steep
tracks of their homeland. They mostly wore brightly-coloured cotton
dresses and many of them had heavy wire rings hanging in the lobes
of their ears or bound round their dark-skinned necks. Some carried
a bag or satchel of some sort and many others had babies slung on
their backs. It was a fine day and the sun glinted on the blades of a
thousand pangas.

Getting the women spread out round the selected bit of forest was
a major undertaking, which was ultimately accomplished. Kikuyu
Guard armed with shot-guns or rifles were posted at intervals along
the line. Police with walkie-talkie wireless sets stationed themselves
at strategic positions around the cordon. Eventually all was ready
and the Superintendent of Police gave the signal to get going. I did
not see the operation start because I had been told that some Tribal
Police had shot a terrorist just outside the cordon while the women
were assembling. A group of three had been ambushed, but the
other two had got away. I picked up the body and returned to the
scene of events as quickly as I could, fearing to miss some interesting
occurrence.

There was not long to wait. Soon after my return I noticed a great
commotion at one point in the line. From where I stood it looked
like a rugger scrum out of which steel blades flashed rhythmically in
the sun. For one awful moment I thought that the women had come
upon a terrorist and were chopping him up. I ran to the scene, but
on arrival found that the victim was a small buck. By this time the
girls had stopped chopping and were standing there, panting and
sweating: blood streaked their arms and legs and dripped from their
long sharp knives. The lucky ones were stuffing bits of flesh into
bags and satchels presumably looking forward to the unaccustomed
luxury of venison for supper, although strictly speaking the eating of
wild animals was not permitted in the usage of the tribe.

The next incident occurred about half a mile from the first one and
this time a terrorist was shot and killed by Kikuyu Guard interspersed
in the line of cutters. The incident took place in a much thicker part
of the forest and the women were unable to concentrate on the body
in large numbers. A District Officer managed to get possession of the
body quite quickly and he had it carried out to the edge of the
forest. I met the bearer party coming along a narrow track between

the thick, tangled undergrowth and a moment or two later we were joined by Eric and some of his men. Although the terrorist had been cut about a good deal and one of his legs had been severed at the knee, he was immediately identified as the leader of a supply party, the man who had written the letter which we had found earlier.

The next contact was rather more exciting and occurred about an hour and a half later. This time three terrorists were involved. They had evidently been falling back before the oncoming line of cutters, but had got worried when they heard chopping behind them as well. They decided to open fire at the cordon and dash through it. Unfortunately for them they had left it a bit late because by the time they took the decision they had retreated out of the thickest cover and were in a part of the forest where the big trees had been cut so they were relying on undergrowth alone.

Eric and I were standing about two hundred yards away when the terrorists opened fire. Immediately the women hurled themselves to the ground and the terrorists jumped up to break the line. But ranges were short and there were plenty of Kikuyu Guard around. A moment later all three were down and we ran forward to prevent the women from chopping up the bodies. By this time we had armed ourselves with sticks and we managed to keep the girls at bay. It was as well that we did so because two of the three were important men, one being the gang leader himself, a fact which made us all feel that the operation had been worth while.

In fact this was by no means the end of the business. By the time the operation was called off in the evening eighteen terrorists had been killed and we were all exhausted. The greatest surprise came when the body which I had picked up in the morning turned out to be none other than the senior gang leader from Kiambu District.

Altogether the results of this one day achieved far more than most of the big military operations. Admittedly this was partly due to the killing of this particular gang leader which was luck rather than good management. But also the result was due to the destruction of the senior men of the gang which the District Emergency Committee had set out to destroy. We also recovered a number of documents and took a prisoner which enabled us to build up a much more detailed picture of what had been going on in the gangs than anything we had had since the days before operation Dante. This information also served as a jumping-off point for a series of pseudo-gang patrols which piled success upon success during the next six weeks. By the end of this time all except one of the main Kiambu gangs had been broken up and their leaders captured or killed.

These operations served as a culmination to my tour of duty in Kenya which finished at the end of 1955. As the gangs broke up and the members of them were taken prisoner, I was able to meet many of the people we had been thinking about and chasing for months, which was an interesting and pleasant experience. The worst aspect of the final few weeks was the severing of so many friendships, but by the time I left most of my original companions had left the Security Forces to return to their civilian occupations because they had only been called up for two years' service in the first place. Apart from Eric, who had returned home soon after the last operation described here, Kamau had been my closest friend and associate. He it was who saw me off from the airport on the sunny morning when I left for England and for my next job which was to be a student at the Staff College in Camberley.

Chapter 5

❊

Time for Reflection

A shaft of sunlight came through the window and picked out the paper, pencils and india-rubber lying on my desk. There was also a full ash-tray of cigarette ends, and a couple of photographs: one of Eric and one of Kamau. Outside, small white clouds were chasing each other across a blue April sky. The oak trees round the lake were tinged with a yellow-green promise for the month of May while birches already in full leaf swayed with the breeze. Far beneath my third-storey window beds of wallflowers looked up from the edge of the lawn, scenting the air with their fragrance. This was the Staff College, but even after four months in England, Kenya and the Mau Mau were seldom out of my mind. At night I dreamed about them and early each morning lying in bed in the first moments after waking I imagined myself back in my rickety old house wondering what the day would bring. But soon reality forced itself upon me and I knew that I should spend my time confined to a class-room instead of running my little army. It was a bit of a come-down and in any case my mind was teeming with ideas about Kenya and its problems. The Commandant of the Staff College evidently understood my predicament because he asked me to write a paper about my experiences which he could forward to the War Office. Unfortunately he did not tell me exactly what my paper should be about and I was having trouble in deciding on a subject which would yield a worthwhile return.

Although I did not know it at the time, the campaign as a whole had been well handled. The series of committees starting with the Governor's council at the top and working down through Provinces and Districts had enabled economic and political advances to be made in conjunction with the operations of the Security Forces and the Administration had taken advantage of the crisis to force through many progressive measures which would have been bitterly opposed by the settlers under normal circumstances. This fact greatly strengthened the hand of those Africans who advocated progress in co-operation with the Government, rather than in opposition to it and the internment of the nationalist politicians who wished to follow a different line further damaged the cause of the extremists.

The military campaign was also well planned by the Commander in Chief, General Erskine. Appreciating the fact that the Kikuyu could not respond to the Government's approach unless they were adequately protected, he gave first priority to the establishment of the Kikuyu Guard as a defensive force in the tribal area and to the removal of the Mau Mau cells and committees which were directing the coercion of the loyalists. As his second priority he broke up the Kiambu and Nairobi base complex by isolating the one from the other and by removing the cells and committees which were organizing the collection of recruits and supplies for the forest. Only then did he launch his main attack on the forest gangs and by this time they were beginning to wither as their support waned. During the first two phases the gangs had of course been harried in the forest by sweeps, bombings and patrols.

An important aspect of the campaign had been the massive use made of internment to rid the tribal areas and Nairobi of the Mau Mau cells and committees. In Kenya internment without trial was used in conjunction with an efficient system of rehabilitation designed to turn a Mau Mau supporter into a loyalist by removing him from the pressures of his environment and by explaining the realities of the situation to him. Those interned were segregated into groups according to the extent of their commitment and then moved from one group to another as their opinions altered. As soon as they were considered to be free of Mau Mau influence they were released into the care of their locational Chief who watched them and incorporated them into the loyalist community. Altogether possibly as many as 75,000 Africans went through this process and in many cases a man would only be away from his home for a short time. A relatively small number would not respond to treatment, of whom about 1,000 remained in detention for a few years after the fighting ceased. Internment without trial is not an attractive measure to people brought up in a free country, but in Kenya it undoubtedly saved many lives by shortening the conflict and by removing from the scene people who would otherwise have become involved in the fighting. It was as well that it did reduce casualties since the scale of bloodshed was sufficiently horrifying as it was. In the three busiest years of the Emergency something like twelve Kikuyu were killed in Kenya for every one man killed in Northern Ireland in the years 1971, 1972 and 1973, although the population and geographical area were roughly the same in each case. There is no doubt that Kenya was the most violent of the counter-insurgency campaigns in which I have taken part.

When it came to writing my paper my first reaction was to overlook the efficiency with which the campaign had been conducted and to draw attention to all the intolerable circumstances which had surrounded us in our attempts to get information. The time spent investigating fictitious atrocities allegedly committed by loyalists, the hours wasted waiting to give evidence in court, the difficulties involved in getting people in the rear areas to support us energetically, all clamoured for attention and seemed to be matters worth mentioning. But they led nowhere because they were all troubles which were by the very nature of things bound to happen.

Then my thoughts went back to the ways we used for getting men to change sides. It seemed to me that the carrot and stick method which we adopted was capable of a wider application. The first aim of a government in an Emergency is to retain or regain the allegiance of the population. Perhaps this too should be handled on the basis of a policy of rewards backed up by threats of unpleasantness on a nationwide scale. There seemed to be something in this point worth writing about and arising out of it were such subjects as population control and the resettlement of communities in the interests of security. But after careful consideration I decided to leave these matters alone. I had not been personally involved in formulating Government policy in Kenya and was not qualified to write about it.

This left intelligence, but even this field would need narrowing down carefully before it could be expected to yield anything worthwhile, so I tried to concentrate on one or two fundamentals. The first point which stood out clearly was that the sort of information needed by the Government of a Colony after terrorism has started is of a different nature to that required beforehand, which might best be described as political information. Once an active enemy takes the field the Government wants the sort of information that will enable the Security Forces to round up or destroy the terrorists and those people who are supporting them. This might be described as operational information. The machine which exists in peace-time for getting political information is not organized for getting operational information and in any case the requirement for getting political information will continue and may even be increased. The second point which seemed to be of cardinal importance was the question of speed. When a terrorist organization first starts to operate it is extremely vulnerable because it only has the support of a small proportion of the people as a whole. Even if most of the population is in sympathy with the general aims of the movement they will not necessarily be prepared to help men whose business is murder and sudden death. Plenty of people will come forward with information at this stage providing an organization exists for collecting it and acting on it. But if this is not the case the terrorists will quickly gain the allegiance of the people by the simple expedient of killing or torturing all who oppose them. Once this has happened it is twenty times more difficult to get the information necessary to enable the Security Forces to destroy the terrorists and their supporters. Based on these two main points I decided that the aim of my paper would be to show how a colonial government gets operational information, to examine the short-comings of the system and to suggest a better one.

The paper started by pointing out that there is almost as much difference between the methods used to collect political information and those used to collect operational information as there is between the way in which an agent in England tracks a treacherous Admiralty official and the way in which a reconnaissance patrol in conventional war gets information about an enemy defensive position. The main reason for this is that political information can be built up over a period of days, weeks or months while operational information has to arrive in time to enable Security Forces to strike at a fleeting target. A good practical example of this difference of methods can be found by examining the sort of informer required to do the two jobs. High-grade and long-term agents are required in order to get political information of value and, as such people are hard to find, it follows that there will never be very many of them operating. On the other hand, the one essential when looking for operational information is to have a wide coverage and this in turn means that the informers are bound to be fairly low-grade people.

In one case therefore a few top-class men are needed and in the other, a mass of low-grade people are far more useful. An even wider divergence of method becomes apparent when consideration is given to the operation of pseudo-gangs and similar sorts of field-work.

The paper went on to show that the type of man needed for getting operational information was one who could lead, organize and administer a motley collection of local Europeans, informers and ex-terrorists. Such a man should be capable of inspiring confidence in, and co-operating with, officers of the Administration, police and army. The qualities required were energy, determination, imagination and leadership. Remembering the long hours spent trekking round the countryside by day and night I added that the suitable man must have an affection for his job overriding all other interests. Someone with a family in the theatre of operations would be unable to devote himself sufficiently to the task. From this point I went on to show that policemen who happened to be in the Special Branch of the Colony concerned were not necessarily the best people to take on the job of getting operational information. However well suited these men might be to getting political information they might not have the qualities required for getting operational information and even those who were suitable in this respect would need to be trained from scratch for the new job. Finally the requirement for getting political information does not come to a halt when terrorism starts and the people getting it cannot be spared. The paper next discussed the suitability of army intelligence officers for the job, but they too are trained for quite a different purpose. Their business is to put bits of information together, work out what it means and pass it around. They do the staff work involved in gathering information and some of them are needed for this purpose in Emergency situations. But they are no more qualified to pick up the information in the first place than are the policemen in Special Branch: less so if anything.

My solution to the problem was to raise a special unit of soldiers and policemen which could be held centrally and sent to any Colony which looked as if it were about to erupt. Each Colony was to earmark a number of local men who would receive part-time training on Territorial Army lines during periods of peace and who would reinforce the Special Unit when it arrived. My idea was that the Special Unit would provide the officers to work in District and Provincial Headquarters and that the local men would provide the equivalent of the Field Intelligence Assistants. I reckoned that in this way information would start coming in within days of trouble breaking out. The paper went into some detail regarding the problems of language and of training the Special Unit before it was deployed to a Colony. It also discussed important administrative problems such as the provision of adequate funds and transport. Above all it stressed over and over again that the key to fighting terrorism lay in getting enough operational information quickly.

When the Commandant received my paper he decided not to send it to the War Office. The trouble was that it cut across accepted principles in several important respects and he reckoned that it would be a waste of everybody's time to send it outside the Staff College. As an alternative he decided that it should be discussed within the College during the term set aside for the consideration of irregular warfare. The time appointed for this discussion was the second half of the morning of November 26th and the paper was issued to my fellow students a few days earlier. Realizing that my ideas represented some departure from accepted military practice I decided to try and acclimatize the minds of my colleagues. To this end I arranged for a leaflet to be printed which was circulated anonymously to all the students and directing staff, although the identity of the author did not long remain a secret. The leaflet purported to be an official Staff College publication written one hundred years in the future and it was dated October 1st 2056. It read as follows:

WORLD WAR III

World War III started shortly before the end of World War II. It was fought by both conventional forces and partisans.

The actions of the conventional forces were few and of comparatively little importance.

Even in World War II some people could see that where Communism was involved the action of guerrillas was already taking over to some extent.

Nations had practised partisan war for centuries but the Communists were probably the first people to teach it systematically as an integral part of operations. Certainly the Communists were the first to see that nuclear weapons made the old sort of war impractical and that in future the best way to wreck their opponents was by a mixture of people's uprisings and economic chicanery. They kept their armies as a threat and as a weapon with which to finish off the work of their partisans when no risk attached to their employment.

The leaders of the West were slower to understand. For many years bemused and bemedalled parties of the hydrogen hierarchy were talking petulantly about private armies. Their natural reluctance to grasp anything new was accentuated by their ability to see that promotion prospects were at best uncertain in a partisan force. Furthermore the whole idea was a little vulgar.

And so for many years the peoples of a hundred tribes fought in hate at the bidding of the Communists' leaders, knowing neither why, nor for whom, they struggled. In the first decade of World War III (1945–1955) the Communists succeeded in actuating partisans in North Africa, East Africa, Indo-China and Malaya, to mention only a few places. In each case the Western Powers countered with conventional forces which were totally unsuited to the task. They called it the 'Cold War' (though they found it so hot in Indo-China that they baled out). A few people realized that it was not the Cold War but *the* war. A terrific battle raged in the Western camp while these people tried to persuade their countrymen that information was the key to fighting modern war. (Even the elementary difference between intelligence and reconnaissance was unknown at that time.) The Old Guard stamped on the upstarts in a frenzy and ground many of them into paste.

Eventually daylight dawned. What started in 1945 as a collection of odds and ends known as Special Forces, developed into the main offensive and defensive weapon of the Western World. The West was in a position to turn the Communist weapon of popular uprising against its inventor, in the same way that the Communists had turned the tables on the West with nuclear missiles many years before.

CAMBERLEY
1 October 2056.

When my paper was discussed I naturally hoped that most of the time would be devoted to considering the main points of my case. It was quite clear to me that information was the key to fighting terrorists and that the right sort of people would not be available to collect it during the early stages of an Emergency unless something was arranged in advance. I was equally sure that long drawn out operations could only be avoided if an effective intelligence organization could be built up in time to eliminate the enemy before they could terrorize the population into supporting them. For these reasons I thought that the only solution lay in maintaining a suitable organization capable of going to any scene of trouble at short notice. Somewhat rashly I had suggested the form which such a unit might take. Unfortunately nearly all of the discussion period was taken up in arguing about the details of the plan for raising the force. Although most people paid lip-service to the need for good information, they were quite unable to do more than find fault with my proposals and no alternative ones were produced. Altogether it was a depressing performance.

The Staff College course finished in the middle of December. Some months earlier I had decided that the main lesson to be learnt at Camberley was to keep off the Staff and I lobbied hard in an attempt to return to my regiment at the end of the course. In this I was successful and my instructions were to report to the battalion in Malaya after Christmas and take over command of one of the companies. During my time in Kenya I had of course absorbed a lot of basic knowledge about fighting terrorists. I knew how the machinery for directing the activities of the Security Forces worked and how the various committees fitted in together. This knowledge would be of some use to me in Malaya. I had also worked out a number of ways for getting information about terrorists and I had been relatively successful in making contacts with them. But these methods mostly involved the use of special techniques which were not suited to the operations of a straightforward infantry company.

I have already shown that most of the company and battalion commanders in Kenya seemed to think that unless Special Branch could provide them with the sort of pinpoint information, which would enable them to bring their troops into contact with the enemy, they would have no alternative but to send their soldiers out to search large areas on a hit-or-miss basis. They did not seem capable of using the background information which we had collected, concerning enemy identities, habits, supply systems, weapons and organizations in such a way as to bring their men into contact with the enemy. Officers at Camberley who had served in Malaya told me that the same feeling existed among the company and battalion commanders there. Although I knew very little about the Special Branch in Malaya, I realized that my share of pinpoint information was likely to be small. At the same time I had no wish to spend most of my men's time searching vast areas of jungle on a hit-or-miss basis. I was sure that there must be a better way of doing business and it seemed likely that the key to the problem lay in exploiting the mass of background information which I hoped would be available. I had no clear idea as to how this might be done, but I intended to concentrate on this line of approach when I arrived in Malaya. In Kenya I had learnt how to develop background information using special methods. I went to Malaya intending to work out how to do this with ordinary soldiers.

Part II

Malaya

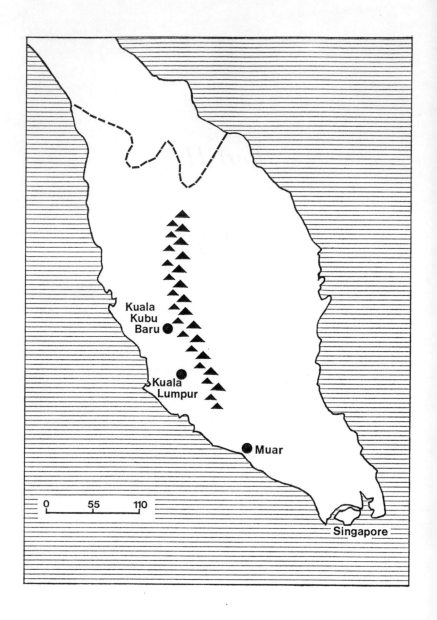

Kuala
Kubu
Baru

Kuala
Lumpur

Muar

0   55   110

Singapore

Chapter 6

❋

The Malayan Emergency

It can be argued that the Mau Mau Emergency happened more by accident than design in that it resulted from a loss of control on the part of those nationalist politicians who were organizing opposition to the policies of the Government. The same can never be said of the Malayan Emergency which was deliberately planned and executed by Communists for their own political purposes. Another important difference between the two Emergencies relates to the scale of the violence. In Kenya something like 12,500 people were killed over a period of three and a half years in an area which was about 150 miles long by 100 miles wide. In Malaya a slightly smaller number were killed over a period of ten years in an area which was about 500 miles long by 250 miles wide. In Kenya nearly all those killed came from the one and a half million members of the Kikuyu, Embu and Meru tribes. In Malaya, although the majority came from the Chinese population of two million, an appreciable number came from other races. In short, even allowing for the fact that many of the fatal casualties occurred in the first four years of the trouble and that 70 per cent of the geographical area concerned was covered in thick, uninhabitable jungle, the general level of violence was never comparable to that experienced in Kenya.

In 1786 Britain acquired Penang in the north-west corner of the Malay Peninsula thus starting her association with the country. At that time Malaya consisted of a number of Sultanates under varying degrees of influence and pressure from the Dutch who had a coastal settlement on the shores of the Malacca Straits. During the Napoleonic War the British proceeded to oust the Dutch and soon afterwards acquired Singapore. In 1824 Britain's paramount interest

over the whole Malay Peninsula and her possession of the Straits
Settlement was recognized by treaty. Meanwhile the Malays continued to be ruled by their Sultans to whom they were attached by
ties of affection, loyalty and the Mohammedan religion.

In 1867 the Straits Settlement, which had formerly been governed
from India, became a Colony. A few years later the British started to
inrease their influence in the four neighbouring Malay States by
obliging the Sultans to accept Residents whose 'advice' on all
matters, other than those concerned with religious observance, they
were required to accept. In 1896 these States became part of a
Federation. In 1909 the four Northern States of Malaya which had
formerly been Siamese dependencies accepted British Residents and
in 1914 Johore, the last remaining Sultanate, followed suit.

Tin-mining and rubber planting grew up in the wake of British
expansion and these two activitives gave Malaya an importance in
the world which she had never had before. They also dramatically
affected the racial structure of the population. For many years
Chinese and Indians had mixed with other foreigners in Malaya
where they had been active in commercial affairs and these people
were closely concerned with the development of the tin and rubber
industries. One of the problems facing them was the fact that
Malays were not, for the most part, prepared to operate the mines
and the plantations. As a result, there was a considerable influx of
Indian and Chinese labourers into the country during the second
half of the nineteenth century and the first three decades of the
twentieth. The Chinese in particular arrived in large numbers and
the mine owners and traders, who brought them in initially, resorted
to the traditional Chinese method of maintaining control over them,
that is to say they established a network of Secret Societies which
combined the functions of local government and welfare with varying degrees of economic management and domination. The Secret
Societies also fostered a sense of national unity within the growing
Chinese community which survived the break-up of the Societies
themselves at the hands of the British-run Administration towards
the turn of the century. The feeling of national unity amongst the
Chinese together with their addiction to Secret Societies was as important a factor in the development of the Emergency as was the
attachment of the Malays towards their Sultans and their religion.

After the demise of the Secret Societies the main national influence within the Chinese community was exercised by the Kuo-

mintang. In China the Communists split with the Kuomintang in 1927 and one of the effects of this was that a separate Malayan Communist Party was established within the Chinese community in 1930. Soon afterwards the world economic recession hit Malaya and a large number of Chinese labourers were thrown out of work, many of whom set themselves up as squatters along the edge of the jungle in places where they could scrape a living from the land and from the rivers. When Malaya was occupied by Japan in the Second World War the Malayan Communist Party, aided by the British, built up a guerrilla force known as the Malayan Peoples Anti Japanese Army which operated from the jungle. For its support it depended largely on the squatters who lived along the jungle edge. Some of these people gave their support willingly, but others had to be coerced and the Malayan Peoples Anti Japanese Army had to devote a lot of its efforts towards maintaining the solidarity of the Chinese community behind the movement. The Japanese set about breaking up the Chinese support organization with their customary brutality. Having less cause for conflict with the Malays they treated them more leniently, which naturally did little to cement good relations between the two communities.

The Malayan Communist Party had every intention of taking over the country in the wake of the Japanese withdrawal, but the end of the War came suddenly before their plans were complete and the British were able to re-establish their position, disbanding the Malayan Peoples Anti Japanese Army with expressions of goodwill, supplemented by gratuities and an appropriate issue of honours and awards. The British plan for Malaya at this time was to set up a unified multi-racial republic which could ultimately become an independent country within the Commonwealth, but this proposal, involving as it did a transfer of sovereignty from the Sultans, was strongly opposed by the Malays and was therefore dropped. Instead a new Federation of Malaya which included all nine States together with the settlements of Penang and Malacca was established, but this left the Malays in a favoured position in relation to the immigrant races and was therefore unpopular with both the Indians and the Chinese who together by this time formed nearly half of the total population. Had Singapore with its predominantly Chinese population been included in the Federation there would have been a comfortable Chinese majority, but for this reason among others it was not included.

But although Singapore was not brought into the Federation so far as the Government was concerned, it was included in the area covered by the Malayan Communist Party. Having failed to gain control of the country at the end of the War, the Communists set about developing new plans for the achievement of their aims. Surprisingly perhaps, they decided to switch their main effort away from the rural areas and to concentrate on building up a campaign of urban subversion in Singapore, which would be followed by similar action in the cities and towns of Malaya. The plan involved overt political activity by the then legal Malayan Communist Party in conjunction with infiltration of such organizations as Trade Unions and Youth Leagues. In the event, the Communists had a certain amount of success in fomenting strikes and riots, but they were obliged to resort to a high level of intimidation, especially within the Unions which did not help their cause. Furthermore, in concentrating on the cities the Communists tended to let their organization amongst the Chinese rural population lapse which was a mistake for which they later paid heavily.

In 1947 the Secretary General of the Malayan Communist Party absconded with the funds and was replaced by Chin Peng. This man was young and enthusiastic and he wasted no time in stepping up the campaign in the cities. But he soon saw that the urban campaign was not going to work and that disruption, violence and intimidation was causing the Communists to lose much of the support which they had formerly enjoyed. At the same time to call off the campaign so soon after the defection of the previous Secretary General would look like weakness and might even result in a general break-up of the Party. In fact, although the Communists had lost support in the cities, there was still a chance of capitalizing on the discontent which some of the Chinese in the rural areas felt for the new Federation of Malaya: at this time there were nearly half a million squatters around the jungle edge who might reasonably be expected to support a rural campaign. In May 1948 a decision was taken to launch a full-scale rebellion designed to seize control of Malaya and although this decision may have owed something to a series of high-level Communist meetings which had recently taken place in Prague, London and Calcutta, it is more likely that it resulted from a feeling that something drastic had to be done to hold the Party together.

Chin Peng's plan was to seize certain base areas and to expand outwards. In March 10,000 members of the old Malayan Peoples

Anti Japanese Army had been asked to return to the jungle and 3,000 had done so, calling themselves the Malayan Peoples Anti British Army. A further 7,000 part-time guerrillas organized themselves outside the jungle in what was known as the Self Protection Corps. The 3,000 regulars were formed up into eight regiments which soon increased to ten. State, District and Branch Committees of the Malayan Communist Party were also set up to control the activities of the guerrillas. Action against mine owners, rubber planters and those working for them started at once, the main emphasis being placed on building up support within the Chinese population by a mixture of persuasion and coercion.

It is difficult to believe that Chin Peng really expected to be able to take over a country such as Malaya by a quick grab of this nature. The British-run Administration reacted slowly, but predictably. A state of Emergency was declared in June and the Malayan Communist Party was made illegal in July. Laws were passed concerning registration of men, control of fire-arms and the detention of suspects. By the end of the year over 2,000 people had been either detained or deported and Chin Peng acknowledged the fact that it would be necessary to settle down to a long drawn out war. In December the Malayan Communist Party issued the directive which governed the form which that war would take. The Malayan Peoples Anti British Army was renamed the Malayan Races Liberation Army in order to give the impression that the campaign was one in which all the inhabitants of Malaya were combining to free their country from the imperialist yoke. The ten regiments were broken down into platoons affiliated to the Branch Committees for the purpose of carrying out tasks allotted to them by these Committees, most of which concerned terrorizing the local population into providing support or damaging the mines and rubber plantations. It was realized that the idea of seizing base areas was impracticable and efforts were directed at establishing a firm political base among the population instead. This was to be achieved by the setting up of a Masses Organization among the squatters directed by the Branch Committees and known as the Min Yuen.

The Communist campaign was fraudulent from first to last. Although there was some discrimination against the immigrant races, it in no way constituted justification for a campaign of insurgency; the Communists merely used it to further their own ends. Despite their best efforts they never succeeded in getting significant support from any but the Chinese, although in the early stages of the Emergency about 10 per cent of the full-time jungle terrorists were Malays. The idea of fighting against the British for the purpose of achieving independence from colonial rule also cut very little ice because ever since the end of the War the British had made no secret of their intention of granting independence to Malaya as soon as a satisfactory system of government could be organized. All these facts combined to ensure that nearly all of the Communist effort would have to be devoted to terrorizing the people into supporting them and this they did with the utmost ruthlessness. It is almost impossible to describe the methods used without straining the credulity of the reader to breaking point. This was not a case of savage people being carried away by passion into doing things which they would not do under normal circumstances. In Malaya terror was planned and executed coldly and efficiently. If a community opposed Communist demands, one or two of the leading members would be dismembered in front of their families or pegged out in the sun for the ants to eat. Several instances of pregnant women being disembowelled in front of villagers as an example are on record. There was a clear purpose behind every one of these atrocities. It was no coincidence that the members of the insurgent gangs were known as Communist Terrorists.

In retrospect it is permissible to wonder why the Communists achieved as much as they did, bearing in mind the poor material from which they had to construct their campaign. But there were a number of things working in their favour and the first of these was the terrain. With so much of the country covered in dense jungle they had plenty of cover in which to hide. Another point in their favour was the weakness of the Government's forces in the early stages. The police were not very strong on the ground and were still recovering from the effects of the Japanese occupation which had, amongst other things, created a rift between that part of the force which had stayed at their posts and been interned and that part which had fled the country to fight in the War and had thereby escaped internment. Another help to the Communists was the fact that there were not many soldiers in Malaya in 1948 and those that were there had little experience of handling insurgency. Altogether the Communists' initial success, such as it was, owed as much to the weakness of the Government resources as it did to the strength of its own campaign.

It took about two years of trial and error for the Government to develop a reasonable strategy. Initially the army, which had been built up to a strength of fifteen battalions by the end of 1948, operated under the command of the Commissioner of Police for the Federation: this was done in order to establish the fact that they were operating in aid of the civil power, but co-ordination proved difficult. In early 1950 a retired general was appointed as the High Commissioner's Director of Operations and he quickly devised and established machinery for conducting affairs which served for the rest of the campaign. Under the arrangements set up by General Briggs, a Federal War Council was established with councils subordinate to it in every State and District on which sat the local police and military commanders under the chairmanship of the senior officer of the Administration. General Briggs also caused the police to separate the Special Branch which was responsible for the gathering of intelligence from the Criminal Investigation Branch. Most of the officers of the uniformed branches of the police were either British or Malays, but Special Branch was largely manned by Chinese and was reinforced by Military Intelligence Officers from the army.

General Briggs not only set up machinery for conducting the campaign, he also produced the plan on which it was to be based. This plan called for action designed to provide a measure of security for the population followed by a break-up of the Communist organization outside the jungle by arrest and internment. The terrorists themselves were to be dealt with by interfering with their food supplies and by forcing them to expose themselves to action by the Security Forces. The most spectacular part of the plan consisted of an ambitious project of resettling the 400,000 squatters into new villages protected by a Home Guard specially raised for the purpose which reached a strength of 200,000 within four years.

It took some time for the Briggs plan to start working, but by the autumn of 1951 the Malayan Communist Party was getting very worried. In particular the Communists had come to the conclusion that the cruelty and terror which they were employing against the local Chinese were doing more harm than good and that the damage which they were inflicting on mines and rubber plantations as part of their programme to bring pressure on the Government was also turning the population more firmly against them because it was destroying their livelihood. An edict was therefore issued by the

Malayan Communist Party calling for a general de-escalation of the methods being used. This loss of confidence on the part of those directing the insurgency did not become known to the Government for many months. In fact in the autumn of 1951 the Government was itself suffering from a crisis of confidence amongst its own supporters who had so far seen nothing but the chaos and devastation which the Communists were inflicting. This was brought to a head in October when the High Commissioner himself was ambushed and murdered whilst driving along a main road.

It was now felt that some dramatic move was needed to restore faith in the Government and it was decided that the new High Commissioner should be a soldier who could personally direct both the civil and military aspects of the campaign. General Templer was chosen for this task and arrived in February 1952. During the next two years this man transformed the situation entirely. So far as the conduct of operations was concerned he built on the foundation laid by General Briggs using his exalted position and his energy and determination to put real impetus behind the programme. In the wider sphere of government he made important advances in several directions which greatly helped the operational situation. In this respect perhaps his two most important moves were the granting of full Malayan citizenship to the immigrant races, subject to certain conditions being fulfilled and the fixing of a firm date five years ahead for Malayan independence. With these two measures he removed the last remaining planks of the Communist Party's platform. Towards the end of his time General Templer was able to introduce a system under which certain areas which had been freed of terrorist influence were declared 'White' and when this happened many of the Emergency restrictions were lifted on the understanding that the people of the area would immediately report any resurgence of Communist activity so that it could be prevented from developing.

In 1952 the strength of the Security Forces reached a peak. By this time there were twenty-three battalions operating and the total number of soldiers in Malaya had risen to 40,000. Of these rather more than half came from the United Kingdom, the rest being from the Gurkhas, the Kings African Rifles, Fiji and from Malaya's own army which had now grown to seven battalions. As pressure on the Communists mounted, their strength started to decline. The party leadership decided that at all costs they would retain their political structure and District and Branch Committees were kept up to strength at the expense of the independent platoons. Soon the number of platoons had fallen to such an extent that there were only enough left for them to be allocated to District Committees instead of to Branch Committees, as had formerly been the case. The part-time guerrillas, who had previously operated outside the jungle, left their homes and were attached to the District and Branch Committees inside the jungle as general assistants. Outside, the Min Yuen also shrank in size, only the senior leaders being allowed direct access to the Branch Committees to guard against betrayal.

Meanwhile the Security Forces were developing tactics designed to take account of the ever changing situation. As the years went by, the problem became more and more one of finding the enemy, who doggedly persisted in their campaign, despite the fact that it was clearly going to fail. A system of concentrating resources against a particular Communist District was introduced and such concentrations were known as Federal Priority Operations. These were carried out in two parts: in the first part the normal military and police forces in parts of the area selected would arrest as many Communist supporters as possible in order to force the Committees and the independent platoon into another and smaller part of the area. This area would then be flooded with troops from outside who would conduct intensive patrolling and ambushing to break up the gangs. These operations were supplemented throughout the country by other operations designed to cut down the flow of supplies to the Communists and this involved food rationing, a limitation on the amount of food which a householder could keep at any one time, road blocks and searches.

There is no doubt that these measures gradually paid off and a great deal of effort was put into the training of soldiers and police so that ambushes and patrols were carried out as efficiently as possible. But despite the ingenuity of the plans and the dedication of the men on the ground the process was a very slow one. In tactical terms the problem was the same as it had been in Kenya. Troops given pin-point information operated economically and effectively, but when they were given background information they were unable to make the best use of it and fell back on patrolling and ambushing in likely areas. Federal Priority Operations and all that went with them could help by reducing the size of likely areas and by raising the number of troops inside them at special times, but the general principle remained the same. It was either operations on information or a sophisticated variety of hit-and-miss.

By the time I arrived in January 1957 the Malaya Emergency was little more than a mopping-up operation carried out in accordance with closely regulated procedures which had been refined over a period of nine years. It is probably fair to say that the Emergency had been reasonably well handled after a somewhat shaky start and this was particularly true of the political and administrative aspects of the campaign. From an operational point of view it had been thorough rather than inspired, but at least the Security Forces had enabled the Government to reap the benefit of its overall measures. However it is necessary to point out that relatively large military resources had been needed to defeat an insurgency which had little in its favour from the start. From what I had heard at the Staff College and from my experience in Kenya I knew that the army's weakness lay in the field of exploiting background information. I was anxious to see whether I could contribute anything in this field.

Chapter 7

❋

Jungle Experiment

One morning early in February 1957 a platoon of the Rifle Brigade dismounted from a lorry and headed off into the Malayan jungle. Dawn was still half an hour away, but the platoon was on a well-worn track. Each man carried a huge rucksack in addition to his rifle and equipment. It was difficult to stand up straight so they walked with a stoop. In the darkness it was impossible to see more than the back of the man in front and the black wall of vegetation rising sheer from the edge of the track. The Platoon Commander came fifth in the line. Having just joined the battalion I was under instruction and followed close behind him.

There was none of the shrill coldness of an early morning in the Aberdares. Instead we moved in an atmosphere of sticky warmth which had seemed pleasant enough when we were in the lorry, but which caused us to drip as soon as we started humping our loads along the track. Even before it was light enough to see the sweat soaking into the clothes of the man in front, its curious smell had pervaded everything. By the time that the platoon sat down for a ten-minute halt everyone was as wet as if they had waded through a stream. The men took it entirely for granted and probably failed even to realize that it had happened. We tramped along in this fashion climbing as we went. Every now and then we came to a dead tree lying across the path and had to struggle through a tangle of branches and creeper, but on the whole the going was not too bad. Gradually daylight filtered through the dense jungle canopy sixty feet above us and colour seeped back into the world; mainly shades of green or brown. Being unfit I could hear no more than the noise of my own breath while we were on the move, but when we halted the creaking and buzzing of thousands of insects provided a back-cloth of sound which was slightly uncanny until one got used to it. With this sound went the jungle smell which some people think of as a rank stench of rottenness. To me it seemed more subtle; a compound of dampness, earthiness and slow decomposition which is difficult to describe and impossible to forget.

The Platoon Commander's task was to patrol a certain area of jungle and in accordance with normal procedure his first act was to set up a base camp. After we had been walking for three hours we reached the place which he had selected and set to work. Sentries were posted and the rest of the platoon started to make waterproof shelters out of ground sheets pegged out and supported by poles cut from the jungle. Under these shelters the men slung hammocks and unpacked dry clothes, gym shoes and such other kit as they had brought with them. Within an hour the camp was prepared and the men sat down to make themselves a cup of tea and smoke a cigarette. The plan for the rest of the day was for two patrols to go out in different directions and start searching the area. The Platoon Commander was to lead one of them and a section commander the other. The rest of the men were to stay behind under the platoon sergeant to finish off work in the camp. Latrine trenches had to be dug and a vine cut from the jungle and stretched round the perimeter.

The Platoon Commander's patrol left at about 10 a.m. with the idea of making its way to the top of a steep ridge about half a mile away and I went with them. There were eight soldiers and two Iban trackers in the patrol. The Ibans, together with two riflemen moved in the first group and acted as scouts. The main body followed along about fifty yards behind. All the heavy kit had been left in the base camp and we only carried our weapons, ammunition pouches and a small haversack containing some light refreshment. We hoped to bump into an enemy camp or perhaps come across tracks in the jungle which we could follow. Being unencumbered, movement was much easier than it had been earlier and it was possible to stand up straight and move around. On the other hand we were no longer following a track, but were cutting straight through the jungle on a compass bearing. This meant that we spent most of the time sliding down banks or pulling ourselves up the sides of the numerous precipitous valleys which ran across our route. Frequently we were held up while the leading group hacked their way through some otherwise impenetrable tangle. Progress was slow and exhausting. On several occasions we halted for a breather and drank a mouthful or two from our water bottles. Once we had a long rest during which we dissolved some Oxo cubes in water and drank the result at the same time eating a Mars bar, some nuts, raisins and boiled sweets. We got back to the base camp by 4 p.m. and prepared to settle down for the night.

Spending a night in the Malayan jungle with the British army was very different from spending one with a pseudo-gang in Kenya. There was no need to roll up on the ground in an overcoat after eating meat toasted over a wood fire and a maize cob similarly treated. This time there was a water-proof shelter, a hammock, dry clothes and a hot meal of steak and kidney, treacle pudding and tea. The only drawback was the mosquitoes, but they were reasonably well controlled by insect repellent.

During the afternoon the sticky heat had become increasingly oppressive. At about 6 p.m. it started to rain and a thunderstorm soon developed. The daylight faded rapidly and by the time the storm had passed it was dark. Neither the storm nor the darkness made much difference to us because we were comfortably settled on our hammocks; warm, dry and full of food. I shared a shelter with the platoon commander whose name was Mark Scrase Dickins. Our hammocks were slung between the same two trees, one above the other. It was much too early to go to sleep so we talked in the darkness with the water dripping off our ground sheets and the mosquitoes humming around us.

Mark had joined the battalion just before it had moved from Kenya to Malaya nearly a year earlier. For most of the intervening months he had been going in and out of the jungle on patrol, but neither he nor his platoon had been in action. As a rule the platoon would go in on the first day, patrol for the following three days and come out on the fifth day. They patrolled areas selected by the Company Commander off a map. The length of patrols was governed by the fact that a man could carry five days' rations into the base camp in addition to his other kit. Beyond the fact that there was supposed to be a small group of terrorists who moved around within the battalion area, Mark knew little of the enemy. The whole battalion had only killed about twelve terrorists during the time that they had been in Malaya and the chance of any individual being involved in a contact was very small. Sometimes word was received that a larger group of enemy were in the area and then the pattern of operations would be slightly different. On these occasions all three platoons and the company Headquarters would disappear into the jungle, with the other companies of the battalion doing the same thing on either flank. So far as each platoon was concerned, the procedure was the same as usual in that the men made a base camp and patrolled from it. The main difference was that the operation might last for longer than five days, in which case further supplies of food were carried into the jungle by men from the administrative part of the battalion, or they might be dropped by parachute

When the platoon was not on patrol it lived with the rest of the company in a hutted camp on the outskirts of a village a mile or so outside the jungle. One of the worst jobs the platoon had to do was to man the gates round the village and search the population when they left in the morning to work in the rubber plantations. The idea was to prevent food from reaching the terrorists. Another thoroughly unpopular occupation was the manning of ambush points along the jungle edge or at river crossings.

Mark was young, keen and very anxious to make contact with the enemy. He had practised his platoon in all the procedures which would ensure success should an opportunity ever arise and they conscientiously obeyed the rules for living in the jungle which had been worked out and taught at the Jungle Warfare School. He did not seem in the least discouraged by the fruitless months which lay behind or by the indifferent prospects held out for the future. In due course we ran out of conversation and went to sleep.

Next morning the sentries roused the camp half an hour before dawn and the men crept into their defensive positions for the first light 'stand to'. The clouds had gone and stars were bright in the sky. Even the air seemed fresh compared with the humid heaviness of the previous evening. Above the trees, sunlight soon chased away the night, but our separate world took longer to come alive. Once it did so, the men returned to their shelters and cooked breakfast on hexamine blocks. When everyone had finished eating, washing and shaving, the platoon was ready to resume operations. The plan was for three patrols to go out and on this occasion our task was to visit a bit of the jungle which the terrorists had cleared and planted with tapioca. We took with us a tracker dog and his handler in case we found signs of recent occupation.

We reached the plantation soon after midday, but unfortunately there were no terrorists tending the crops. The Ibans searched carefully and found what could have been recent tracks of three or four men, although they did not seem particularly confident. As there was nothing more urgent to do, Mark decided to try the dog which was duly set on the trail. Tracker dog Glen sniffed around for a few moments and then turned towards his handler, as if to ask whether he was seriously expected to follow such a stale line. On being convinced that this was indeed the case, he trotted off slowly into the jungle on the end of a long rope. Both dog and handler were covered forward by two riflemen and the rest of the patrol followed along behind. For half an hour the dog led the patrol, but it was soon obvious that he was just wandering around and had no idea where to go. In the end we gave up and sat down by a stream for some sweets and a drink. Most of the men set about removing leeches, but I sat and watched five large, green-and-black butterflies which were avidly feeding on some decaying vegetation at the edge of the water.

Back in camp Mark plotted on the map the routes which each patrol had taken. He decided that he had covered his area adequately, so he contacted his Company Commander on the wireless and arranged to leave the jungle on the following day. We passed another comfortable night, packed up the camp next morning and started the long haul back, weighed down once more by our full scale of kit. During the course of the march I thought about the lessons of the past three days. First, it was obvious that flogging around in the hopes of finding an enemy camp was an uneconomical way of employing troops. Second, if by a miracle the patrol did bump into an enemy camp it would be unlikely to do more than kill the sentry because the stationary enemy would have a better chance of detecting and avoiding a mobile patrol than the patrol would have of engaging and destroying the enemy. Third, the system of carrying such an immense amount of kit into the jungle meant that most of two days out of the five days spent on the operation would be taken up in establishing or dismantling the base camp, or in moving in and out of the jungle. It was of course easier to see what was wrong than it was to know how to put it right.

After the patrol my education was considered to be complete and I took over command of 'S' Company a day or two later. The 'S' stood for 'Support' which meant that I had not got one of the four proper companies but had been given the one which was designed to provide mortar and machine-gun fire to back the operations of

D

the others when required. In addition, short courses were run in 'S' Company to prepare reinforcements from England for their life in the rifle companies. To carry out its role 'S' Company was organized into a mortar platoon, a machine-gun platoon and a draft training platoon. From the operational point of view I had a very poor job. Both the mortar platoon and the machine-gun platoon were lent to other companies by the Colonel as required. Sometimes they fired their weapons into the jungle which was reasonably good training, but a complete waste of time from all other points of view. At other times they acted as infantry and carried out patrols or ambushes as required by the Company Commander to whom they had been lent. To make matters worse 'S' Company lived with battalion Headquarters, which meant that life was governed by a barrack-like routine, as opposed to the freer atmosphere that existed in the detached rifle companies. It was annoying to find that I should have no part to play in the direction of operations because as a result of my activities in Kenya I was far better qualified than the other Company Commanders. Unfortunately the Colonel allotted the companies by seniority. In an attempt to find a worthwhile job I decided to try out some of my ideas about operating in the jungle on the men who were undergoing training in 'S' Company.

A few weeks later I went back into the jungle with two riflemen called Russell and Handley from the machine-gun platoon. This time we took no more than we could carry wrapped up in a waterproof sheet slung on our belt. We spent the first day watching patrols from the draft training. As darkness fell, the men under training returned to their camps for the night. The three of us pooled our ground sheets and made a basha a few hundred yards from one of the camps. We had neither hammock, nor dry clothes, but we reckoned that we would be comfortable enough if we stripped off, wrapped ourselves in pieces of parachute silk and lay on a ground sheet.

Russell was a large man with ginger hair who had been a stevedore before joining the army. Seen in the half-light cutting sticks to support the shelter he seemed immensely powerful. Handley squatted over the stove preparing the meal, his jungle hat tilted back over his fair hair and a cigarette stuck in the corner of his mouth. Both of them came from the East End of London and their conversation, which was carried out in a hoarse whisper, was in accordance with the best cockney traditions. Talking in whispers was one of the rules of jungle life and it soon became second nature. The only problem was trying not to laugh too loudly at the cracks and sallies which passed between the two men. After the meal we lay chatting for a time before we fell asleep. Russell and Handley had no special feelings about the jungle and it certainly never occurred to them to think of it as eerie or sinister. They merely lumped it together with everywhere other than London as being thoroughly unsatisfactory. All they wanted was to get back to their 'birds' and their families.

We slept fairly well during the night, although one or other of us kept waking up as our insect repellent wore off and the mosquitoes settled down for a meal. At about 5 a.m. we were all awake because it was cold. We realized that we needed a bit more than parachute silk to see us through the last hour or so before dawn. We got up as soon as we reasonably could and cooked breakfast. During the day we again watched the soldiers under training, attaching ourselves first to one group and then to another. We carried all our kit with us and found it no inconvenience. During the next night we carried out a further experiment.

Both in Kenya and Malaya the army took it for granted that operations in the jungle did not continue at night. This was strange because even by day it was necessary to steer by compass, so presumably it would be perfectly possible to do the same by night providing that there was enough moonlight to enable one to slide and scramble around. Obviously it would be no good from the point of view of looking for enemy tracks, but there were a lot of other things which could be done. For example, it would be useful to be able to deploy men in the dark, to re-supply them, to concentrate two patrols or to move men into ambush positions surreptitiously. On this occasion we waited in one of the base camps until it got dark and then left, telling the men that we intended to make our basha a short distance away as on the previous evening. Instead of doing so we set off on a compass bearing for the other camp. There was a reasonably bright moon and we experienced no particular difficulty in getting along provided we went slowly. Soon after midnight we guessed that we were somewhere near the second camp, so we made a basha and went to sleep for the rest of the night. Next morning we found that we were within a hundred yards of our destination.

By the end of the exercise it was clear that operating on a light scale of equipment was feasible and in many ways preferable to the normal system. There were several items of kit which we wished we had left behind and others which we wished we had brought, but all that could be taken care of by minor adjustments. It was also clear that under certain circumstances movement by night in the jungle was possible. Both techniques needed developing further and the soldiers would have to practise before they could be committed to operations of this sort. The possibilities opened up by operating at night and by cutting free from the base camp concept were of course considerable.

At the end of the exercise the men of the draft training platoon were graded and passed out to the companies. I selected one man called Pascoe to be my batman. He was small and young and had closely-cropped fair hair. At first sight he did not look as though he would be particularly well-suited to the rigours of jungle life, but I had noticed that he was determined and a good shot. Russell, Handley and Pascoe operated with me for the rest of the time we were in Malaya and together formed a pleasant and effective team.

It was one thing to test my ideas regarding night movement and the use of light scales of equipment on Russell and Handley, but it was obviously desirable to try them out on a larger and more representative group. The draft training platoon was not altogether suitable, but an opportunity arose when the Colonel gave 'S' Company the job of running a course to select new NCOs from twenty or thirty candidates put forward by the Company Commanders. The climax of this course was a two-sided exercise which lasted for four days. During this time we made both sides move by day and night, ambushing and searching for each other. At one stage, one party forded a fast flowing river by moonlight using ropes and floats made of clothes wrapped in ground sheets. The men covered great distances and were tired by the end, but they were very pleased with themselves and with the new method of operating. Most of the riflemen taking part in the exercise had been in the battalion for some time, but they had never done more than move into the jungle, make camp, patrol for a few days and move out again. They had come to regard the business of living in the jungle as an achievement in itself and what they did there as being of lesser importance. It had never occurred to them that they could live for four days on less than four days' rations, or that they could sleep quite happily without hammocks and dry clothes.

From my own point of view the exercise further confirmed my ideas regarding night movement and light scales. It also showed that much more could be got out of soldiers in the jungle than most people imagined. What it did not do was to get me any closer to the point where I could try out my ideas against the enemy, but in fact an opportunity was approaching and would present itself in due course.

Chapter 8

❦

Cold War Reconnaissance

It was planned that the whole battalion should move to a new area in the state of Johore early in June so that it could take part in a Federal Priority Operation called Cobble. Battalion Headquarters was to be at Gemas and the companies were allotted permanent camps in and around the Cobble area. Although 'S' Company's role was to remain unaltered, the Colonel decided that we would live with 'B' Company and not with battalion Headquarters.

In due course advance parties set off to take over the new camps and it is almost certain that the plan would have come into effect, but for an incident which occurred during the night of May 28th, when a rubber planter was attacked by some terrorists a few miles from the new 'B' and 'S' Company camp at Bukit Serampang. The attack had taken place outside the area of Operation Cobble and was, strictly speaking, nothing to do with out battalion. As soon as I heard of the incident I drove to the new camp on the pretext of delivering further supplies of ammunition to our advance party. I arrived in the evening of May 29th and heard that the Brigade Commander intended to hold a meeting next day with the local police and the District Officer. The purpose of the meeting was to decide how best to deal with terrorists in the districts bordering the Operation Cobble area. It seemed to me that the battalion should be represented at the conference, so I went along.

The aim of Operation Cobble was to remove Communist influence from a sizable part of North Johore so that the area concerned could be declared white. In order to do this, territory outside the area of the operation had to be ignored, despite the fact that it might contain plenty of terrorists, so that the maximum number of

troops could be used for the achievement of the main aim. When the
enemy carried out their attack on May 28th they presented the
Brigadier with a problem. He called the meeting to decide whether
it was safe to ignore the incident and continue to concentrate the
maximum number of troops on Operation Cobble, or whether it
would be necessary to disperse a part of the force to deal with the
threat.

During the discussion it became clear that in the part of the
Cobble area allocated to our battalion there was only one Communist Branch Committee operating and that even including the
Armed Workers who were attached to the Committee the total
number of terrorists did not exceed twelve. In the territory bordering
the battalion's area to the south and west, however, there was one
Communist Area Committee which corresponded to a State Committee, two District Committees and four Branch Committees, all of
which had varying numbers of Armed Workers attached to them.
Although there should have been one or two independent platoons
backing up these committees, none existed because they had by this
time been broken up to maintain the strength of the Committees
themselves. This constituted a relatively large concentration of
terrorists for 1957 and although the Brigadier was reluctant to disperse his force, the local administrative and police officers wanted
some soldiers to be made available. Bukit Serampang was in the
middle of the disputed area and although the Brigadier was not prepared to release 'B' Company from Operation Cobble, he did not
mind detaching 'S' Company.

'S' Company therefore found itself with an operational role at
last; and a very good role it was. From an army point of view we
would be responsible for a bit of country stretching for thirty miles
from north to south and twenty miles from east to west. It consisted
of jungle, swamp, rubber plantations and patches of cultivation. A
number of enemy groups were busy spreading their poisonous doctrine and terrorizing all who opposed them. The task of destroying
these people was greatly preferable to that of training recruits. 'S'
Company's new area covered most of one administrative District
and I was made the military member of the District War Executive
Committee. District Headquarters was on the coast at Muar. Our
area also covered part of another District based on Segamat. I had
access to the police and intelligence facilities at Segamat, but was
not made a full member of the District War Executive Committee

because most of this District came into the area of Operation Cobble
and in any case it would be difficult to be a full member of two of
these Committees and command a company at the same time.

When the Brigadier's meeting broke up I paid a flying visit to the
Colonel, who was still in the old battalion area 150 miles away to
the north. I returned early next morning and visited the Special
Branch Officers at Muar and Segamat in order to get an outline of
the enemy position. I also had a quick look at the countryside.
When it got dark some men of the 'S' Company advance party
collected themselves together in a room of the rubber planter's
house at Bukit Serampang, which had been commandeered to serve
as our Headquarters. Russell, Handley and Gillard, the company
clerk, pinned maps to the wall so as to provide complete large-scale
coverage of the company area. Pascoe and Green, the driver of my
Austin Champ, cooked a meal in the corner of the room. I tried to
work out a method of tackling our problem, but it was an uphill
struggle. Gillard was a fat and forceful Londoner who was constitutionally incapable of keeping quiet. Wisecracks flowed continually between him and the others – particularly Handley – so
that it was impossible to concentrate. On the other hand it was too
good to miss.

The aim, as laid down by the Brigadier, was to destroy the terrorists in the company area. In practice no one at the meeting, least of
all the Brigadier, expected that we would achieve as much as this.
They hoped no doubt that we would prevent the enemy from causing
trouble and with luck we might kill one or two. It was generally
reckoned that a battalion should on average account for one
terrorist a month, which meant that one company should get one or
two of them in a period of just over four months, which was the
time left to us before our scheduled return to England in November.
I personally felt that the total elimination of all the terrorists in our
area was perfectly possible and this was the aim which I set myself
to achieve. In practice the task was nothing like as hopeless as it
seemed at first sight. Although 'S' Company only consisted of two
platoons it represented a relatively small part of the force available.
Two platoons of Malay policemen operated in the area on tasks
allocated by the Muar District War Executive Committee, of which
I was a member. In addition there were Home Guard detachments
in each of the villages, who were capable of defensive tasks. Most
important of all was the fact that the Brigadier had agreed that up

to one platoon of 'B' Company could be lent to 'S' Company providing that they were not wanted for Operation Cobble.

Examination of the enemy position also showed that circumstances were a great deal more favourable to us than appeared on the surface to be the case. The Special Branch Officers at Muar and Segamat had given me details of the Communist organization which is shown on the chart on the next page. The senior terrorist leader was Ah Chien, who was the Secretary of the Johore Malacca Border Committee Area. For some reason the Communists had interposed this 'Area' between the States of Johore and Malacca: it covered parts of both these States and had the status of a State in its own right. Ah Chien moved around within his Area with a headquarters of six men making contact with the District Committee Secretaries. Neither he, nor the members of his headquarters, ever left the jungle and information regarding his whereabouts was seldom forthcoming. He was thought to spend some of his time in the territory given to my company. The Johore Malacca Border Committee Area was divided up into Communist Districts, two of which impinged on my company's area. One of these was the Communist Malacca District which had been badly broken up over the years. None of its former Branch Committees remained in operation and the District Committee Secretary called It Hiong lived in the jungle with six other terrorists making occasional contact with leaders of the Min Yuen in an attempt to rebuild his battered organization. The other Communist District which concerned me was called the West Segamat District. It consisted of three Branches all of which operated in my area. The three Branches were the Kebun Bahru Branch, the Grisek Branch and the Jementah Branch. Leong Tek Chai was the leader or District Committee Secretary and he lived with the Kebun Bahru Branch because there were not enough terrorists left for him to have his own headquarters.

In effect this meant that there were five separate gangs living in my area each consisting of a leader and his henchmen and totalling thirty-six terrorists. With the exception of Ah Chien's group, they could not live in deep jungle because they had to come out into the rubber plantations in order to meet the people and spread their doctrine. Even if they had been prepared to abandon their responsibilities in this respect they would still have been obliged to leave the jungle in order to collect food. It seemed likely that my best opportunity for making contact with the terrorists would come from

JOHORE MALACCA BORDER COMMITTEE AREA

(as at 6 June 1957)

J.M. BORDER COMMITTEE SECRETARY

*AH CHIEN

WEST SEGAMAT DISTRICT DISTRICT SECRETARY
*LEONG TEK CHAI

JMBC AREA HEADQUARTERS
†LIM TUAN
†KIANG SIN
†WU SAN
†SIOW LIEW
†CHUA SEE CHAK
†CHAN YOKE ENG

MALACCA DISTRICT DISTRICT SECRETARY
*IT HIONG

*HO LIM SENG
*PIONG CHOON
†AH KUT
†WONG CHAN FOOK
†KWAI CHING
†CHAN KIONG CHAN

KEBUN BAHRU BRANCH
*KAM BOON PIOW
*CHAN AH FOOK
†LEONG HIAN
†KAM KIM CHAR
†LEE CHOR
†HAN YING
†KWAI YING
†SIOW KWONG
†KUAN SUEN

GRISEK BRANCH
*SEET HO CHING
*HAN LEONG
*CHAN AH HIONG
*TAY BOON HUI
†KAM SAN
†WU KUAY
†AH HENG
†LEE AH KUAN

JEMENTAH BRANCH
*LEE MENG
†CHOW ENG SU
†HOOT CHENG
†TIEN WEI CHING

---

* Area, District and Branch Committee Members   † Armed Workers

exploiting their need to leave the jungle for one of these reasons.

Because of our shortage of men it was necessary to consider an order of priority for dealing with the various enemy groups so that enough of our own force could be concentrated to produce results. This meant considering each of the Communist groups in turn. The best results would obviously come from getting the enemy leader Ah Chien, but this would be difficult because his little group of seven men did not contact the population direct and they usually got their food from one of the Branches. Ah Chien could only be approached once the Branch organization had been broken up. Of the potential targets, the Jementah Branch of four men was the smallest and least influential so it could reasonably be afforded a low priority. In Malacca District the Branch organization no longer existed and, although it was important to eliminate It Hiong and his gang to prevent them from reorganizing, there was no particular hurry. Furthermore they operated in a distant part of my territory and information about them was even more scanty than it was about the rest of the groups.

That left the Grisek Branch of eight and the Kebun Bahru Branch of ten. The Grisek Branch operated exclusively in Muar District and any information would come from Inspector Boey, who was in charge of Muar Special Branch. The Kebun Bahru Branch was based in the jungle of Mount Ophir which was in Segamat District, so most of the information about it would come from Inspector Cheong of the Segamat Special Branch. This gang did however operate to some extent in rubber and vegetable plantations which were across the border in Muar District. For this reason Inspector Boey might also provide information about it, which meant that if one Special Branch dried up for a bit the other might be able to give us a lead. Finally more was known about the Kebun Bahru Branch than about the Grisek Branch, so I decided to concentrate on it initially. A map showing the 'S' Company area, and the general division of territory between the Communist branches is opposite page 94.

It was one thing to decide to concentrate on the Kebun Bahru Branch, but quite another matter to decide how this should be done. Both Special Branch Inspectors had warned me that there was very little information about the future intentions of the terrorists, although they had a lot of background information about personalities, old camp sites and so on which they had built up over the years. My position was thus much the same as that of the Company Commanders in Kenya, who had relied on our organization there, and my first reaction was to echo their cry that nothing worthwhile could be done without better intelligence. At the same time I was determined not to send soldiers into the jungle on five-day hit-or-miss patrols, which was the method normally adopted by commanders who had no intelligence system. Some vague ideas were already forming in my head, but as the soldiers were not due to arrive in the new area for another four days it seemed wise to think matters out more carefully before making a detailed plan.

During the next few days I paid several more visits to the Special Branch officers and gathered as much background information as I could about the Kebun Bahru Branch. Their records went back for years and we carefully plotted positions of old hides on a map to see whether any pattern appeared which could be related to known factors, such as rainfall variations, availability of crops, the activities of logging teams or the movement of aborigines.

We then went through the back history of every one of the thirty-six terrorists in an attempt to guess the most likely areas from which they would try and get food. This check involved going into the details of all the friends and relations of the terrorists, where these were known, but it proved a somewhat abortive exercise because most of the old villages had been abandoned during the past seven years and the population resettled elsewhere. All the same it was valuable in one respect in that it made me familiar with the background of our opponents and helped to create an atmosphere against which to judge their probable reactions to events. Obviously many of the rank and file were good old-fashioned bandits, but the leaders had impressive records of devotion to the Communist cause stretching back into the war against Japan. These men had been in the jungle for most of the past fifteen years, having emerged briefly in 1945 and then returned in 1948. They were men who deserved respect for their loyalty, toughness and resource. Pictures were available of some of the terrorists and I asked that these should be reproduced in sufficient quantities for all the men in the company to have a set, but this was turned down as being a waste of money. I took the matter up time and again with the District War Executive Committee and brigade Headquarters and eventually they were produced.

A new fact, which emerged from my visits to Special Branch, was

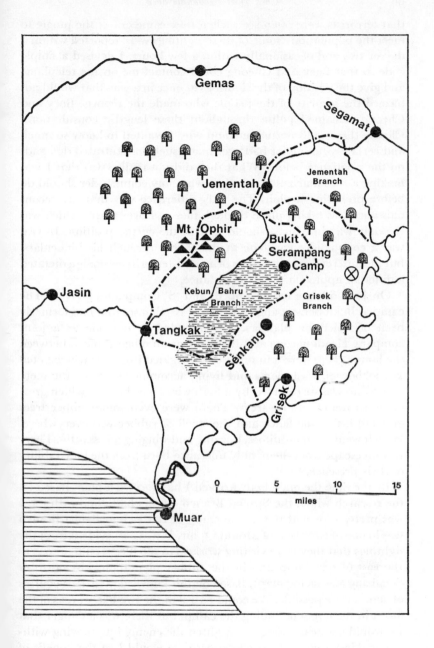

Gemas

Segamat

Jementah

Jementah
Branch

Mt. Ophir

Bukit
Serampang
Camp

⊗

Jasin

Kebun Bahru
Branch

Grisek
Branch

Tangkak

Senkang

Grisek

0   5   10   15
miles

Muar

that terrorists were often seen when they came out of the jungle to meet the population. Some of these sightings were reported within a day or two and occasionally within a few hours. I devised a simple code so that Boey and Cheong could contact me on the telephone and give the position of the sightings at once in a way that would not hazard the security of the people who made the reports. Boey and Cheong remained polite throughout these lengthy consultations. Clearly they could not understand why I wanted to know so much and certainly no soldier had ever made such concentrated demands on their patience before. What they did not realize was that I was making a reconnaissance, which is what any commander should do before preparing a plan. The only difference was that my recon-naissance was taking place through files and over maps, which was the only way in which I could look at the enemy position. In real war a commander can look at the enemy through his binoculars, but the different circumstances of an anti-terrorist campaign dictated a different approach to reconnaissance.

On June 6th the balance of 'B' and 'S' Companies arrived. The camp at Bukit Serampang consisted of two houses that had formerly been occupied by planters. We intended to use one as a joint company Headquarters and the other as an officers' mess. Between the houses there were a number of corrugated iron huts which acted as cookhouses, washrooms and living accommodation for the men. The camp was surrounded by a high wire fence beyond which grew endless rows of rubber trees. There were even some rubber trees growing inside the fence and the smell of rubber was everywhere. With it went the mosquitoes, buzzing and stinging incessantly. There was no escape from them, only tolerance born from the inevitability of their presence.

By the time the main body arrived I had formed a plan. Based on the research which the Special Branch officers had done with me I was pretty sure that the jungle camp of the Kebun Bahru Branch was in one of two areas of Mount Ophir. It was also evident from the sightings that they were visiting workers in the illegal cultivations to the east of our camp and in the rubber plantations just north of Sengkang (see facing map). Based on this knowledge various courses of action were possible. We could patrol in the two likely areas of the forest in the hopes of finding the camp, but there was a danger that we would get near enough to frighten the enemy into moving with-out making a contact, in which case we would lose the benefit of

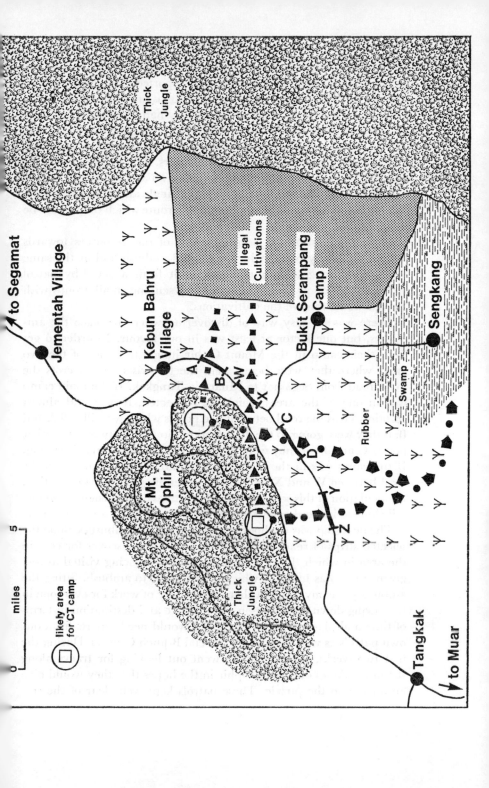

much of our research. Another possibility was to get a petrol to the
scene of a sighting soon after it was reported. It might then be
possible to follow tracks with dogs and Ibans and come up with the
gang while they were resting or after they had reached their camp.
As an outside chance it might be worth putting patrols in suitable
vantage spots around the illegal cultivations in the hopes that they
might observe terrorists through binoculars. The best chance of an
effective contact undoubtedly lay in siting an ambush in the path of
a group which was moving between the jungle and the cultivations,
but to do so involved knowing exactly the route which they would be
likely to take.

My plan consisted of devoting most of our resources towards
finding out likely routes which we could ambush and at the same
time trying to get an immediate result from a stand-by patrol
organized to follow up sightings and by sending small groups with
binoculars to observe the cultivations.

There was no easy way of discovering where to place the ambushes, but one factor at least was in our favour. In order to get
from their camp in the Mount Ophir jungle to either of the two
areas where they were being seen, the terrorists had to cross the
main road from Segamat to Muar via Tangkak. If the main camp
was in one of the areas which we suspected, they would almost
certainly cross the road between two points which we will call A and
B, if they were going to the illegal cultivations, or between two other
points C and D, if they were going to the rubber round Sengkang.
If the camp was in the other probable area, they would cross the
road between W and X or Y and Z depending on their destination.
A calculation of this sort suggested four strips of road each about one
mile long as being the most likely places on which to site ambushes.

The next step was to choose exact sites for the ambushes along the
selected strips of road and at the same time to discover for certain
the area in which the camp was and the area being visited at any
given time so as to know which of the strips to ambush. Siting the
ambushes was my job, but there was plenty of work for everyone in
narrowing down the selection of camp site and destination in terms
of time and place. For this purpose I would need reports from our
own patrols as well as from the Special Branch Officers. During the
first two weeks, several patrols went out looking for tracks along
the lower slopes of Mount Ophir in the hopes that they would give
an answer to the puzzle. These patrols kept well clear of the sus-

pected camp sites, but were none the less able to get a good idea of the lie of the land, which was to prove valuable later on.

The job of selecting ambush positions was not altogether easy. There were literally dozens of tracks running to the road through the rubber and the terrorists might use any of them. But not all of these tracks ran the whole way from the road to the edge of the jungle and it was these that were most likely to be used, especially if they continued on into the jungle itself. It would have taken months of patrolling to discover which tracks were the best ones to ambush on this basis. A far better way to find out was to be told by a sur-rendered terrorist, who was prepared to co-operate, and two such people were eventually produced by Inspector Boey. Both of these men had been members of the Kebun Bahru Branch in the past and both had trooped backwards and forwards across the road for years. They were months out of date regarding the actual whereabouts of the gang, but they could tell immediately whether a particular track was likely to be one that was used or not. After a few days in their company I had chosen ambush positions along all four of the selected strips of road. There were about eight likely places on each stretch which was a practicable number to man.

One further difficulty had to be overcome. If the men were seen getting into their ambush positions, word would probably reach the enemy by one means or another. The men would therefore have to get there in the dark. But they could hardly take up satisfactory positions in the dark unless they had seen them before by daylight. At the same time it was not possible to show each man in 'S' Company each of the selected positions on each stretch of road be-cause it would take too long and it would also attract attention. Furthermore when the moment to man the position arrived we might find that the men selected to do the job were from 'B' Com-pany or from a Malay police platoon. We got round the difficulty by taking pictures of each position from several different angles. When an ambush party was picked they could refer to the pictures and from them select their positions on the ground. Within a few days of choosing the positions, there were thirty-two sets of photographs safely filed away in Gillard's cupboard.

The value of the two ex-terrorists was not confined to pointing out likely ambush positions. During the days which we spent on reconnaissance we talked continuously about the individuals in the gang, their motives, beliefs, hopes and fears. We discussed life in the jungle, the relationships that existed between the various members of the gang and the contact which the terrorists had with the population outside the jungle. After a few days I felt that I knew almost as much about the Kebun Bahru Branch as I did about my own two platoons. I became intensely interested in every little detail and arranged with Inspector Boey to keep one of the men after the business of selecting ambush positions was finished. He remained in our camp and I used to go off and talk to him whenever I had a free moment. His name was Ah Meng.

June seemed to flash past at a great speed. In addition to the measures already described we embarked on a concentrated training programme to ensure that there would be a satisfactory outcome to any contact which we did manage to make. This involved practising all the soldiers in firing their weapons at moving targets at short range in the jungle by day and by night. In the latter case we fired by moonlight and by the light of torches and flares. Soon after the middle of the month our calculations showed that it might be worth manning some of the ambush positions. The men lay there for four nights running, but nothing happened. After that they were withdrawn because it was clear that we had made a mistake somewhere in our reckoning. We reverted to patrols looking for tracks and to observation of the illegal cultivations.

Shortly afterwards Inspector Boey told us that the Grisek Branch was collecting food from Grisek village every two or three weeks. Apparently a small party from the gang came through the perimeter fence at the same spot each time: he hoped to be able to let me know the time a day or two before the next visit and he could show us the spot, if we could think of a way of getting to the village without arousing the suspicions of the villagers. It looked as though we were going to get some very high-class contact information and we took great pains over the reconnaissance. First, we got hold of a river launch and steamed slowly up and down the Muar river pretending that we were on a picnic. We stacked beer bottles all over the cabin roof and sat around in relaxed attitudes. Paul Greenwood, who was the second in command of 'B' Company, Sergeant Bagley of the mortar platoon, Russell and Handley, accompanied me on this jaunt. A day or two later Inspector Boey and myself together with one or two others crowded into the back of the Government information van which was due to give a film show in Grisek village. We jumped out a mile outside the village just before dark and had a good look at the perimeter fence while the show was in progress. The van picked us up on its way home.

At the end of June our position was much stronger than it had been a few weeks earlier, but we had failed to make contact with the enemy, despite the fact that the stand-by patrol had been out on two or three occasions following reports of sightings. By this time it was pretty clear that the Kebun Bahru Branch had its camp in the eastern part of Mount Ophir and that they were visiting the workers in the illegal cultivations, although there were no recent sightings to confirm this assumption. If this was the situation, our calculations showed that a party of terrorists should cross the main road from east to west between July 1st and 5th. There was one weak link in the chain, which was that they might be visiting a small area of rubber to the west of the road near Jementah instead of the cultivations. In this case they would not have to cross the road and our ambushes would draw blank. Cheong thought that he could find out whether the terrorists were visiting the rubber and promised to ring me on the afternoon of June 30th. If his report was satisfactory, we would man the ambush positions.

That afternoon 'B' and 'S' Companies were due to receive a visit from the battalion padre and one of the corrugated iron huts was rigged up as a church for the occasion. By 5 p.m. the two Company Sergeant Majors had rounded up most of the Church of England members who were not otherwise employed. The padre's batman handed round hymn-books and a bandsman took his seat at the portable organ which had been sent from battalion Headquarters for the occasion. In due course the service started and it was immediately apparent that the padre had no intention whatsoever of following the order of service laid down for use by the troops. He chatted away making up his own prayers as he went along and missing out anything he did not like. These omissions included the confession, absolution and creed. When he decided to have a hymn he asked the men what they would like. The subsequent discussion went something like this:

> PADRE: 'Well, lads, what hymn would you like to sing?'
> MEN: Stony silence.
> PADRE: 'Come along now, don't be afraid to speak up. Choose a good one.'
> RIFLEMAN: 'Let's 'ave "The 'eathen in his blindness", sir.'

SEVERAL MEN: 'Yes, yes, "The 'eathen in his blindness".'
PADRE: 'No, I'm not sure that's very suitable nowadays.'
RIFLEMAN: 'Then why is it in the book?'
ANOTHER: "'E asks yer what yer wants and when yer says 'e says yer can't 'ave it.'
A THIRD MAN: ' "The 'eathen in his blindness." '
PADRE: 'We will sing "The Church's One Foundation". It has the same tune.'

The organist struck up, the officers and one or two sergeants started to sing and the men began laughing and chattering among themselves.

When we reached the sermon, the dialogue between the padre and the men was resumed because he kept asking oratorical questions which they answered. At this point the weather took a hand, as a sudden storm hit the camp. Torrential rain splattered onto the tin roof of the hut making a deafening racket. A Malay labourer, who normally helped in the kitchen, backed into the entrance out of the rain. He stood in the doorway with his back to the altar, holding a tray of jam tarts, totally unaware of the service which was going on behind him. The men started to laugh which added fuel to the flames of the padre's wrath. At that moment Gillard appeared in the doorway with water streaming from his green poncho cape which was flapping round him in the wind. He had arranged to man the telephone in my office so as to avoid the service and his message was that I should come at once because I was 'wanted by a wog what said it was urgent'.

I left the service with relief and found that Inspector Cheong was on the other end of the telephone. His message was that the Kebun Bahru Branch had not been operating in the rubber to the west of the road near Jementah. As soon as it got dark an officer of 'B' Company took his platoon out of the camp and put them into the pre-arranged ambush positions. Our period of preparation was nearly over.

Chapter 9

❋

Yonder Hill

At half past ten the engine which provided light for the camp spluttered and died: it did so every evening at this time. As always, the occasion was marked by a barrage of abuse from the soldiers who had not been watching the clock and who found themselves unprepared for bed. Paul Greenwood, the second in command of 'B' Company and his dog Wuzza, came into this category as they had been dozing in a corner of the mess. Paul reacted in much the same way as the soldiers had done as he bumped into various articles of furniture on his way to bed.

Jonathan Peel and myself were the only other people there at the time. Jonathan commanded the mortar platoon and had just returned from a week in the observation post overlooking the illegal cultivations. We had a lot of things to discuss and we did not need a light, so we sat talking in the dark while the rain pelted down outside and mosquitoes jabbed at our ankles through sweat-dampened socks.

It had been a depressing week for both of us. Jonathan had seen nothing to compensate him for the long hours he had spent in the observation post and none of the dispositions which I had made had produced a contact. The ambushes had been in position since the day of the church service. This was their sixth night and the last one on which anything was likely to happen. For the first time since we moved into the new area my faith in the system, which I had devised for the conduct of operations, began to waver. Apart from Jonathan it is doubtful whether anybody else had any faith in it at all. There was no particular reason why they should.

'S' Company did not have a second in command because under

normal circumstances there would be nothing for him to do. Although Jonathan was only just twenty, he was the next senior officer to myself and I treated him as a second in command to the extent that we discussed everything together when circumstances permitted. He seemed to have an instinctive understanding of the business of hunting terrorists, which I had carefully fostered during the past few months. Professionally this was useful and it also enabled him to fill the gap in my personal relationships which had been there since Eric drove out of our camp at Kamiti to work in his uncle's sawmill. There were other similarities between Jonathan and Eric besides their awareness of the ways of terrorists. Both were tall, thin and fair and both were by nature quiet and reserved. Their backgrounds were of course different, but both were countrymen whose chief interest was the pursuit of game of one sort or another. Jonathan's conventional upbringing had more in common with my own than with Eric's wild youth, but I felt equally at ease with either of them. So far Jonathan had not been in action and this worried him because he was not sure how he would react when the great moment arrived.

At some stage during that hot, damp evening I went to bed, but it seemed that I had scarcely fallen asleep before I was awake again. A huge shape was leaning over the bed with news that one of the ambushes had made contact and that a terrorist had been killed. At that moment Pascoe, who had heard the commotion, appeared with a pressure lamp and the shape took the form of Andrew Foley, the officer who commanded the 'B' Company platoon which had been manning the ambush positions. His face and hands were covered in camouflage cream and rain dripped from the brim of his jungle hat onto my bed.

Together we made our way to the shed at the entrance of the camp which served as a guard room. A sodden bundle of wrecked manhood lay on the floor encased in the remains of a faded khaki uniform. The Guard Commander bent down with a lamp and I looked into the dead man's face trying hard to recognize him from photographs I had been studying during the past month. But a bullet had gone right through his forehead and the resulting distortion made identification impossible.

Then we got down to business. Inspector Cheong had to be rung up and Ah Meng was sent for to come and have a look at the body. Andrew Foley and the corporal, who had been in charge of the ambush position, which had made the contact, gave their account of events. It appeared that three men had walked into the position from the direction of the illegal cultivations. They had come so quietly that no one heard them until the leading terrorist was half-way across the road and therefore within a few feet of our riflemen. In the split second that it takes for a flare to blaze into light two of the three were back across the road and had disappeared into the undergrowth. Only the leader presented a fleeting target and he fell at once.

When Ah Meng arrived he said that we had killed Leong Tek Chai, the District Committee Secretary and the most important leader in the company area with the exception of Ah Chien. We did not dare believe this piece of news because it seemed too good to be true. At that moment we would not have minded if he had said that the man was the gang cook; we were so pleased to have been successful at last.

While Andrew Foley and his men were rejoicing over their success, I was thinking about the next stage of our campaign. My system was based on the assumption that the first contact would provide a clue which would lead to further action. A prisoner would be the best basis for this, but it did not look as if one would be forthcoming. Another possibility was that there would be some tracks which we could follow, so a patrol was sent to the scene of the incident to have a good look as soon as it got light. It was possible that some guide to future action would result from a careful examination of the dead man's belongings. Perhaps a document would be of value, or a food source might become apparent from a careful study of the supplies carried.

Soon Inspector Cheong joined us and took finger-prints. His first reaction was to agree with Ah Meng about the identification. We were still looking at documents and discussing the situation when it got light. Shortly afterwards we went to the scene of the ambush to see whether the follow-up party had found anything. A thorough search is always necessary and often pays dividends. It is not unusual to find abandoned equipment, documents or weapons and some-times a blood trail leads to a dead or wounded man. But in this case nothing was found. Even the tracks leading into the ambush had been obliterated by the rain.

Inspector Cheong returned to his office at about this time and rang up later on to confirm that the dead terrorist was Leong Tek

Chai. Congratulations flowed in from various quarters, but although it was gratifying to receive them, it did not solve the problem of what to do next. One of the difficulties lay in the fact that my superiors were anxious that something should be done at once. Phrases like 'striking while the iron is hot' and 'exploiting success' were in their thoughts and on their lips. But the survivors of the ambush might lie low for a day or two, then meet up with the rest of the Kebun Bahru Branch and it was quite possible that the old pattern of activity would be resumed. Having taken so much trouble to discover this pattern it would be a pity to frighten the terrorists away from their base by crashing around in the general area of their camp at a time when the chances of a successful contact were no greater than they had been in the past. A further possibility existed, which was that one of the survivors from the ambush might take the opportunity of being separated from the leaders to surrender. There was a better chance of this happening if he could get to the nearest village undisturbed by the passing of soldiers to and fro along the jungle edge.

Next day something did turn up. A member of the Kebun Bahru Branch surrendered to a policeman in Jementah and was taken to Inspector Cheong. My immediate reaction was to assume that it was a survivor from the ambush and Jonathan got a patrol ready in the hope that the prisoner would be prepared to lead us back to the main camp. My objections to operating against their camp did not extend to this sort of situation because the prisoner could prevent us from blundering into the sentry and could indicate the exact position of the camp so that it could be surrounded. Under these circumstances there was every chance of eliminating all the occupants.

As it happened, my assumption about the surrendered terrorist was wrong. The man concerned was Han Ying. He had only recently joined the gang and he had not been involved in the ambush. He arrived with Inspector Cheong during the morning and we then heard the full story. Soon after Leong Tek Chai had taken his party off to the illegal cultivations another group had gone towards Sengkang leaving Han Ying and one other man in charge of the camp. When Leong Tek Chai failed to return, Han Ying had become very worried supposing that some disaster had occurred and fearing that the position of the camp had been compromised. He urged the other man, whose name was Leong Hian, to abandon the area, but Leong Hian was a veteran terrorist and merely told him to stop worrying. But Han Ying continued to worry and in the end he decided to murder his colleague and surrender. He described how he waited until Leong Hian went to sleep, smashed his head with a lump of wood and made good his escape. He gave his account with some relish – he was little more than a boy – and it was clear that having made his decision he had acted with speed and resolution. We readily accepted his offer to lead a patrol back to the camp as an earnest of his changed allegiance. For reasons best known to himself, Han Ying seemed to be out of sympathy with Communism.

If Jonathan and his patrol left at 2 p.m., he should arrive at the camp about one hour before dark. He would then be in a position to attack at once if circumstances were favourable, or delay until first light if that seemed to offer a better chance of success. Should he find that neither of the two enemy groups had returned, he was to ambush the camp. Han Ying reckoned that the Sengkang party must be back within a couple of days at the most, but the patrol took four days' rations to be on the safe side.

After Han Ying had been dressed up like a soldier and the men had eaten a good meal, the patrol disappeared into the dense jungle which covered the steep sides of Mount Ophir. A corporal led followed by Han Ying, his Special Branch escort, an interpreter and Jonathan. Next came seven riflemen, a couple of Iban trackers and Sergeant Bagley who brought up the rear.

Intense optimism frequently results from a favourable turn of events following a long period of expectation. On this occasion I was confident that the patrol would have found the camp by sundown and that a bloody and decisive battle would take place. I even visualized the complete elimination of the Kebun Bahru Branch and my thoughts turned towards the men of Grisek. For our men, who had gone into the jungle, the patrol was like so many others which they had embarked on in the past. Perhaps the knowledge that they were heading for a known enemy position made them tread with extra care and perhaps the thought that they expected to reach their destination within a few hours and be back home within a day lent some extra lightness to their step. But for the most part it was the same back-breaking, sweat-making flog as usual as they struggled up the steep slopes of the mountain through the eternal tangle of greenery.

By 4.30 p.m. Jonathan was beginning to get worried about the amount of daylight left. Han Ying kept saying that the camp was just ahead, but each crest disclosed another one ten, twenty or fifty yards ahead and still there was no sign of the enemy. Soon after 5 p.m. it was obvious that no attack could be made that night and as it would be foolish to blunder into the camp in the dusk, the patrol halted. They were only carrying light equipment so they soon settled down. The signaller tapped out a situation report on the morse key which ended up by saying that the patrol intended to continue the search in the morning. Because they might be within a few yards of the enemy they had to be extra careful about lighting stoves and smoking was not allowed. It rained steadily all night.

Next morning the patrol packed up their few belongings at first light and started to search once more. It was obvious that Han Ying had missed the way, but he was a recent recruit and it was probably the result of a genuine mistake rather than an attempt to default on his undertaking. Everything pointed to the fact that the camp was close at hand and the men set off happy in the knowledge that the march in front of them was likely to be over quickly. But no camp appeared as they pushed through the jungle from crest to crest, sliding down banks, splashing through streams and dragging themselves up the far side. Throughout the day Jonathan was conscious that the hopes of the whole company were moving with his patrol. He knew that he had set off with better chances of success than usual and he felt that failure to contact the enemy was in some way his fault. The men, having started with the idea that they need do no more than walk for an hour or two to take part in a first-class punch-up, had sunk into the apathy which normally accompanied them through the jungle. They did not grumble – they had no spare breath for that – they just retreated into their shells and plodded on through the damp heat as they had done so frequently in the past.

Jonathan did not take the whole patrol on this occasion because there were too many men for a search. He left the signaller and one or two others at the place where they had spent the night and re-joined them in the evening. Later on, the signaller tapped out the depressing account of the day's proceedings for the benefit of those of us who were waiting at Bukit Serampang. At the end of the report came the statement that the search would continue next day unless I wanted them to call it off. If it was to continue I was to send the letter 'R' for Romeo on the morse key. Realizing that they had already disturbed the area thoroughly, I saw little point in withdrawing the patrol so sent them a Romeo. Keeping the men going in the face of such disappointment would be extremely difficult for Jonathan, but he was well capable of doing it.

The next day was worse still, with incessant rain from dawn to dusk and afterwards. The men struggled on, but this was the third day of the search and the patrol had only set out with four days' rations. By all the rules they should come out of the jungle next morning. That evening when the men had settled down in their bashas, Jonathan moved around among them as usual. The interpreter was in a bad way complaining bitterly about his feet, back and stomach, but he was over fat and got no more sympathy than he deserved. Sergeant Bagley was quietly efficient as always. He had fought throughout the War in Europe and had been with the battalion in Kenya. He had been in dozens of contacts with the enemy, was fifteen years older than Jonathan and was very much more experienced. From Jonathan's point of view this was usually a great help, but there were times when it was rather uncomfortable.

The men had long since given up thinking about whether they were likely to find the enemy camp. They squatted on the ground trying to coax their hexamine stoves into providing a meal and as they fiddled with their tins and mugs they crooned their cockney songs under their breath. At the best of times these songs are sung on one or two notes in a minor key. They recall in lyrical terms the poverty of the slums and most of them deal with the persecution of the very poor at the hands of the landlord's agent. The theme running through them all is pleasure for the rich and blame for the poor. They are dreary and piteous to a degree, but the men used to enjoy singing them. When the signaller sent through the report that evening, I told them to continue with the search. In order to have some food in hand against an emergency Jonathan told the men to eat half a day's rations only and then to bed down and get what sleep they could.

Next morning the sun shone through the leaves out of a cloudless sky. The patrol set off as usual and started to scramble up and down the seamed face of the mountain. They had not been going for long before Han Ying started to show signs of recognizing trees and rocks. Soon it was evident that he was no longer lost and that the camp really did lie just ahead at long last. In another half hour they had crept up to a ridge from where they could just see the outline of an attap shelter about fifty yards away, but it was not possible to know whether any terrorists were there. Jonathan acted on the assumption that they were and made a plan to assault from one side, whilst leaving a party to cover the rear of the camp in case anyone tried to escape in that direction.

In the last few moments excitement rose to fever pitch, mouths went dry and men who had been sweating for hours began to feel cold. Then the word to advance was given and they pushed up the steep side of the hill towards the camp. They reached the crest and stood on a small plateau which was the camp site. All around were little attap shelters over benches of interwoven sticks and creeper. A strong, sweet smell of rot hung on the air, but nothing moved.

And then they saw the cause of the stench. The grossly bloated body of a man was lying on one of the benches. His stomach blown up like a barrel had forced its way out of his shirt and a hugely distended belly-button winked at the roof of the shelter. His face was black and his head was battered and bloody. A large lump of wood lay close by, a further witness to the truth of Han Ying's story. The sight was not a pleasant one and it is possible that some of the younger men felt sick. But Jonathan gave them little time to ruminate. First sentries had to be posted and then the body buried. The job of digging a grave was given to Corporal Harris and Rifleman Smith, but the selection of a suitable site proved difficult. On one side of the plateau the mountain rose sheer for many feet and on the other it dropped away almost as steeply. It was not possible to carry the body far, so in the end they decided to bury it in the open space in the middle of the camp.

Finding the camp empty had been another disappointment, but a systematic search showed that no one had been back since Han Ying had left four days earlier. Clothes, papers and even some bags of rice were stowed away in different places. There was therefore a reasonable chance that one of the two groups would appear eventually and Jonathan decided to ambush the camp in accordance with the original plan.

Next came the moment for moving the body, with each man looking at his neighbour and hoping that the grisly task of undertaker's mate would not fall to him. In due course a small group of retching men laid Leong Hian to rest and speedily piled earth and stones on top of him. When all was finished there was nothing to be seen, but the body was only just underground. The burial party knew only too well that the patrol would continue to suffer from the smell.

And then they settled down to wait. Four days in ambush had been Jonathan's instructions when he set out, but we had not visualized the business starting after four days' exhausting search and with food supplies reduced to almost nothing. But Jonathan reckoned that by combining what rations the men had left with the rice found in the camp, he would be able to manage for four days. At any rate he would try. Few jobs are more demanding than manning a twenty-four-hour ambush. Part of the time is spent on the alert, but when this is over one can do no more than relax in position. Sleeping, eating and all the other things that go towards existing as an animal have to be done on the spot. Four days is a long time under these circumstances.

The first day of the vigil passed pleasantly enough. The men were tired and were only too happy to be lying down warm and dry. Early next morning Smith was on watch as it became light. He was installed in one of the terrorist shelters and was covering the track leading into the camp. Nothing stirred in that direction, but he was puzzled by something about the size of a rabbit which was sitting in the centre of the camp roughly on top of Leong Hian's grave. It was only a few feet away, but he could not make out what it was in the twilight. The stench had not abated during the night, rather it seemed to have increased, although the creature evidently did not mind. Smith turned back to watching the track and did not look round again until it was fully light. When he did so he saw that the object which had puzzled him earlier was one of Leong Hian's feet. Some muscular contraction had forced it up through the thin covering of earth and there it had to stay, macabre and malodorous.

The second day passed like the first with no sign of the terrorists returning and the men began to wonder whether the Sengkang party had not come back earlier, seen Leong Hian's body and bolted without waiting to collect any of their belongings. By the morning of the third day the suspicion had become almost a certainty.

And then at about 10 a.m. a faint scuffling noise was heard coming up the track. The men on watch alerted their comrades and they all lay waiting, hearts thumping with excitement. Soon there was no doubt about it: someone was approaching the camp. Perhaps there were some more following along behind.

Sergeant Bagley's position covered the track leading into the camp and he was the first man to see the small khaki-clad figure, who was edging gingerly through the jungle. Every now and then the terrorist stopped and looked from side to side; he was obviously taking nothing for granted. Soon he was only a few yards from the men, but still they held their fire, hoping that there were other terrorists following along behind. Next time he stopped he half turned round and it seemed foolish to wait any longer. If he decided to bolt, there would only be a split second in which to fire before he had disappeared into the undergrowth. Sergeant Bagley squeezed the trigger of his rifle and the intolerable tension was shattered by the shot. The terrorist spun round from the impact of the bullet and as he fell three or four other men opened fire. After seven days of jungle silence the noise was deafening. Jonathan had to shout at the top of his voice to stop the fire and even after this was accomplished the racket went on for a few moments, as echoes of the fusillade were thrown back and forth between the innumerable gullies of Mount Ophir. Gradually they died away and the usual background sounds of the jungle reasserted themselves. Only the bleeding corpse of a terrorist, lying in the entrance to the camp, remained as proof that the incident had taken place and that 'S' Company had at last achieved success.

At first the patrol thought that the terrorist must be a courier because he had arrived by himself, but Han Ying identified him as Kam Kim Char, one of the men who had gone to Sengkang. Elated by the success and hopeful of a further contact, Jonathan settled down to continue the ambush having first sent a man off to find his other group, so that word could be passed to us at Bukit Serampang by wireless. He suggested that we should send a patrol with extra rations who could also remove the body. He was evidently disinclined to arrange for another funeral on the spot.

The ambush party remained in position for another two days, but I could guess that it must be somewhat of an anti-climax for them after the events of the past week or so. It also seemed very unlikely that any further visits would be made to the camp and so reluctantly I sent word for them to withdraw. During the final two days of the vigil they made up a song about their adventures which they sang to the tune of one of the cockney dirges. They called it 'Yonder Hill' and it became the 'S' Company anthem from then onwards. They were singing it when I met them at the jungle edge. It went something like this:

'YONDER HILL'

One day twelve men and Mr Peel
Set off to climb up yonder hill.
They climbed and climbed until last light
And then they Basha'ed for the night.

They found the CT camp one morn,
Just as another day was born
And from the camp there came a stench
Of one dead CT on a bench.

'Oh Smudger, Smudger,' said John Peel,
'Go dig his grave on yonder hill.'
'Oh Sir, Oh Sir, why pick on me,
I'm no grave-digger as you can see.'

They dug his grave both broad and deep
And buried him all but his feet.
They knew the boys would go through hell
Because there was a ghastly smell.

At 10 a.m. in three days' time
The hill, a courier did climb.
With thumping hearts we waited 'till
With lead we could his belly fill.

As he came walking down the track,
The sergeant shot him in the back,
And round and round and round he spun.
We fired until he hit the ground.

Oh shiny, shiny, shiny 'S',
At last you have achieved success.
And we're as pleased as we can be
'Cos we're the boys of 'S' Company.

Chapter 10

❈

Frustration

A few days later Inspector Beoy rang up and gave the codeword which meant that the terrorists were planning to send a food party into Grisek village that evening. Having done the necessary reconnaissance some weeks earlier and having also selected the men for the ambush party, we had no problems regarding the preliminary moves. There were three gaps in the village fence through which the enemy might pass, so our force was divided into three groups. Paul Greenwood of 'B' Company was in charge of one group, Sergeant Bagley was in charge of another group and I was in charge of the third. The gaps in the fence were only ten or fifteen yards apart.

We reached our positions just as it was getting dark, set up our flares and settled down to wait. Immediately in front of the fence was a ditch, which obviously played an important part in the drainage arrangements for the village, judging by the smell. Soon the last of the light had gone and we were left sweating in the damp, stinking darkness with an even greater concentration of mosquitoes than usual humming round our ears. The terrorists were expected to arrive between 8 and 8.30 p.m. so for the first hour and a half our discomfort was offset by hope. From 8.30 onwards hope began to fade, but there was no compensating reduction in our discomfort.

Suddenly a flare burst into light from the direction of Sergeant Bagley's group and we waited tense and expectant for the shots, but no shots came. Soon afterwards Sergeant Bagley himself crawled up to say that his flare had gone off by mistake. There was nothing to be done except to collect up the men and slink off home. We had a long and cheerless walk back to our vehicles which we had hidden about three miles away. It rained steadily all the time.

1 Original team: Kitson third from right

2 George

3 Hooded men: Eric Holyoak (smoking), Denis Kearney (jungle hat)

4 Kamau

5   Pseudo-gang on move

6   (*left to right*) Handley, Sergeant Bagley and Russell carrying out reconnaissance of River Muar banks under cover of pleasure trip on police launch

7 Jonathan Peel bringing men out of jungle after 'Yonder Hill Patrol'. Surrendered terrorist in lead, then Jonathan Peel, Sergeant Bagley and two more soldiers

8 Re-supply party with bicycles leaving transport in rubber plantation on way into jungle

9 (*left to right*) Rifleman Smith, Corporal 'Bunny' Bryan, Corporal Skillet, Corporal Solly, Rifleman Egbert Henry

10 Surrendered terrorists: Tay Boon Hui, Ah Kui and Kim San with Jonathan Peel

11   A view of the Sumayl Gap

12   General Carver sorting out a problem in Nicosia, March 1964

13 UN
position on
Radio Hill
after the
Greek
attack,
November
1967

14   Bob Pascoe and Mr Rolz Bennett (one of U Thant's two deputies), November 1967

There is no sin more complete and unforgivable than to make a mess of an operation laid on by Special Branch. In the first place, all the work is done by somebody else. One only has to sit where one is placed and do the job. Another reason is that by making a mess of it an informer or group of informers may well lose faith in the Government and cease to give information. Some of them may become compromised and lose their lives. Finally Special Branch loses confidence in the soldiers with the consequences which I remembered so well from my time in Kenya. Matters were not improved by the fact that we had made such an appalling mess of it. Anyone can miss when firing at a fleeting target in the dark, but we had not even made contact. I dreaded the thought of explaining the situation to Inspector Boey, the District Officer, the Colonel and the Brigadier.

Although I was feeling pretty low, Sergeant Bagley must have been feeling even worse because he was the man who was responsible for the flare which had gone off. He could not understand how it had happened. He was prepared to swear that he had not touched the button and no one else could have reached it. So far as he was concerned it must have gone off by itself. Had anyone else come up with such a story I should not have believed him, but Sergeant Bagley was so reliable and experienced that I found it hard to doubt him. Later we did some experiments with the flare firing mechanism and found that damp in a certain part of the circuit could bring about accidental ignition and this is almost certainly what happened.

Events during the next few days were reassuring from my point of view. Mr Moloney, the District Officer, heard about the fiasco in the morning and came straight out to Bukit Serampang to tell us, on behalf of the District War Executive Committee, not to worry. It was a very nice gesture and confirmed us in the high opinion which we already had of this man. The Colonel and the Brigadier were also very reasonable, which was fortunate, but best of all was the news which we got from Inspector Boey a few days later. He told us that the terrorists had come as arranged but had entered the village by a different route. The flare had gone off while they were actually inside the house of one of Boey's informers, who had evidently persuaded them that it was only the Home Guard hunting wild pig. They must have been convinced by the story because they returned to pick up some more stuff the following evening. It seemed that no lasting damage had been done, but we had taken a good jolt and the incident served to remind us how close is the gap between

E

triumph and disaster. Also, time was beginning to run out. We were nearing the end of July and there was a lot still to be done, if we were going to eliminate all the enemy in our area by the time we were due to leave in October.

At the end of July, 'B' and 'S' Companies received a visit from General Bower, the Director of Operations. I explained our plan and the course of the operations so far. He evidently thought that our activities were likely to bear fruit because he told the Brigadier that he could release the whole of 'B' Company from Operation Cobble so that it could work with 'S' Company. This decision more than doubled our strength, but it brought a complication in its train. The difficulty arose from the fact that the Commander of 'B' Company – Dick Worsley – was senior to me and should from that point of view have taken command. On the other hand, I had been running the operations so far and had done all the planning and had gained the confidence of the police and administration, so the Colonel decided to leave me in command.

But Dick did not like this arrangement, which was not in the least surprising. The Colonel therefore worked out a compromise under which Dick would be in command, but which provided for me remaining on the District War Executive Committee and dealing with the outside world. Such a solution was quite hopeless because the man who dealt with the outside world and had the access to Special Branch was the only person capable of making the operational plans. For a time we tried to work on the lines laid down by the Colonel, but neither of us liked it. It is all very well to compromise over command in the secure surroundings of Tidworth, or to govern by committee in Whitehall, but men engaged on operations must know exactly who is directing their efforts. There is no substitute for the impulsion of a single will. Both of us were agreed on this point.

After a few weeks it was obvious that the situation could not continue. We therefore went to the Colonel and jointly proposed the only other acceptable solution, which was that I should work under Dick's command. The Colonel however decided for various reasons that I should continue to conduct operations, but said that when using platoons of 'B' Company I should issue instructions through Dick. Otherwise I was to have sole command. Thereafter we continued to work on these lines, but it was not altogether satisfactory, especially for Dick. For some time I had been living at a great rate and every second of my time was fully occupied. As a result I was tense and not very easy to live with. The fact that we remained on speaking terms was entirely due to Dick's even temperament and considerable charm.

The command question is relevant to the story because it formed the background to all our operations and because it came near to wrecking them.

It is also worth recording because it illustrates on a very small scale one of the oldest of all the lessons of war. From an operational point of view there is no room for compromise over the position of the commander because he is the man that counts. From all other points of view it is often highly desirable to compromise over the commander's position. Weakness in this matter has been one of the major causes of disaster since time immemorial.

Although I had been obliged to concentrate my resources of manpower against the Kebun Bahru Branch during June and July, I had none the less been trying to build up a picture of the movements of the Malacca District group under It Hiong at the same time, using the same sort of approach in terms of research and discussion with Special Branch and others. The release of 'B' Company from Operation Cobble came at a moment when it seemed that constructive action was possible, so I proposed a plan to the District War Executive Committee under which a Police Field Force platoon and a 'B' Company platoon would jointly operate on the south-west slopes of Mount Ophir.

A few days after this operation started, Dick Worsley was in the wireless room at Bukit Serampang when a message was received to the effect that a patrol under Sergeant Cassidy had contacted three terrorists and killed them all. Dick immediately came to tell me about it and was very generous in his praise of the plan. Although I was naturally pleased at this success, my immediate reaction was to make sure that the operation did not stop. The Malacca District gang numbered five and the other two might be close at hand. Sergeant Cassidy realized this only too well, but unfortunately the officer commanding the police platoon was in overall command of the operation and he considered that a successful contact should be followed by a return to camp and a celebration. This was in fact common practice and he disregarded my request that he should carry on.

I immediately raised the matter with the other members of the District War Executive Committee and the Superintendent of Police issued the necessary orders to the police officer, but it was some time before he received them and the follow-up was delayed by nearly twenty-four hours.

Even then it was not carried out with much enthusiasm, except by the soldiers. A few days later a re-supply party went in commanded by another police officer. This party got lost and the officer decided to attract attention by firing a few shots and by blowing his whistle. By these means he did eventually reach his destination, but only at the expense of disturbing the whole area. It was obviously useless to continue with the operation under such circumstances, so we called it off.

Although the behaviour of these two police officers was maddening, it is perhaps worth mentioning two points. First, they were not regular policemen, but were men serving on contract as commanders of police field units. There were lots of these people dotted around in Malaya and most of them had been there for years and were planning to stay for as long as the Emergency lasted. They were not fresh from a period in England, nor could they look forward to a change of employment after a few months. The second point is that these officers were not commanding British soldiers. Their platoons were made up of Malay policemen who had no intention of exerting themselves more than was necessary. In this particular case the fault lay not so much with the police officers as with me because I should have known better than to employ them on a job of this sort. Thereafter I arranged for police platoons to carry out separate operations and did not try and use them in conjunction with our own units. On the other hand we did attach individual Malay policemen from these platoons to our own patrols to act as guides and interpreters and they were very useful in this way.

The operation had been intensely irritating, but some comfort was to be had from the fact that the leader of the Malacca District terrorists – It Hiong – was one of the men killed. In days gone by he had been an extremely important man and he was still, in theory, second in command to Ah Chien. In practice his influence had waned because nearly all of his organization had been destroyed. All the same, he was a good man to get out of the way. Another cause for satisfaction lay in the professional skill shown by Sergeant Cassidy's patrol; to kill three out of three terrorists in a jungle engagement was no mean feat.

The fiasco of this follow-up was followed shortly afterwards by another cause of annoyance. One day, out of the blue, I was told by battalion Headquarters that the Brigade Commander wanted to draw a line through the middle of Mount Ophir and give all the country to one side of it to a battalion of Gurkhas who were based at Segamat and who evidently had too little to do. The drawback to this idea was that it split the Kebun Bahru Branch's area between us and the Gurkhas. They would have the jungle in which the terrorists made their camps and we would have the area in which they operated. In consequence no sensible plan of operations would be possible and we would all have to revert to the old hit-and-miss methods of the five-day patrol and ambushing by guess-work. I had barely recovered from the frustration of the Malacca operation and was furious. I immediately wrote a lengthy and impolite appreciation of the effects of the order which I sent to the battalion second in command, the Colonel being away. Soon afterwards I heard that the Brigadier was coming to see us and that I should be prepared to explain my case to him.

When he arrived, he was extremely reasonable, as was always the case. He said that his idea was merely to employ the maximum number of troops to the best advantage, but that in the light of our arguments he was prepared to leave things as they were for another month and that he would reconsider the matter in September, if we had not succeeded in eliminating any more terrorists by that time. And so this incident came to a satisfactory conclusion, although it had caused me to waste a lot of time preparing my case. As a matter of fact, it is unlikely that the Brigadier had ever intended dividing up our area in such a senseless way. In all probability he had merely told his staff to work out a plan that would give the spare Gurkhas something to do and at the same time relieve the pressure on us, but the result was a piece of prep-school strategy which was well in keeping with the outlook on terrorist hunting held by most regular officers at that time.

Strangely enough we got our next elimination two days after the Brigadier's visit. This time it was Kam Boon Piow, Branch Committee Member and senior survivor of the Kebun Bahru Branch, who had decided to retire from the fray and we were full of hope at the prospects opened up by his surrender. But once again hope crumbled to frustration in our hands. We never discovered whether Kam Boon Piow was mad or whether he was merely pretending to be so, but something like him must have crossed Shakespeare's path

when he was writing *The Tempest* because he was the living image of
Caliban. Kam Boon Piow must have been past his first youth when
he went into the jungle at the time of the Japanese occupation and
it is doubtful whether he had emerged at the end of the war. If so,
he had not taken the opportunity of having a bath. He shuffled
around like a baboon with a stupid smile on his face and agreed
with everything anybody said, which made interrogation difficult.
Thus, if he was asked whether the balance of the Kebun Bahru
Branch had returned to Mount Ophir he would say yes. If in the
next breath he was asked whether they had joined up with the
Grisek Branch he would say that they most certainly had done just
that. Getting useful information out of him was impossible. He did
however say that he would be willing to lead us to the camp of the
Jementah Branch. He maintained that Lee Meng, who was in
charge of this gang, was a terrible rascal and that he deserved to be
shot every day for a fortnight. He was accordingly taken to the base
camp of the 'B' Company platoon which was working in the area.

During the first evening that he was with this platoon Kam Boon
Piow managed to get hold of the water bottle which contained the
rum ration and he drank the lot before he was discovered. His an-
tics thereafter delighted the soldiers to such an extent that they considered themselves compensated for the loss of their rum. Later he
found another bottle containing what he thought was gin. Unfortunately for him it was insect repellent which burned him badly.
Next day the patrol set out in search of Lee Meng's camp, but it
was soon obvious that Kam Boon Piow had no intention of taking
the patrol there, even supposing that he knew where it was. After a
couple of days the platoon commander returned him to us.

I was reluctant to abandon all hope of getting anything useful out
of Kam Boon Piow and I discussed the matter with Ah Meng, the
surrendered terrorist who lived at Bukit Serampang. He had known
Kam Boon Piow on and off for many years and said that he had
always been a bit simple. On the other hand he was not nearly as
mad as he pretended to be, or if he was, he had deteriorated greatly
during the past year. Although it was now clear that he was not
going to help us intentionally, there was a chance that he might
accidentally provide some useful information about recent events,
food sources or jungle routes, if he was living with one of our groups
in the field. We therefore sent him off to join Jonathan Peel, who
was living in a jungle base camp at that time. In the event nothing

came of this plan either. Kam Boon Piow lived with the patrol for nearly a week and showed them all sorts of things which were obviously wrong. One evening an appalling noise came from the basha where he was supposed to be sleeping and it turned out that he was singing Communist songs. Jonathan sharply reminded him that by his own reckoning he was working for us, thereupon he said that he was very sorry. A few minutes later the racket started up again, but on this occasion he met Jonathan's onslaught by saying that he was now singing anti-Japanese songs which he was sure the soldiers would appreciate. Soon afterwards we handed Kam Boon Piow over to the police.

There is no doubt that the exercise of command during operations is unlike any other activity. Nothing can compare with it in terms of the demands it makes, or of the satisfaction it can yield in return. Every ounce of energy and every scrap of intelligence and imagination is focused in one great effort to achieve the tactical aim whatever the cost mentally or physically. People who spend their lives in more settled surroundings cannot begin to understand what is involved and probably never realize what they have missed. In that respect it is like being in love. I had been lucky in having a very good command in Kenya and I knew that I had been lucky again in getting the job of operating against Ah Chien and his friends. At the same time my temper was getting pretty short, as a result of the pace of the past few months. The frustration engendered by the failure of the Grisek ambush, the command issue, the question of our boundary with the Gurkhas, the mess we had made of the operation against the Malacca terrorists and the disappointment suffered as a result of Kam Boon Piow's uselessness did nothing to improve it.

Had I but known it, I had better cause for satisfaction than I supposed. In the first place we had, in a relatively short time, killed five terrorists and caused two more to surrender, one of whom had murdered his companion in doing so. In other words, of the thirty-six terrorists who formed our target in early June, eight had already been neutralized including both the District Committee Secretaries. More importantly, in terms of the long-term consequences, was the fact that I had almost by accident hit upon a method of developing the background information, which I had been able to acquire from many sources, into contact information. At the time I was only vaguely aware of this. Although I had made a conscious effort to analyse the background information and make calculations from it, and although I had deliberately cross-checked the result of these calculations by sending out patrols to seek further positive and negative information before setting out the ambushes, the killing of Leong Tek Chai and all that followed from it could have been luck. But when the system worked a second time in roughly similar circumstances against the Malacca District gang I realized that this was what I had been groping after at the Staff College. I now had to take matters a stage further in an attempt to make further contacts with the terrorists with whom we now seemed to have lost contact.

Since the saga of the operation on 'Yonder Hill' we had lost sight of the Kebun Bahru Branch altogether. While the 'B' Company platoon had been engaged against It Hiong, the two 'S' Company platoons had concentrated on the old areas of Mount Ophir, the illegal cultivations and Sengkang but we had not had any sort of lead. I came to the conclusion that the key to the puzzle lay in the question of the leadership of the Kebun Bahru Branch. There were two officers who might have taken over from Leong Tek Chai. One was Kam Boon Piow and the other was Chan Ah Fook. Even before he surrendered, it seemed unlikely that Kam Boon Piow would be able to command a gang and Ah Meng did not consider that Chan Ah Fook would be a great success in that role either.

The question therefore arose as to what would happen to the survivors of the Branch and three possible answers seemed worth considering. Firstly one of the other members might seize power over the head of Kam Boon Piow and Chan Ah Fook and run the Branch in the same way as Leong Tek Chai had done. In this case terrorists should be showing up in the same sort of places as they had done formerly. The second possibility was that Ah Chien would pick them up and add them to his followers. In this case we would not see them again because Ah Chien's gang made no contact with the outside world either by visiting the population or by collecting food: they were provided with food by the other Branches. This seemed an unlikely course for events to have taken because it would have made Ah Chien's group unwieldy and it would have put a very large burden onto the other Branches with regard to food collection. The third possibility was that the survivors had joined up with one of the other Branches in the District, that is to say, the Grisek Branch led by Seet Ho Ching or the Jementah Branch led by Lee Meng. Seet Ho Ching was known to be younger, more enterprising and better educated, but it was quite possible that these characteristics were not those most sought after by the Kebun Bahru survivors.

Early in August we decided to leave Mount Ophir and go in search of these two Branches. We already knew enough about the Jementah Branch for some troops to go into the jungle in search of them and this task was given to Robin Alers-Hankey's platoon of 'B' Company.

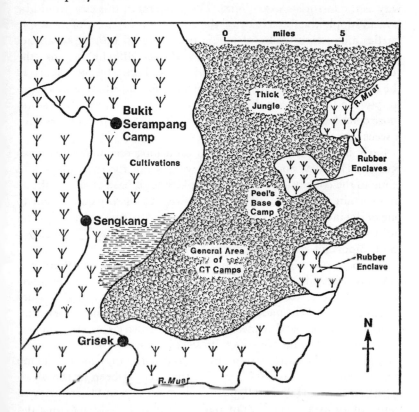

Operating against the Grisek Branch was more complicated because the jungle in the area which belonged to them was interspersed with patches of rubber. This was due to the fact that the river Muar ran along the southern and eastern edge of the region and rubber tappers from the villages along the river bank could go to work by boat. The existence of these rubber enclaves made our task of finding the enemy more difficult than ever because the enemy need never come to the jungle edge at all in order to meet the population: they could contact them at work. Furthermore this part of the jungle was at the extreme range of operations based on Bukit Serampang and the five-day patrol would have been less likely than usual to achieve success. Clearly a better system would be to make a long-term base camp on the eastern edge of the area near the river and operate towards the rubber from within the jungle in the same way as the terrorists were doing. The problem in this case would be how to supply the force because the constant movement of re-supply parties along eight miles of jungle tracks would be sure to attract attention. Re-supply by boat would also be difficult because the river banks were so swampy that men could only be put ashore at the landing stages used by the tappers. A third alternative was to re-supply the force by air drop, but few things give away a position more completely than a shower of brightly coloured parachutes once a week.

Early in August therefore I went on a long reconnaissance with Russell, Handley and Pascoe. We were away for three days and came to the conclusion that the best place for a base camp would be in a certain part of the jungle, which was reasonably convenient to one of the landing stages, which was not too far from a track leading ultimately to Bukit Serampang and which was close to the three most important rubber enclaves.

We spent one night in this bit of jungle during which there was the most fantastic thunderstorm. It had been an oppressive afternoon, but there was no reason to suppose that anything unusual would happen. We made a small shelter out of ground sheets and poncho capes, cooked a meal and settled down as usual with our insect repellent to talk ourselves to sleep. Soon after midnight some wild pig started routing around in the undergrowth, which woke me up. It seemed even more oppressive than it had been in the afternoon and flashes of distant lightning lit up the sky. But the storm was many miles away and I went back to sleep. Two hours later the storm reached us. When I woke up it was raining hard and the gap between lightning and thunder was down to two or three seconds. During the next few minutes the wind rose to a crescendo driving the rain in front of it. Our ground sheets flapped and torrents of water flowed around our recumbent bodies. We lay there praying that no branch torn from its parent tree would crash upon our shelter.

By this time Handley and Pascoe were both awake, but in some unaccountable way Russell slept on. Suddenly it seemed that our worst fears were about to be realized as a flash of lightning tore through the steamy heavens and bit into a huge tree almost immediately above us. As a result the whole top half of the tree broke away and crashed into some bamboo near to our position. The noise of the thunder was deafening and the subsequent cracking of bamboo stalks sounded just like a machine-gun. Russell chose that particular moment to wake up and evidently thought that we were being attacked because he grabbed his rifle and made as if to man his 'stand to' position. We just managed to restrain him in time.

Gradually the storm passed us. Next morning it was so fresh and sunny that the jungle seemed like a veritable paradise. Great butterflies reflecting bright metallic colours from their wings flapped contentedly from one patch of rotting vegetation to the next. Raindrops sparkled in the shafts of sunlight, which managed to penetrate the jungle canopy and occasional flowering creepers provided a blaze of orange colour from where they hung way up in the trees. It seemed that we alone, in our drab and sodden clothes, failed to live up to the glory of that morning.

On our return I decided that Jonathan should take both the mortar platoon and the machine-gun platoon into the area and stay there until the Grisek Branch was destroyed. We thought that the re-supply problem could be managed, if we sometimes took stores in by boat and sometimes took them in through the jungle. We also reckoned that if we could get hold of some bicycles on which to suspend the packages, each man could push in about three times as much as he could carry on his back, thereby reducing the number of occasions on which re-supply would be necessary. Although one could not push a bicycle through virgin jungle, it is perfectly possible to push one along a track, however narrow, and many such tracks existed because of the presence over the years of loggers and aborigines. Strange as it may seem, it was more difficult to get the bicycles than it would have been to get aircraft to deliver the supplies by parachute. We had to answer all sorts of questions, but in the end the bicycles arrived.

When planning the operation Jonathan and I had agreed that the first phase should be taken up in trying to establish the pattern of movement of the gang. As a result of careful research with Inspector Boey, we had a very good idea of the general area in which the main enemy camp must be and we knew of the expeditions made from it to Grisek village every month or six weeks for food.

This was our one sure source of information and we had no intention of disturbing it again until we could be sure of a really good contact. We based our hopes for the immediate future on the movement which was obviously taking place between the suspected camp area and the rubber enclaves. It was for this reason that we had put our own base camp nearby. Because of the considerable distance between these enclaves and the suspected area of the enemy's main camp, it seemed likely that they would spend some nights in temporary camps near the river.

We did not expect to get any sensational information from Inspector Boey, but we hoped that his contacts in the villages along the river would get to know about visits made by the terrorists to the rubber tappers in the enclaves. Sightings of this sort were valuable in working out the pattern of enemy movement, even if the reports took several days to reach us. The arrangement was that Inspector Boey would pass this information to me and I would pass it on to Jonathan by wireless or by visiting him. At the same time Jonathan intended to send his own patrols out to look for tracks in likely areas so as to confirm or deny our theories of the enemy movement pattern. When he had collected enough information from his own sources together with anything I could give him, he would be ready to lay ambushes or send out patrols into areas through which the enemy should be moving at the time. It was the same system in outline that we had used against the Kebun Bahru Branch, that is to say, we intended first to narrow down the problem in relation to space and time by means of reconnaissance and deduction. Then we would take offensive action within these narrow limits which would have a fair chance of success. The difference between our operations against the Grisek Branch and those which had taken place in June and July was that on this occasion we would be working from a jungle base camp instead of from Bukit Serampang and it would be Jonathan who would be in immediate tactical control of events rather than myself.

Jonathan took the two 'S' Company platoons into the jungle during the first half of August and struck oil almost before he was ready. Two days after the start of the operation one of the platoon commanders, called John Starkey, who was leading a patrol looking for confirmation of a terrorist route, ran into a small gang. Unfortunately the contact was abortive, but the enemy left their haversacks behind and we got a great deal more information about the Grisek Branch from an examination of their contents.

This incident was followed by nearly three weeks during which no further contact was made. After the first ten days I was subjected to pressure from various quarters outside 'S' Company to withdraw Jonathan and his men on the grounds that young conscripts without specialist training could not be expected to stay in the jungle for long periods without detriment to their physical and mental health. At the same time Jonathan was himself subject to pressure from some of the senior NCOs, who had not yet come to trust his tactical judgement and who considered that no good would come from staying there indefinitely. But Jonathan and I knew that progress was being made in the form of a steady build-up of information and we had no intention of calling off the operation.

Despite all the muttering about the evil effects of jungle life, the riflemen were enjoying themselves: they always like to get away from the Sergeant Major's influence. After the operation had been going on for three weeks the sickness rate in 'S' Company was the lowest in the battalion. This was partly due to the fact that if a man contracted some minor ailment such as a jungle sore he had to report to Jonathan who treated him with a poultice made of biscuits mushed up in boiling water. Most men preferred to conceal their scabs and cankers.

To give the men an interest and to reduce the risk of skin disease Jonathan started a beard-growing competition in the company. Another popular pastime was learning all about the terrorists in the Grisek Branch. Each man had a complete set of pictures and they constantly discussed the characteristics of the members of the opposing team. By this time we had unearthed a great deal of information about the enemy and most of the riflemen knew as much about their history, tastes and habits as they did about each other. An indication of the amount of detailed information which the soldiers had picked up was brought home to us when they found some old bits of rag which a female had used in connection with one of her monthly periods. These were unearthed in a temporary camp which had been used by four terrorists. There were two women in the Grisek Branch, one of whom was the wife of Seet Ho Ching, the other being a rank and file member. At some stage we had discovered that this other woman was pregnant, from which the patrol commander deduced that the camp must have been occupied by Seet Ho Ching's wife and therefore, probably, by Seet Ho Ching since they usually moved around together. This particular discovery, added to a lot of other information that we had collected, led to the next contact.

Chapter 11

────────── ✻ ──────────

Cause and Effect

By this time it was the end of August and we only had a little more than two months left, but Jonathan was now ready to strike. He knew the general area of the enemy's main camp and he had worked out that Seet Ho Ching, with his wife and two other terrorists, were likely to be visiting the rubber tappers in the enclave to the north of his base camp. In view of the distance between the main camp and the enclave Jonathan reckoned that the terrorists would be spending a few nights in a temporary camp in a certain strip of jungle. The area was small enough to give a patrol a good chance of success, so while a number of ambushes were placed in the rubber plantation itself Sergeant Bagley took a patrol to look for the suspected temporary camp.

On the second day of the search Sergeant Bagley and his men suddenly came under fire. The jungle was immensely thick at this point and the men had not seen the enemy camp until they were right in it. After a few moments the enemy withdrew leaving one dead man behind them. Sergeant Bagley reported the action on the wireless to Jonathan, left two men to hold the fort and guard the body and set off in pursuit.

On hearing of the incident I made my way to the base camp. Jonathan took me to the scene of the engagement and we discussed future moves. Considering how thick the jungle was at this spot it was amazing that Sergeant Bagley should have killed any of the terrorists. The dead man turned out to be Seet Ho Ching's second in command, a Branch Committee Member called Han Leong.

There was nothing for me to do with regard to following up the

contact because Sergeant Bagley and Jonathan had taken the necessary action. But there was one other matter requiring urgent attention, if our future operations were to have any chance of success.
After John Starkey's contact three weeks earlier, the enemy had
continued to visit the rubber enclaves which showed that they had
not been unduly alarmed by the experience. They probably thought
that our presence on this occasion was the result of a normal five-day
patrol from Bukit Serampang. We had now contacted them again
in the same general area and there was a danger that this would
frighten them away altogether unless we took some positive steps to
reassure them. We decided that the best course would be for me to
send a large re-supply party into the base camp secretly two nights
later. The following day they would come out looking as though
they were returning home after a long patrol and walk through the
rubber to the landing stage. From there they would go down the
river in a police launch and land at one of the villages, where they
would be met by army transport. In this way we hoped that the local
people would think that the re-supply party was the main patrol
coming out of the jungle and get the impression that our operation
was over. Such an impression would soon be communicated to the
terrorists.

After seeing Jonathan, I returned to Bukit Serampang and waited
for news of the follow-up patrol. I also made the arrangement which
we had worked out for deceiving the enemy. Two days later I went
in the police launch to fetch our re-supply party. By so doing I would
be able to have another talk to Jonathan and I thought it would lend
colour to our cover plan if I was seen welcoming the men back as
though they were returning from a long sojourn in the jungle. On
arrival I heard that word had just been received from Sergeant
Bagley to the effect that he had overtaken the terrorists and had
killed two more.

It soon became apparent that the chase had been extremely
vigorous. The terrorists had travelled in a large circle after the first
contact hoping to throw Sergeant Bagley off the trail, but his
trackers had not been fooled. Eventually the terrorists had tried to
ambush our men, or so it seemed, because they were waiting in some
thick cover when the patrol came up with them. They opened fire
first with a sub-machine-gun and two rifles, but they did no damage.
The patrol quickly killed two of the three terrorists seen and the
third man made good his escape after dropping the magazine of a

tommy-gun. There was only one such weapon with the Grisek Branch and it belonged to Seet Ho Ching.

Sergeant Bagley set off once more after the fugitive and Jonathan sent a party to collect the bodies. They arrived in time for us to take them out with the re-supply party. One was a woman, later identified as Seet Ho Ching's wife, Chan Ah Hiong. The other was Lee Chor, who had formerly belonged to the Kebun Bahru Branch. This was the first occasion on which we had proof that the Kebun Bahru Branch had broken up.

After this incident there was a further period during which we had to search for more information and for just over two weeks Jonathan's men made no further contact with the enemy. A notable development in this period was that Inspector Boey arranged for one of his informers, who was a rubber tapper, to contact Jonathan direct, if he had a sighting to report. This represented a considerable act of faith on the part of Inspector Boey and the informer because any carelessness on Jonathan's part would almost certainly result in the murder of the man concerned. It also represented a risk on our part because the informer might let the cat out of the bag regarding our continued presence in the area, in which case all our efforts would be wasted. Having heard how the man's brother had been tied to a tree and bayonetted by Ah Heng and Kam San, two members of the Grisek Branch, we thought that the risk was worth taking.

In the days immediately following Sergeant Bagley's great patrol my attention was largely directed towards some operations being carried out by a platoon of 'B' Company against the Jementah Branch. These culminated in a contact early in September, but luck was against our men and the enemy escaped. A day or two later, I was told to go to Kuala Lumpur for discussion with members of the Special Branch and the military operations staff, who were interested in the system which we had been using to make contact with the terrorists. I was to catch an aircraft in Segamat next morning at 7 a.m. I wanted to visit Jonathan before I left, but could not see how I could get to his base camp and back in time. Luckily there was a very bright moon at the time so I decided to try bicycling as an experiment. Pascoe and Gillard came with me as escorts and we left Bukit Serampang as soon as the moon was up at about 8 p.m.

The first part of our journey lay through the illegal cultivations and here we made good time along a very reasonable track. There was also a passable track for a short way inside the jungle, which had been used by logging vehicles, and we managed to pedal along it after a fashion although visibility was uncertain and we had several misfortunes. This track soon petered out and thereafter we were reduced to a footpath which was so narrow that the trees met overhead with the result that very little moonlight penetrated at all.

We managed to ride occasionally, but were on our feet for most of the time. All the same when we arrived at the base camp we found that we had completed the journey much faster than we would have done had we walked all the way.

Our only serious set-back occurred on the return journey. When we reached the logging track we started pedalling recklessly, spurred on by the improved visibility. Moonlight and shadow alternated alarmingly as we hurtled through the night and the wind of our passage blew the heavy jungle scent into our faces. Suddenly we came to a log bridge over some water. Gillard, who was leading, got over safely and my front wheel was on the bridge before I had time to brake. Sheer momentum carried me across, but I fell off on the far side. Pascoe started to brake as soon as he saw the obstacle, but the only result was that he skidded on the bridge and both he and his bicycle fell into the scum-covered muck with a splash. Luckily no damage was done, but it was a thoroughly unusual experience. On our return I had plenty of time for a wash and change before catching the aeroplane at Segamat. I returned a few days later, but it was more than another two weeks before we had our next contact.

The morning of September 20th was fine and hot. As Corporal Bunny Bryan and Rifleman Egbert Lancelot Henry lay concealed in some rough grass on the edge of one of the rubber enclaves, the sweat trickled off their backs and legs. Corporal Bryan was a burly Englishman, steady as a rock. Rifleman Henry came from the West Indies. He was small and dark, a great favourite with the other men and one of the best shots in the company.

According to Jonathan's calculations a terrorist was likely to approach to within fifty yards of their ambush position at some time between 7 a.m. and midday. He would be there to talk to the tappers who were working on the rubber trees. A great deal of skill and effort had gone into the making of these calculations, but it would all be in vain if Bunny Bryan and Egbert Henry proved unequal to their task.

The job which these two men had got to do also required a high degree of skill and effort. They would have to lie absolutely still for several hours despite the goading of the mosquitoes, the irritation of the undergrowth and the slowly moving shafts of sunlight which baked first one part of their body and then the next. They could not wipe away the sweat or move their stiffening limbs because tappers were working within a few yards of their position. At the same time they had to remain on a razor's edge of alertness because the target, if it came, might only present itself for a few seconds. Furthermore both Bryan and Henry had lain in ambush on numerous occasions in the past without ever seeing a terrorist and this made it even more difficult to maintain the intense degree of readiness required.

Although he could not look at his watch, Corporal Bryan estimated that the time must be about half past nine, judging by the position of the sun and the fact that some of the tappers were drifting away towards the river. He had managed to achieve a certain detachment from his body, so that he could leave it lying under its covering of undergrowth, limp and unfeeling, while at the same time remaining on watch with his eyes, ears and nose. This was a condition which most of the soldiers managed to achieve eventually, but only after several months of experience and hard training.

Rifleman Henry lay in a similar state next to the Corporal, but facing the opposite way, so that between them they could cover as wide a field of fire as possible. He was trying to work out what the odds were against his ever having a shot at a terrorist, but gave up after a time because he realized that the necessary facts on which to base the calculation were not available. For a moment he looked down at his own brown hand as it lay coiled around his rifle butt. A mosquito was gorging itself with blood from his thumb, but Henry looked at it with as much detachment as if the hand belonged to someone else. Automatically his eyes returned to their work of scanning the rubber plantation and checking on the position of the tappers.

At that moment he became aware that something unusual was happening. One of the tappers had stopped work and was talking to another man. He could hardly see them, but they were walking fast through the trees. He got a glimpse of them for a moment and got the impression that the other man was wearing a khaki uniform. Judging by their course, he would see them once more for a split second between two bushes slightly to his left and then for rather longer in a wider gap to his front. The next glimpse convinced

Rifleman Henry that a terrorist was about to appear in his sights.

Deep down in most people lies the natural computer of the primitive hunter, rusty and disused. In Henry's case it had been brushed up and exercised by many hours of practice on the jungle range. As a result, information regarding distance, angle, speed and light was processed automatically, his rifle came into the aim; there was a loud crash which echoed around the trees and the target fell to the ground and lay there concealed in the long grass.

'Bunny, Bunny, I've shot a terrorist,' said Henry excitedly.

'Oh Egg,' said the Corporal, 'it was a tapper and we'll both be court-martialled.'

'No, no Bunny. It was a terrorist and I shot him,' said Henry.

'Well, we might as well go and see,' said Corporal Bryan.

The two men crawled stiffly out of their concealed position and walked over to the body. Long before they arrived all the tappers had disappeared from the plantation and were legging it back to the landing stage as fast as they could go.

Rifleman Henry had indeed shot a terrorist for a small, oldish yellow man lay at their feet wearing breeches and crossed puttees, a khaki tunic and a cap with a red star in the front. By his side lay a carbine. Henry's bullet had passed through his brain killing him almost at once.

There was rejoicing in the base camp that evening. It was three weeks since the previous contact and the men needed the encouragement of success. Only Rifleman Henry failed to share in the general elation. He mourned for his victim and wondered what his father would say, if he knew that his son had killed. He was not only a first-class soldier, but a sensitive man as well and this was his first experience of killing.

The dead terrorist was soon identified as Chua See Chak, a relatively unimportant person in his own right, but one of Ah Chien's personal followers. He was a member of the team whose job it was to work the portable printing press, which turned out propaganda. The significance of his death lay in the fact that one of Ah Chien's followers should be visiting the tappers at all. Admittedly this might have come about because Ah Chien had got tired of him and sent him off to join the Grisek Branch, but it might equally well be that Ah Chien himself had been obliged to join the Grisek Branch for one reason or another. This opened up some interesting possibilities.

Although the ambush itself was a very minor affair, it represented a considerable achievement on the part of Jonathan Peel, Bryan and Henry. Just as certainly, but rather less obviously, it represented a success for the system of training which the Colonel had forced on the battalion. Through many long and weary months he had insisted on the rigid discipline and constant practice which could alone produce the necessary degree of excellence. His intense preoccupation with detail in all matters to do with minor tactics had often maddened the Company Commanders, but time and again we had reaped the benefit in the form of successful contacts as opposed to abortive ones. According to the records kept at Muar Police Station the contacts made by 'B' and 'S' Company were three times as productive as those achieved by any other battalion that had operated in the area.

As the crow flies the main enemy base camp was about four miles from our own. Although we had no proof of it at the time, Ah Chien and his followers had joined forces with the Grisek Branch two or three weeks earlier and on the evening of September 20th they were sitting around waiting for the return of Chua See Chak. Ah Chien had delivered himself of a short speech on some doctrinaire subject earlier in the evening and had then gone to his basha. Next door his two bodyguards, Lim Tuan and Kiang Sin lay talking quietly together, while immediately opposite was a bigger basha which housed the staff of Ah Chien's press.

Of the original members of the Grisek Branch, five men and a heavily pregnant woman remained and they, together with one survivor from the Kebun Bahru Branch, accounted for the rest of the people in the camp. Kam San and Ah Heng were on guard, Wu Kuay sat with the girl and the others lay in their bashas.

Seet Ho Ching had become very silent and preoccupied since losing his wife a few weeks earlier and he was in no mood for talking to Tay Boon Hui, the only other officer in the Branch and the joint occupant of his basha. They therefore lay silently in the damp, dank darkness. Although he was not saying anything, Tay Boon Hui's mind was turning over at a good rate. He had been in the jungle for nine years and was fully accustomed to the risk involved. During that time there had been occasions when one or other of his friends had failed to return from patrol. There had been one ghastly moment when he himself had been chased through the jungle by a huge Fijian, but he had managed to escape unscathed. But the events of the past few months had been altogether different. It had all started with the death of the District Committee Secretary, Leong Tek Chai, and the break-up of the Kebun Bahru Branch. Most of the survivors had gone to Lee Meng at Jementah, but two had joined Seet Ho Ching, one of whom was already dead.

Then, one evening when he had gone to collect food in Grisek village he had heard about the death of the District Committee Secretary for Malacca, It Hiong, and his two followers. This had been followed by the disaster which had overtaken the patrol led by Seet Ho Ching. Han Leong had been one of Tay Boon Hui's particular friends. Now it seemed that Chua See Chak would not return. For nearly six months Tay Boon Hui had been in charge of getting supplies from Grisek. To start with he had made the journey into the village about once a month, but since Ah Chien had billeted himself on the Branch he had been obliged to go nearly every week. He did not like the idea at all. Every time he went he felt that he was bound to run into an ambush. The chances of survival were just not good enough.

And then he fell to wondering whether there really was much point in going on forever. Certainly the cause did not seem to be making much headway in Ah Chien's area and his contact in Grisek had said quite recently that there had been a number of surrenders further north in the State of Perak. Both he and his contact had condemned this backsliding in words, but Tay Boon Hui was astute enough to realize that his friend had only mentioned the subject in order to suggest surrender as a possible course of action.

The night wore on and Seet Ho Ching lay sunk in thought. Tay Boon Hui went out for a last look round before turning in. Ah Heng and Kam San had been relieved by two of Ah Chien's men and were talking and laughing together under their breath. Tay Boon Hui often wondered what those two thought about the cause. Very little he imagined. They would be perfectly happy in any group of outlaws where there was good company, enough food, a bit of excitement and not too much work. Since Ah Chien's party had joined them there was less work around the camp because there were more men to do the chores.

Eventually Tay Boon Hui lay down to sleep, but sleep did not come. He was having a big decision forced on him by the pressure of increasing risk. He had to go to Grisek tomorrow evening and then again only six days later. Chua See Chak's empty bed-space danced in front of his eyes as he had seen it earlier in the evening when doing his rounds. In the end he made the decision. If Chua See Chak was not back by the time he left for Grisek he would definitely broach the question of surrender with his friend in the village.

Three days later Tay Boon Hui's intentions were made known to Inspector Boey.

Chapter 12

❋

Climax in Malaya

At midday on September 27th Inspector Boey told me that Tay Boon Hui wanted to meet a representative of the Government that evening in order to surrender himself. The business was complicated by the fact that he would be accompanied by another terrorist who could not be told of the surrender plan until Tay Boon Hui was safely in our hands. Another problem arose from the fact that Tay Boon Hui would not come into Grisek village to surrender in case we took advantage of the enclosed surroudings to kill him and his companion. He had stipulated that the meeting should take place at a point in the jungle known only to his contact, who would lead us to the spot.

Together with Inspector Boey I made a plan designed to meet all of Tay Boon Hui's requirements together with some of my own. He was naturally reluctant to trust in our good faith until he had broken the ice. At the same time I was disinclined to present myself as a target in any ambush that he might possibly be preparing. Our plan entailed getting to the meeting place some time ahead of Tay Boon Hui and his friend and concealing Rifleman Pascoe and Green close by, so that they could lend a hand if things went wrong. Inspector Boey together with a Special Branch Officer from Johore would wait nearby and join us once the formalities were over. Tay Boon Hui's contact man and I would greet the two terrorists at the rendezvous.

We arrived at the place where we intended to leave the car soon after dark and started walking up a track in the jungle. I was not armed, but carried the hammer from my Landrover tool-box, wrapped around with sacking, just in case Tay Boon Hui required any help when it came to convincing his friend that surrender was a good thing. We had only got about half-way to the meeting place when I suddenly walked into a terrorist who was coming down the track in the opposite direction.

Tay Boon Hui was as surprised as I was. Whereas he was in the wrong place, I was much too early. All the same we obviously could not disengage and start again and it was clear that his motive was to surrender and not to ambush us, so I held out my hand and said good evening. There was no sign of a second man.

By this time Inspector Boey had come up and he started talking to Tay Boon Hui. It soon became apparent that he had left his companion, who turned out to be Kam San, a hundred yards down the track on some pretext or other because he did not want to risk an incident taking place while he was surrendering. Once he was satisfied with our behaviour, he said that he would go back and persuade Kam San to surrender as well. Having got Tay Boon Hui's rifle there was no likelihood of his changing his mind so we let him go, albeit with some misgivings.

For the next ten minutes we squatted by the track wondering whether we had made a mistake. From past experience with the Mau Mau I knew that Kam San would need time to get used to the idea of surrender because he might never have given the matter any thought before. But the others were afraid that something had gone wrong and were all in favour of setting off down the track to see what had happened. In the end we decided to send Tay Boon Hui's contact man because he could at least join in any discussion that might be going on without frightening Kam San away.

His departure was followed by a further agonizing period of waiting after which it was decided that I should go and find out what was happening. Grasping the hammer firmly at the point of balance, I edged my way through the darkness, but it transpired that my decision to act had coincided with a similar decision on the part of Kam San. For the second time that evening I experienced the unusual sensation of bumping into an armed and uniformed terrorist in the middle of the track. Once again we exchanged politenesses and the business was over.

The next job was to try and find out enough about the intentions of the rest of the gang to carry out an operation against them before they discovered what had happened and changed their plans. The best results would come from being taken direct to the enemy camp early next day. Inspector Boey would do the necessary interrogation as soon as we got back to camp, but we had two miles to walk before we reached the Landrover and it seemed well worth trying to establish some sort of relationship with the men at once so as to save time later.

From the very start I treated Tay Boon Hui as if he were an officer visiting 'S' Company from another unit. As soon as we started the walk back, I gave both men their weapons to carry and chatted away about the Grisek Branch, Ah Chien and the rest of their men, as if they were no more than the members of a rival football team. In this way I aimed to build up a confidential feeling of trust and at the same time demonstrate that we knew all the background to their lives already so that at least this part of the business would be taken for granted when the interrogation started and would not be the cause of endless delay as we winkled the information out of them bit by bit.

On arrival at Bukit Serampang we went straight to the officers' mess and I installed Tay Boon Hui and Kam San in my own bedroom so that their presence would not become known. It was immediately clear that although Kam San was trying to be pleasant he would do no more than he was told to do by Tay Boon Hui. From him we could expect co-operation, but not initiative. Tay Boon Hui, on the other hand, seemed anxious to help eliminate his former associates and ostensibly fell in with suggestions which would result in their destruction. He said that it would be no good trying to lead us back to the camp because the gang had left it that afternoon. They intended to move to a new one and the arrangement was that Tay Boon Hui and Kam San were to remain near Grisek for the night and that Seet Ho Ching and another terrorist would meet them next evening and lead them back to the new camp.

Kam San corroborated the story independently so it seemed that it might be true. We decided that the best arrangement would be to station Tay Boon Hui at the meeting place with instructions to kill Seet Ho Ching and capture the other terrorist, who could then lead us to the new camp if we could persuade him to do so. We would lie in ambush round the meeting place and set off flares as soon as Seet Ho Ching was killed so that the other man would realize that escape was impossible and submit to being captured. Tay Boon Hui approved of the plan. He said that he understood the necessity for killing Seet Ho Ching, who was a fanatic. There would be no chance of getting him to surrender, let alone lead us back to the camp. If we took him alive, he would probably manage to prevent the other man from helping us.

The next job was to get together a force to carry out the ambush. If all went well we would go straight on to the main camp and any success there would involve us in a follow-up, the whole operation being conducted in Jonathan's area. Accordingly I got on to the wireless and told him to bring out a force of ten men to join us at Bukit Serampang and carry out the operation. They were to arrive as soon as possible.

I did not like our plan very much because it was too complicated. It is all very well in theory to talk about shooting one man and capturing another, but it was asking a lot of Tay Boon Hui. Furthermore, if the man refused to be captured, our soldiers would be obliged to open fire with Tay Boon Hui stuck in the middle of the target area! On the other hand, 1 was not prepared to risk losing Seet Ho Ching and I was determined that the meeting place should be well and truly covered in case anything should go wrong with Tay Boon Hui's part of the job. Whereas it was not a good plan, I could not think of a better one. Next day we would rehearse as much of it as we could. Meanwhile Kam San and Tay Boon Hui spent the rest of the night sleeping as best they could on the floor of my room.

Three things had to be attended to before we went to the meeting with Seet Ho Ching. Firstly we had to make sure that Tay Boon Hui's rifle would work properly at the critical moment. Secondly we had to be sure that he would keep his head. Thirdly we had to be sure that the soldiers would prevent anyone getting away, but at the same time would not kill Tay Boon Hui or the man whom we needed to lead us to Ah Chien.

The first real horror came to light when we inspected Tay Boon Hui's rifle. He said he had not fired it for about five years and it looked as though he had not cleaned it during that time either. In due course it responded to treatment and within an hour or two he was practising on our jungle range. The next part of the training programme was designed to acclimatize Tay Boon Hui to the sound of battle. For this purpose, he and I lay on the ground in the target area while men fired rifles and sub-machine-guns over our heads. Finally, after Jonathan arrived with his patrol, we staged a rehearsal of the ambush and ran through with the men what we hoped was going to happen.

That evening we moved into our ambush positions and settled

down to wait. Tay Boon Hui sat on a fallen log, which was the agreed meeting place. We all lay in a semi-circle around it astride a track. We were about half a mile inside the jungle. We had arrived in daylight, so that at first everyone seemed close together, but as the light faded distances between us lengthened. After half an hour each one of us lay alone in a dark and sticky world with nothing to occupy our attention but the buzzing of insects and the incessant irritation of their endless probing.

For the first half hour it was very uncomfortable, but I was sustained by the expectation of imminent triumph. Gradually the discomfort and the hope ebbed away, as I began to free myself from my surroundings. Ever since childhood I have spent long hours waiting in hides trying to shoot things and whenever this is going on I get the feeling of it being one, continuous wait. Only the waiting is real; events since the last period of waiting are telescoped into nothingness. My thoughts on these occasions wander haphazardly over the years between the recent and the remote past. At one moment I am a boy standing stock-still under a Douglas fir waiting for pigeons. Large numbers of them are being blown across a cold, grey sky – out of range. The light begins to fade and a goldcrest flutters up the side of a young pine tree searching for food along the needles. I watch intently as its tiny body is held stationary in mid-air for a moment before darting across to another tree. Subconsciously ears and eyes keep watch for the pigeons.

At other times I am hiding in the rushes by the side of a pond on a hot September evening, waiting for duck, or perhaps lying half-frozen in some dyke on a January morning ready for the geese to fly in off the estuary. Always I seem to be waiting; acutely uncomfortable, but incurably hopeful. Occasionally the vigil is crowned by success. More often I bring home no more than a memory of the sun sliding up over the horizon to chase away grey twilight and paint the frosted landscape pink or, on a more restricted scale, the reward may be the perfect colouring of a newly hatched butterfly, as it floats over the rabbit-hole in which my ferret has elected to go to sleep for a hot, summer afternoon. Time of year, surroundings and quarry are forever changing. The waiting, the discomfort and the hope remain the same.

Seet Ho Ching was supposed to be meeting Tay Boon Hui at 8.30 p.m., but it was at least three hours later before anything happened. I had long since given up hope and was lost in my thoughts when I noticed a very slight murmuring from the direction of the log on which Tay Boon Hui was sitting. Straining through the gloom I could just see the outline of three shapes where formerly Tay Boon Hui had been alone. I waited for the crash which would mean that our new colleague had murdered his one-time leader, but instead two of the shapes separated themselves from the third and started to walk down the track past me and out of the ambush. This was puzzling. A few minutes later one of the shapes returned. There was another period of subdued whispering and then both men started walking out of the ambush in the opposite direction. This was altogether too much of a good thing. If we went on any longer we would lose the lot. A decision had to be taken. It was now or never.

The first flare was followed immediately by three more. Suddenly the whole area was drenched in brilliant light. One man ran for all he was worth down the track and through the ring of waiting soldiers. This was Tay Boon Hui making use of the pre-arranged escape route. The other ran in the opposite direction, darting in and out of the trees and bushes in an attempt to get away.

There was a moment of complete silence as the men brought their rifles into the aim. Pascoe and John Starkey were the first to fire because they were stationed on the left of our position, which gave them the earliest opportunity for a shot. The man staggered and lurched forward. There was a further burst of fire from other men who had by then identified the target and this in turn was followed by a lot more firing from men who just had to let their rifles off now that the tension was broken. I stood up and shouted to them to stop. The terrorist was down and still. Huge shadows leapt and tumbled as the magnesium guttered and blazed. Firing was continuing from one part of our line and I wondered whether there could be another terrorist. I looked round and saw the face of an NCO screwed up with feverish excitement. It was he who was firing and the bullets were hitting the ground not far in front of the place where I was standing. I called to him by name and told him to stop, which he did. I made a note to deal with him next day.

The lights were burning low by the time I reached the terrorist. I was praying that he would not be too badly hurt, so that he could tell us where Ah Chien's camp was. As soon as I arrived I realized that it would be no good. He was rolling around on the ground moaning in a way which I knew meant death. John Starkey and Jonathan joined me and immediately started looking for the wound.

They found a bullet in the groin, administered morphia and applied a field dressing. I watched their efforts for a time and then shone my torch on his face which showed another bullet hole through the forehead. I wandered off to call Tay Boon Hui, who soon reappeared. The terrorist died.

From talking to Tay Boon Hui it transpired that Seet Ho Ching was ill and that one of Ah Chien's bodyguards – Kiang Sin – had been sent to meet him instead. Kiang Sin brought Wu Kuay, but neither of them knew the meeting place exactly and they had waited about a hundred yards away from 8.30 p.m. onwards. Eventually they had decided to scout around and had found Tay Boon Hui on his log. Tay Boon Hui was not sure what he should do, but he thought that if he could separate the two men he might be able to get them to surrender. He guessed that if Kiang Sin gave in, Wu Kuay would certainly do so as well. As a first step, he took Wu Kuay out of the ambush and told him to wait. He then returned to Kiang Sin and started working on him. Kiang Sin appeared to be reasonably well disposed to start with, but was probably suspicious of our presence and had tried to stroll off. This was the moment when our flares went up. The net result of the evening's work was one dead terrorist and no one to lead us to Ah Chien. It was a great disappointment, but Tay Boon Hui said that he was sure Wu Kuay would surrender next day.

We returned to Bukit Serampang and next morning Jonathan and his patrol went back to their base camp. They took Tay Boon Hui and Kam San with them so that they could point out suitable ambush points and other useful landmarks in the terrorist world. A few hours after they had gone I wished that they were back with us. I had just finished luncheon when a message was received from Inspector Boey to say that Wu Kuay had contacted a tapper near Grisek and told him that he wanted to surrender. He said that he would wait in some rushes nearby until we came and met him. I picked up Inspector Boey near Grisek and together we went to the place. Inspector Boey called out once or twice and sure enough Wu Kuay appeared.

Wu Kuay was very slight. He was brown rather than yellow and had a prominent jaw and teeth which made him look a bit like a monkey. We had to talk to him all afternoon and evening before he would agree to lead us to the new camp. It was of course possible that the gang would have moved again as a result of the fact that Kiang

Sin and Wu Kuay had not reappeared with Tay Boon Hui and Kam San as arranged, but there was a worthwhile chance of fighting a decisive action with Ah Chien and his men. Everything would depend on reaching the camp quickly because the enemy would not necessarily move at once. They would only do so if they were reasonably convinced that their position was compromised.

Next day, as soon as it got light, I went with Wu Kuay to a bit of high ground overlooking the jungle so that he could indicate the general position of the new camp to me. Having done this, we returned to Bukit Serampang, picked up a patrol and set off. After a sweat through the jungle which lasted for three or four hours and which was very like any other jungle patrol, Wu Kuay beckoned me to stop and lie down. He then said that we were within a hundred yards of the enemy camp.

We took off our packs and prepared for action. Wu Kuay and I crawled forward until we could see a particularly thick patch of undergrowth, which he said marked the north end of the Camp and which sheltered Ah Chien's basha. I quickly made the plan of assault and then lay down to wait while the men moved into their jumping-off positions. This only took a few minutes, but it seemed like a year. As I lay near Wu Kuay, my mind was already pushing through the screen of leaves which separated us from the enemy. I visualized them as I had thought of them for so long. Seet Ho Ching, the pregnant woman, Ah Heng, Lim Tuan and Ah Chien himself. I prayed over and over again for a decisive engagement.

The prospect of action always makes me feel cold and on this occasion I was almost shivering, despite the torrid heat of the midday jungle. My watch said that there were ninety seconds to go; then sixty, then thirty. At last we were on the move. We burst over the intervening ground and stormed up to the tangled bush. But there was no camp. The anti-climax was ludicrous. We put out sentries and the men sat around looking so disappointed that it was hard to know what to do. My first reaction was to suppose that Wu Kuay had led us up the garden path, but he looked even more miserable than the rest. We later discovered that this was in fact the case: he loved the woman in the gang and had fathered her baby. He tried very hard to lead us to them then and later, in the hope of getting her back.

Suddenly Corporal Gard started to laugh; nothing could depress him for long. He did not worry much about tactics. So far as he was concerned, if we did not shoot Ah Chien one day, we would shoot him another and anyhow it was not worth worrying about. Corporal Gard was the ideal man for bringing up the rear and keeping the men going. His reaction on this occasion was true to form. Soon everyone's spirits were restored and we set off again. Wu Kuay had made a mistake and would have to try a bit harder. We still had four or five hours of daylight.

Wu Kuay found the right place about three hours later and we went through the whole performance again. Unfortunately we suffered another set-back because the birds had flown. So far as we could judge, they must have left the previous day. They had probably decided to move as soon as Kiang Sin and Wu Kuay became overdue.

It was too late to go any further, so we erected a basha a few hundred yards from the deserted camp and settled down for the night. Soon after 1 a.m. I was awakened by the sounds of a quarrel.

'Me man, not woman,' said an angry voice. This was followed by the grating noise of a parang being drawn out of its sheath.

'I cut your head,' was the next remark. Then Corporal Gard moved into action to sort out the trouble which had arisen because Wu Kuay in his sleep had confused the Iban tracker lying next to him for his girl friend. Luckily no heads got cut, but the men of 'S' Company thereafter called Wu Kuay 'The Ponce'.

When we reached Jonathan's base camp next day Wu Kuay was reunited with Kam San and Tay Boon Hui. These two had also been given new names by the soldiers, who evidently considered this to be a necessary adjunct of a change of allegiance. Possibly because of his officer status, Tay Boon Hui was called Mister Wong which was not too bad, but the unfortunate Kam San became Chopper Gleasby.

For the next ten days Mr Wong, Chopper Gleasby and the Ponce took patrols to all the known food dumps, post-boxes and old camps in the area which were searched and ambushed. We recovered a certain amount of material, including Seet Ho Ching's tommy-gun, which he had abandoned after losing the magazine in the contact with Sergeant Bagley, but we saw no more of Ah Chien or the Grisek Branch. In the second week of October a company of the Cheshire Regiment arrived at Bukit Serampang and started to take over from us. During the take-over period we found a new enemy camp in the Jementah Branch's area in which were documents showing that

Ah Chien and the Grisek Branch had moved in to join Lee Meng.

My last week on the District War Executive Committee was largely taken up with making arrangements for an offensive by the Psychological Warfare Team. I am not a supporter of the more starry-eyed manifestations of this type of activity and consider that it is a complete waste of time to tell a terrorist that he is a good man at heart and that he should therefore surrender so as to hasten the day when freedom and democracy can bring peace and plenty to everyone. Unless the terrorist is in imminent danger of being killed, or of starving, he will probably laugh and will certainly lose any vestige of respect that he might otherwise feel for the Government. On the other hand, there are times when the weapon can be used to good effect. Such moments arise when the Government is in a position to put either the carrot or the stick to good use. An extreme example of this is when a group of enemy are completely surrounded in a small area of cover from which they can be winkled out and killed with certainty. Under these circumstances a loud speaker, telling the enemy exactly how they can surrender and explaining the implications of not doing so, represents the simplest and most effective form of psychological warfare yet devised.

Although Ah Chien and his followers were not in quite such a desperate position, they were evidently rattled and it seemed worth trying to combine a little psychological warfare with our other operations. We started by getting Tay Boon Hui to record a message for Ah Chien, which was broadcast by an airborne loud speaker over the jungle. We then asked him in conjunction with Chopper Gleasby and the Ponce to compose a letter to their former comrades which could be dropped from the air in the form of a leaflet. As a result, the three of them produced a document which emphasized the friendliness and affection which they maintained we had shown them. At first this surprised me, but on thinking about it, I came to the conclusion that there was some truth in it. Strange as it may seem we really had received our former enemies as friends up to a point. I have the feeling that we had started to look on them in this light even before we had got hold of them. The very business of learning about them had started it off. It is difficult to know someone well without either liking them or disliking them and this is what happened. Apart from their former calculated brutality, there was nothing much to dislike about Mr Wong, Chopper Gleasby and the Ponce.

F

Wu Kuay in particular was a great character as I discovered one day when I went up to him and said good morning. His answer was to brandish his fist under my nose and say:

'A bunch of five. Rot 'yer.'

At first I was taken aback by this, but then I noticed a group of soldiers standing around laughing. This was apparently a regular source of amusement. To while away the hours of waiting in the base camp Rifleman Neale, the mortar platoon signaller, had taught Wu Kuay to answer good morning greetings in this way. Thereafter we tried to persuade all visitors to 'S' Company to say good morning to Wuy Kuay and, as it was the period of the hand-over, we had a number of distinguished guests who were caught.

We finally left Bukit Serampang on October 19th. From my point of view it was a pity that we could not have stayed for a bit longer because we had not quite achieved our aim of destroying the terrorists in our area, although we had eliminated nearly half of them, including a high proportion of their officers, and had broken up their organization. Within six weeks of our leaving, ten more terrorists, including Ah Chien and Seet Ho Ching, had surrendered. Lee Meng and his gang soldiered on for a month, but then they too retired from the fray and the job was done.

A few nights before we left Bukit Serampang for Singapore and the troopship, we held a company party. The police gave us a large money grant out of cash which we had taken off dead or captured terrorists and which we had handed in, in accordance with the regulations. This paid for several pints of free beer per man and the party was a great success.

A normal feature of such functions is that officers and other prominent characters in the company are made to sing a song. By about half past ten everyone who should have sung had done so and there was a slight pause during which the buzzing of flies and the night song of a thousand frogs and crickets suddenly became very pronounced. Suddenly a rifleman sprang to his feet and made a little speech pointing out how much we all owed to Ah Chien for being such a good enemy commander and for providing, indirectly, the financial backing for the party. This was greeted with immense enthusiasm by the soldiers, so the speaker asked them all to drink Ah Chien's health.

Mr Wong, Chopper Gleasby and the Ponce, who were at the

party, looked a bit surprised, but the toast was drunk. I think that under the influence of the moment we all felt that Ah Chien had been a good captain of the opposing team and deserved a round of applause. In fact, this is rather a dangerous attitude for soldiers to adopt until the war is over, but our war was over, so perhaps it did not matter too much.

The week following the company party was taken up with fare-wells and in saying them I became very conscious of my good for-tune in having had such excellent people with whom to work. In particular Mr Moloney had proved himself to be a first-class District Officer and Chairman of our War Executive Committee and Inspec-tor Boey had been the ideal Special Branch Officer, patient, re-sourceful and truly touching in the trust he extended to us. Both in Kenya and Malaya I had been working within a well-established framework and I had yet to discover how very different life can be when such a framework does not exist.

At the end of the week the battalion sailed from Singapore in a troopship and I leant over the rail to watch the land sink below the horizon. At first the city and the ships in the harbour made up the view, but soon they occupied no more than one corner of the canvas. Once again the all-pervading impression was of a vast expanse of dark green jungle under a streaming grey sky. After a time the land became partly obscured by black thunderclouds which seemed to rise out of the sea itself and spiral up to meet the heavy banks above. I tried to recapture some of the events of the past months, but all I could see was Wu Kuay's clenched fist and furious ape-like face breaking into a grin after he had said his little piece. After a time I went below to my cabin.

During the voyage home I tried to relate the experience we had gained in Malaya to the general problems of fighting insurgents. I had already discovered in Kenya that an intelligence organization such as Special Branch could never hope to provide enough bits of contact information to enable the Security Forces to identify and neutralize the members of insurgent groups, although it could pro-vide a great deal of background information. In Malaya I had received confirmation of this. Despite the fact that the Emergency had been in progress for nearly nine years and that people like Inspector Boey were far more professional and far better backed in terms of resources than we had been in Kenya, the Special Branch was seldom able to give us the sort of information on which we could make contacts. For example, in the whole time we were operating from Bukit Serampang, we only got two pieces of information of this sort, that is to say the report about the terrorists picking up supplies in Grisek, which we bungled, and the news of Tay Boon Hui's intended surrender.

On the other hand in Malaya, as in Kenya, Special Branch had been able to produce a great deal of background information and looking back over the past few months it seemed as if we had managed to exploit it to some extent. In a sense the process was not unlike that by which we had used pseudo-gangs to exploit background information, but whereas in Kenya we had used ex-enemy to trick their former supporters into supplying more information, in Malaya we had used our own soldiers to get it by sending out patrols looking for confirmation of our theories. In other words the background information, sensibly analysed, produced most of what we wanted and our own men got us the little bit extra needed for turning it into contact information.

Based on these thoughts, I formulated the theory for operating against terrorists which I have worked on and taught ever since. Briefly it can be stated in this way. Firstly, if the tactical aim is to destroy a group of terrorists operating from some form of cover, then the main problem will be to discover who they are and where they are, so that they can be neutralized. As a commander cannot be given sufficiently detailed information to enable him to do this, he must get it for himself because the responsibility for achieving a tactical aim must be that of the commander of the force concerned. In practice he can do this by using a chain-reaction process, in which information and deduction lead to action designed to get more information. At some stage in the chain the chance of bringing about a contact arises and if a contact results, then further information automatically becomes available. This is precisely the process which I had used against the Kebun Bahru Branch initially and then against It Hiong. It was also the system which Jonathan Peel had used when intercepting the terrorists of Grisek Branch on their trips between their main camping area and the rubber enclaves along the River Muar.

Naturally this theory works best when there is a lot of background information available and one of the implications of it is that Special Branch should be organized specifically to get background information, rather than contact information. I had been edging towards this view during my time in Malaya and the discussions in which I had been involved in Kuala Lumpur with Special Branch Headquarters and with the army operations staff were based on this idea. The senior army staff officer with whom I had been working on this subject was Lieutenant-Colonel Clutterbuck, who had been one of my instructors at the Staff College. He had visited us at Bukit Serampang and he organized my visit to Special Branch Headquarters, where we discovered that some senior Special Branch Officers agreed with my views, although they cut right across accepted ideas.

Another implication of my theory concerns the handling of prisoners. If the intelligence organization is responsible for providing contact information, then their main interest in a prisoner is to get matters of immediate tactical information out of him as quickly as possible. This usually implies direct interrogation, in which interrogator and prisoner are ranged against each other on opposite sides of the table. On the other hand, if the intelligence organization is responsible for providing background information, the chief use of a prisoner lies in gaining his co-operation and friendship and a different process, which may take much longer, is required. Both in Kenya and Malaya I had found that the second process was much more satisfactory and that the dividends paid by it far outweighed the loss of the odd bits of immediate information which sometimes accrue from formal interrogation.

The third implication of my theory concerns the degree of expertise required of the troops themselves. Our operations in Malaya would never have been successful had it not been for the interest and understanding of our methods displayed by our own soldiers. Of course they had to be highly proficient in their normal skills, such as shooting and moving through the jungle, but in addition they had to learn all about the terrorists, if they were to notice and make sense of the clues which were around them as they went about their business. Our men all became intensely interested and were able to rise to the occasion whenever required. During the early period at Kuala Kubu Bahru, when we had been experimenting with different forms of kit and with night movement, I had realized that we could get far more out of our two-year conscript soldiers than was commonly assumed to be the case, but I had never guessed how great was their capacity for entering into the process of information collection and analysis. The fortitude, enthusiasm and sheer natural ability of the British soldier has to be seen to be believed.

Part III

*

Muscat and Oman

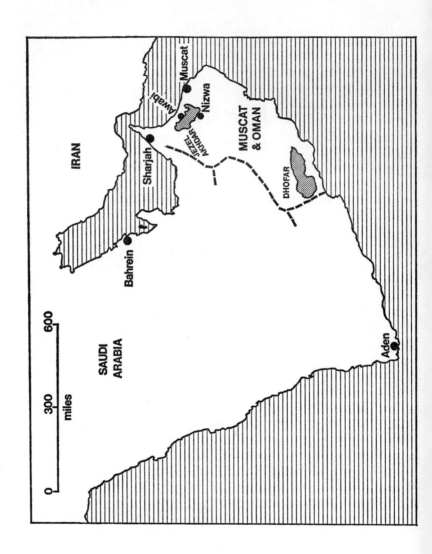

❈

Chapter 13

Rebellion in Oman 1957–1959

In 1958 a rebellion was taking place in the interior of a country which was then called Muscat and Oman and which is now just called Oman. The rebels were the followers of the Imam, or religious leader, and they were contesting the right of the Sultan to exercise his rule in certain parts of the country. In order to see why this had come about and to understand the nature of the rebellion it is necessary to take a brief look at the history of the area.

The country of Oman consists of 1,300 miles of the Arabian coastline and the mountainous land lying between it and the uninhabitable desert behind, known as the Empty Quarter. In an historical sense the importance of the country related to its position on the flank of the trade routes between the Persian Gulf, India and East Africa and for centuries its ports have been centres for trade and shipping. The significance of the mountainous hinterland lies in the fact that it has sheltered tribes which have been in a position to dominate the coast. The heartland of the interior has always been the massive plateau of the Jebal Akhdar and the villages in the surrounding valleys and gaps. The Jebal Akhdar rises in places to over 8,000 feet and lies to the south and west of the port of Muscat.

Arab tribes started to push into this hinterland from the north and from the east during the three or four centuries preceding the birth of the Prophet. At this time the main influence in the country was exercised by the Persians whose irrigation schemes were mainly responsible for the fact that the interior was inhabitable at all. Persian influence fell back before the Arabs, but maintained itself in the coastal ports until the dynamic influence of Islam gave new impetus to the Arab presence. In the years following Mohammed's death a number of movements sprang up within Islam in much the same way as the early Christian Church developed along different lines from place to place. At this time the majority of the tribes in Oman became associated with the Ibadi movement, a sect dedicated to the strict preservation of Islamic purity. To lead them these tribes chose an Imam, who combined the functions of spiritual and temporal leader.

The next few centuries, which corresponded in time with the Saxon hey-day in England, became a sort of heroic age. Hundreds of years later, during successive afflictions, the tribes looked back to the days of the first Imamate with the same sort of longing as the Jews of the Roman occupation regarded King David's Israel, although the function of the early Imams probably corresponded more closely to that of Samuel than of David. But inevitably things started to go wrong; strong Imams were succeeded by weak ones and there were several lengthy periods when no Imams were elected at all. In parts of the country, particularly in the north, the Sunni movement gained adherents at the expense of the Ibadi sect with a corresponding loss of influence to the Imamate. In the south-east the tribes took less interest in the affairs of the Imamate, as they became increasingly preoccupied with their East African trading links. As the tribes became less united, the coastal ports became increasingly subject to pressure from outside. Initially this meant that Persian influence re-asserted itself, but from the sixteenth century onwards Portugal, Turkey and Britain all intervened in the affairs of the country. During the first half of the seventeenth century Oman reached its lowest ebb.

At this time a new and vigorous dynasty of Imams became established who, taking advantage of dissension between the various European powers, cleared the country of foreign influence and largely re-established the prestige and authority of the Imamate. But this was only a start, as the Arabs captured a number of Portuguese ships and used them to raid Portuguese territory in India and East Africa. These Imams even established their rule over Zanzibar and over parts of the East African coast. As a result, they became more interested in trade and maritime adventuring than in controlling the Omani tribes, but in so doing they gave opportunities for intrigue and revolt which resulted in the downfall of the dynasty. However, two aspects of their rule, at that time new to the Oman, survived. The first of these was that for almost a hundred years the office of Imam had stayed within the same family and had come to be regarded by many as hereditary. The second was that the Imam himself had changed from being primarily the spiritual leader of a group of Arab tribes into a maritime merchant prince administering far-flung temporal possessions.

The next significant event in the history of Oman took place in 1749 when Ahmad ibn Said became Imam. The country has been ruled by members of this family ever since. Ahmad ruled as a merchant prince, but was able to control the tribes as well and at his death he was succeeded by his son. This man, however, was not able to maintain his position as ruler and in this capacity he was ousted by his son. But when this happened the son decided that he neither needed nor wanted the spiritual position of Imam which remained with the father for life, after which the office lapsed altogether for many years. Meanwhile the country was ruled by successive members of the Al Bu Said dynasty, who became known as Sultans and who divided their time between the capital port of Muscat and Zanzibar, until Zanzibar passed to a younger son in the middle of the nineteenth century.

The loss of Zanzibar indirectly led to the next round of serious strife. As early as 1822, the Sultan had signed a treaty with Britain designed to curtail the slave trade, but it was not until the separation of Zanzibar from Muscat that hardship really began to be felt by notables throughout Arabia. Within a relatively short time the distress thus caused produced an alliance between the Saudis and certain of the non-Ibadi tribal leaders in Oman which led in 1866 to the assassination of the Sultan by his son who succeeded him. So far the Ibadi tribes of the interior had remained more or less quiescent, although disapproving of the worldly ways of the Sultans and disliking the curtailment of the slave trade. But they were outraged by the new Sultan's association with the Saudis, who in religious terms belonged to the Wahhabi sect. Spurred on by their sense of outrage they chose a new Imam for the first time in half a century to lead them against the Sultan, who became increasingly dependent on Britain for support. In the rebellion which followed the Sultan was killed, but thanks in part to Britain's good offices, he was succeeded by his uncle who stamped out the revolt. The Imam lived on quietly for a few years and when he died the Imamate lapsed once more. The significance of this period lies in the fact that for the first time a

British-backed, coastal-orientated Sultan fought a tribal-backed, interior-orientated Imam.

With the failure of the revived Imamate the leaders of Ibadi thought became increasingly strict and withdrawn from the world, while the Sultans became increasingly lax and worldly. In 1913 the leader of the Bani Riyam, one of the most influential tribes of the Jebal Akhdar area, arranged for the election of a new Imam and after some skirmishing dislodged the Sultan's representative from the traditional seat of the Imamate at Nizwa. The tribal coalition which stood behind the new Imam was very powerful, but British backing for the Sultan prevented his overthrow. Over the next few years a stalemate prevailed under which the tribal chiefs exercised a high degree of autonomy around the Jebal Akhdar without any formal acceptance of the fact by the Sultan. In 1920 the Imam was murdered and replaced by the nominee of the Harithi chief who had by this time become the dominant tribal leader. A few months later the Sultan concluded an agreement with this man, who signed on behalf of the other chiefs, designed to regulate the respective spheres of influence between them. This agreement, known as the Treaty of Sib, led to a prolonged period of relatively harmonious relations between the Sultan and the tribes which continued until the death of the Imam in 1954. It is interesting to notice that in 1952 the Imam even offered to co-operate with the Sultan in dealing with a Saudi incursion into the northern part of the country.

The most important tribal leader at the time when the Imam died was the thoroughly unpleasant chief of the Bani Riyam, Sulaiman ibn Himyar. He had for some years entertained hopes of becoming the autonomous ruler of the Jebal Akhdar and had even made overtures to the Saudis for support. Unable to make much headway while the fiercely traditional and respected old Imam lived, he had seized the opportunity afforded by his death to gain the Imamate for a young man of the influential neighbouring Bani Hinya tribe, called Ghalib ibn Ali. It soon became apparent that the power behind Ghalib was his fiercely ambitious brother Talib. Talib, Ghalib and Sulaiman were the prime movers in the next rebellion and the events leading up to it showed how far this group of dissidents had moved away from the traditional attitudes of the inland tribal leaders.

The incident which sparked off the chain of events leading to the revolt was the arrival of a group of oil prospectors in the summer of 1954. This group came from a company which had many years earlier been given permission by the Sultan to search for oil and the tribe in whose area they were working had made them welcome. But Talib did not want any company, licensed by the Sultan, to find oil in the Oman, since he wished to channel the profit into his own pocket and into the pockets of his friends. He therefore attacked the tribe concerned, which provoked a reaction from the Sultan, whose soldiers guarding the oil company expedition drove off Talib's men. The Sultan also took the opportunity of occupying certain villages in the northern part of the Oman in order to interfere with the links which Talib and Sulaiman were building up with the Saudis. Talib meanwhile applied to the Arab League for recognition of the Imamate of Oman as an independent Arab country and tried to raise a force to attack the Sultan's new outpost in the north. The Saudis played their part by furnishing him with money and weapons, but the Sultan proved too strong for Talib, who enjoyed little support outside the Bani Riyam and the Bani Hinya. In 1955 the Sultan appeared in person and occupied the seat of the Imam at Nizwa. Ghalib and Sulaiman each took refuge in mountain villages of their respective tribes and Talib left the country to build up an army of expatriate Omanis in Saudi Arabia. He also visited Cairo to give impetus to the Egyptian-run propaganda campaign aimed at discrediting the Sultan and at gaining world support for the idea of an Oman independent and separate from the Sultan of Muscat.

Two years later in June 1957 Talib returned to the Jebal Akhdar with a large consignment of arms. Using the Omanis, trained in Saudi Arabia, as the nucleus of his force and backed by Sulaiman and the Bani Riyam he quickly dislodged the Sultan's representative from Nizwa and occupied the villages around the Jebal Akhdar. Meanwhile Ghalib reappeared and resumed the duties of Imam. Talib was now master of the central area of Oman and he declared its independence of the Sultan, whom he claimed had broken the undertakings given in the Treaty of Sib by occupying the interior with his troops in 1955. The Imam's followers also claimed that by long hallowed tradition the very existence of a duly elected Imam rendered rule by a Sultan, or indeed by any other person, totally invalid. This was put forward as another reason for expelling the Sultan's representative from the interior.

But although much play was made of religion and of tribal tradition, the rebel cause was seen to be threadbare and fraudulent to such an extent that few people, beyond the confines of the two tribes concerned, gave it much support. For one thing it was well known that the Treaty of Sib was not an agreement about autonomy between a Sultan and an Imam, but that it concerned spheres of influence between the Sultan and the local chieftains. The Imam was not a signatory of the Treaty, nor was the Imamate even mentioned in it. Furthermore it was not the Sultan who had broken the Treaty of Sib, but Talib and Ghalib who had deliberately tried to disclaim the authority of the Sultan which was plainly laid out and recognized by all parties in the Treaty itself. The second claim, that is to say the assertion that the very existence of an Imam rendered the Sultan's authority invalid, was abject nonsense in terms of the events of the previous two centuries and cut clean across the contention that the Sultan had broken the Treaty, since if he was not a valid Sultan he could never have entered into such a treaty in the first place. Finally, the dealings which Talib and Ghalib had with the Saudis greatly weakened Ghalib's position as the Ibadi Imam since true Ibadis resolutely set their faces against accommodations of this sort.

In practice two separate influences working on the ambitions of Talib, Ghalib and Sulaiman caused the rebellion. The first of these was the Arab nationalist aspirations of Egypt. At the time, Nasser, carried along by the flood of socialist revolutionary fervour, was busily attacking Western influence wherever it presented itself and Muscat with its old-fashioned monarchical regime, closely allied to Great Britain, offered a perfect target for propaganda. The fact that an Ibadi Imamate was even more old-fashioned and inimical to Nasser's brand of socialism was of no account in a situation of this sort. The second influence was the enmity which existed between the ruler of Saudi Arabia and the Sultan of Muscat, as a result of conflicting interests over the Buraimi oasis on the borders of the two countries and rivalry regarding the exploitation of newly discovered oil reserves. Although for religious reasons the old Imam had made common cause with the Sultan when the Saudis threatened Buraimi in 1952, his successor was prepared to work with the Saudis against the Sultan to the disgrace of his religion and at the expense of the Omani people. Likewise for the time being the ruler of Saudi Arabia, whose regime was every bit as reactionary as that of the Sultan, was prepared to work with revolutionary Egypt and the disreputable Imam against the Sultan in order to pursue his nation's interests. Later Saudi Arabia and Egypt became rivals over the Yemen, whereupon the Saudis withdrew their support from Ghalib, but meanwhile all three partners to the rebellion concocted a cause out of the historical divisions of the Sultanate around which they hoped to rally the tribes.

Despite the fact that Talib and the Imam were not supported by a large number of tribes, their position was relatively strong from a military point of view because the Jebal Akhdar dominated the route from the coast to Nizwa and the interior, and Talib's regulars, supported by the Bani Hinya and the Bani Riyam, controlled the Jebal Akhdar. In days gone by, the Sultan would probably have tried to handle the situation by a show of force backed by bribery, but in 1957 the Sultan's army was weak and when it came to cash payments the Sultan could not match the vast resources of an oil state like Saudi Arabia. Ten years had still to pass before an appreciable revenue from oil started to flow into his coffers. The Sultan therefore turned for help to the British, invoking the most recent treaty signed between the two countries in 1951.

It is difficult to know exactly what was the status of Britain in relation to the Sultanate. Britain had concluded a series of treaties with the countries of Arabia during the nineteenth century in pursuance of her efforts to stamp out piracy and the slave trade and to safeguard the route to India. Undoubtedly in 1957 Britain was responsible for the defence and foreign policy of Kuwait, Bahrein, Qatar and of the Trucial States. Furthermore Aden was a British Colony and its hinterland was divided into two British Protectorates. Relations with Muscat and Oman were governed by a series of treaties, the most important of which were those of 1891, 1939 and 1951. It is not absolutely certain that Britain was obliged to intervene directly in an internal dispute, but it is undoubtedly true that all the other countries of Arabia with whom Britain had close relationships expected that she would respond to a call for help by the Sultan. To have prevaricated would have sown seeds of doubt in the minds of the rulers of these states about Britain's resolve to uphold her obligations to them and although at the time Britain had little to gain from Muscat, her relationship with the others, particularly with Kuwait and Bahrein, were immensely important.

On the other hand there were good reasons why Britain should not embark on adventures in Arabia. The Suez operation which had taken place about six months earlier had stirred up a certain amount of opposition both amongst the Arabs, and in the world at large, and it was argued that a further campaign, especially one involving the use of British ground forces on Arabian soil, might add fuel to the flames. None the less it was decided that Britain should honour her obligations to the Sultan of Muscat.

The next point to consider was the form which this help should take. The 1957 Defence White Paper had marked a major change in British strategic thought with its emphasis on an RAF-carried nuclear deterrent and major economies for the army and the Royal Navy. Naturally this philosophy was received with some reservation by these two services and the trouble in Muscat was seized upon as a suitable opportunity for demonstrating the continuing need for a ground intervention capability. On the other hand since well before the War the RAF had been regarded as the most suitable service for carrying out operations in the desert. It was held that the speed and range of aircraft, together with the terror which they were supposed to inspire in the hearts of primitive men, made them particularly suitable for policing the wastes of Arabia. It was not that aircraft were expected to kill or injure large numbers of dissidents, but it was thought that they could interrupt normal life to such an extent that any revolt would come to a rapid end when faced by attack from the air. For this reason the principal Headquarters in the Arabian Peninsula was commanded and largely staffed by officers of the RAF.

In the event, it was decided to try the effect of airpower alone on Talib's force, but it soon became apparent that aircraft by themselves would not be able to achieve the aim. A short time later, an infantry brigade group of the strategic reserve based in Kenya was deployed on the ground. Nizwa and the surrounding villages were captured and Talib, Ghalib and Sulaiman withdrew into the fastnesses of the Jebal Akhdar. At this point it was decided not to mount further operations against them because the worst of the hot weather was approaching and in any case it was felt that the Imam and his henchmen could do little harm at the top of the Jebal once the villages and roads around its base were firmly in the Sultan's hands. In an attempt to avoid being dragged into further operations, the British Government decided to supply the Sultan with massive assistance to build up his armed forces. To this end, arms and equipment were provided and a contingent of regular officers on secondment was sent out to run the force.

Chapter 14

❈

Change of Life

Six months after the battalion returned from Malaya it was decided that I should join the Staff at the War Office. Monday, June 22nd, 1958 was the fateful day on which I reported for duty. I was to be one of two majors in a branch called MO4, the MO in this case standing for Military Operations. Our task was to deal with events which occurred in the Middle East and East Africa. Each of us had two Captains to help us and our immediate superior was a Colonel, who was in charge of the whole branch. Above him was a Major-General who was known as the Director of Military Operations. Responsibility within the branch between myself and the other major was split geographically. He concerned himself with Cyprus and all the countries bordering the southern and western shores of the Mediterranean together with Iraq. I was concerned with the Arabian Peninsula and Persian Gulf and with East Africa. It soon became apparent that my job consisted principally of corresponding with the two overseas Headquarters in my area, acting as the War Office link with other Whitehall departments, such as the Foreign Office and the Colonial Office for matters concerning my area and writing briefs for the Chief of the Imperial General Staff to use at meetings of the Chiefs of Staff Committee. The Chief of the Imperial General Staff at that time was Field Marshal Sir Gerald Templer, who was generally regarded as being a somewhat formidable character.

The first thing to strike me on arriving in MO4 was the unsatisfactory conditions in which we were expected to work. Apart from the Colonel, who had an office of his own, all six of us sat in one room crammed together like sardines. Each of us had one or more tele-

phones and almost always there were at least two people talking at
once: sometimes all six. Under such circumstances concentration
and creative thought were not easy. It was also apparent from the
start that everything was done in a fantastic rush and one's contribution was normally wanted by the day before yesterday. Another
fact that struck home quickly and forcibly was that this life had little
in common with the army. All my experience to date had led me to
believe that performance was directly related to leadership and that
leadership meant, at the very least, involvement with one's men to
the extent necessary for producing an outlook, which enabled them
to give of their best. I took it for granted that a soldier's main concern was with his unit and that any other connections, such as his
family, were of minor importance. Here everything was different.
People turned up in the morning and went home in the evening and
no one knew or cared about what they thought providing the work
got done. The army as a way of life had given place to routine office
work between certain hours on five days a week. The sharp distinc-
tion between being a soldier and being something else, such as a
business man, politician or civil servant, was blurred. It was disturbing and unpleasant.

There were two other differences between life in the War Office
and anything which I had experienced previously. The first was that
everyone seemed very old by comparison with the soldiers in the
regiment. Not a single officer in the whole of the Military Operations Directorate was younger than me: my own two assistants were
slightly older and most of the other Grade 2 Staff Officers were
seven or eight years older. Even the clerks for the most part were
senior NCOs. The other difference was that it appeared on the surface that no one was capable of making a decision, with the result that
most issues were dealt with by committees sooner or later. In the very
nature of things a committee, consisting of ten or a dozen people,
must be a time-waster because a sizable number of the members are
free-wheeling for a good proportion of the time. I took an instant dislike to doing business at meetings and determined to go to as few as
possible. There were of course one or two bright spots on the horizon.
For one thing the Colonel was a proper soldier and the other officers
in the branch were very decent people. None the less I quickly
developed an intense loathing of the job, although I ultimately
learned to tolerate it. Both the office environment and the Civil
Service attitude were the antithesis of all that I had ever regarded as

being worthwhile. To cut a long story short, I was faced with the problem of a major mental readjustment.

If adjustment was the order of the day with regard to my work, it was also important in connection with my life outside the War Office. In the past I had always lived as a member of a community, either at school, or in an officers' mess, or with our team in Kenya. Now I had to learn what it was like to live in London as a civilian, but whereas the office was squalid in the extreme, my living conditions were very much the reverse. Thanks to the hospitality of an old friend, Colin James, I lodged with him in his luxurious flat in the Earl's Court area. We were looked after by an aged but efficient retainer and from the start this flat was my refuge from the horrors of the War Office.

For the first week or two all went well and then on the morning of July 14th I got to the office to find the whole place in a turmoil. All the telephones seemed to be ringing at once and we were required to produce several briefs for an emergency meeting of the Chiefs of Staff at record speed. Apparently the King of Iraq had been murdered and it was necessary to decide what we intended to do about it with particular reference to the forces which we kept in that country. We were also concerned about the neighbouring country of Kuwait because at that time Britain was responsible for her security. The telephones continued to ring all morning and the racket caused by people talking and running in and out was unbelievable: it was more like riding on a fire-engine than sitting in an office. To make matters worse we were in the middle of a heat-wave and the sun poured through the windows of our first-floor office which overlooked Whitehall. Outside a man was digging up the road with a pneumatic drill. At one stage an old fellow came in to water the plants in the window-boxes, which had been put there a day or two earlier in preparation for the state visit of some foreign leader. The old man's face as he took in the situation was worth watching. He went about his duties in an absent-minded way, as though he could not bear to miss a moment of the charade being played out in front of him. Before going, he stood for a moment with his cap pushed back, scratching his sweaty, grey head. It was plain from his attitude that he was saying to himself, 'Are they all mad, or is it me?'.

It was us all right. Day after day the hubbub continued as more and more plans were made to cover every remote contingency. Long after the situation in the Middle East had settled down, we continued to make plans. At every level, officers were working out what they would suggest to their superiors if some new circumstance arose. They were not prepared to wait until it did before making the plan because by doing it in advance they might save a few minutes at a critical moment. During all this period we worked on and on. Sometimes we missed lunch and sometimes we did not leave the office until late at night. We abandoned the Whitehall weekend entirely in favour of an arrangement under which we got one day off, once a week. Although my working hours were as nothing compared to Kenya or Malaya, they seemed far longer because of the frustration of most of the work and because of the foulness of the surroundings.

Nothing more happened in Iraq after the King was killed. Once the British forces which had been in Iraq were safely withdrawn, our main concern was that Iraq should not invade Kuwait and by the end of August it looked as if this danger was receding, at any rate for the time being. By this time too our hours of work were becoming more normal and I was beginning to take an interest in other parts of the area for which I was responsible. In doing so I became aware that the situation in the Aden Protectorates was rather unsettled and that events were not standing still in the country of Muscat and Oman. Unfortunately although the Sultan's army was gradually getting stronger, as a result of our aid programme, Talib was also becoming dangerous again and was conducting a mining campaign along the roads and tracks around the Jebal Akhdar from his sanctuary on the plateau. From time to time he also sent patrols to attack isolated Government garrisons and as early as June it was becoming clear that the Sultan's army was going to need some extra help. For this reason a squadron of the Trucial Oman Scouts and two troops of armoured cars were sent into the country from the north and some Royal Marine NCOs from frigates in the Persian Gulf arrived to stiffen up platoons of the Sultan's army which were operating against the Jebal Akhdar. It was intended that these NCOs should help out until more seconded officers could arrive from the British army.

Despite these reinforcements, Talib continued to improve his position and in London an ever increasing flow of signals from our Headquarters in Aden and in Bahrein told the tale. By September it was clear that stop-gap measures would no longer suffice and the Commander of the British Forces in the Arabian Peninsula recommended a further full-scale operation, using British troops to restore the situation, as had been done in 1957. The problem this time was however rather different as the rebels were now established within the strong, natural defences of the Jebal Akhdar, instead of being in the comparatively accessible villages around its base, as had been the case the year before.

The plateau of the Jebal Akhdar was roughly twelve miles from north to south and eighteen miles from east to west and its average height above sea level was 6,500 feet. But the plateau itself was enclosed within a ring of mountain peaks some of which rose to nearly 10,000 feet. Relatively few tracks onto the plateau existed and those that did, ran through passes which could be held by a handful of resolute men against an army. Talib had about 150 hard-core men whom he had trained and these he used to organize and lead groups of Sulaiman's tribe, the Bani Riyam. In this way Talib was able to dispose of a sizable and effective force well in excess of what was needed to hold the passes onto the plateau.

The military problem of defeating Talib was perfectly straightforward. In its simplest terms it amounted to devising a method whereby a sufficiently strong Government force could reach the plateau. The difficulty arose from the fact that the Sultan's army lacked the numbers, training, and resolve needed for forcing the passes. It was for this reason that the British Commander for the area, based in Aden, was recommending a full-scale operation. One obvious answer to the military problem would have been to use helicopters to land men on the plateau behind the passes, but it was thought that they could not operate at such an altitude in the prevailing climatic conditions. Another possibility was to use parachute troops in the same way, but once again the combination of altitude and likely wind strengths was such that their employment would have been extremely hazardous.

The plan which the Commander of the British Forces in the Arabian Peninsula forwarded from Aden was therefore based on a conventional assault using a British battalion in addition to the Sultan's forces. The operation would be commanded by a British brigadier and would be preceded by a small parachute drop, if the weather was favourable. It was a sound plan and it could not possibly have failed. But there were political objections which could not be overruled. It was decided that the Sultan would have to make do with the help which we were already affording him. Although there was no firm prohibition on the addition of a few odd individuals, there was to be no question of formed British units entering Muscat. The staff in Aden were not very pleased at this decision, but they started to examine ways in which additional help could be brought to the Sultan's forces within the limits set by the Government. It was generally felt that, although the situation might be prevented from getting worse, it would be difficult to bring about any marked improvement.

In an attempt to think of a way round this difficulty, I put forward a suggestion that a small and comparatively simple special operation should be mounted. In outline my suggestion was that four or five specially selected officers should be established in suitable posts around the foot of the Jebal Akhdar. Each one would be provided with a substantial sum of money and a few strong and resourceful soldiers to act as guards, drivers and escorts. Each officer would also need a reliable English-speaking Arab to act as an interpreter and some trackers. The first stage of the operation would be for the officers to install informers in nearby villages by judicious use of the money allotted to them. The job of the informers would be to discover when and where groups of the Bani Riyam, coming down from the plateau, might be contacted. Stage two would be to ambush and capture some of these people. If carefully handled, a proportion of the captives would doubtless change their allegiance and work for us. I visualized forming one or two teams of prisoners augmented by some of our own soldiers in disguise. During stage two we would also build up a detailed and accurate picture of the way in which Talib had organized his force. The third stage would be for one or more of the teams to get onto the plateau. With reasonable luck they should be able to get through the piquet at the pass by virtue of their disguise. If the worst came to the worst, they would certainly get up to the guards before they were spotted and they would then have to overcome them. Once on the plateau, they would discard their disguise and start operating against Talib's irregulars with a view to engaging Talib, Ghalib and Sulaiman in due course.

I judged that the total number of British troops required would not exceed forty and that a cash sum of £15,000 would be required. Obviously there was a risk of casualties, but bearing in mind the effect of surprise in operations of this sort, I thought that the risk was small. A straightforward assault on the Jebal, as originally envisaged, was far more likely to produce them. One drawback would be that any man wounded on top of the Jebal would have a poor chance of survival, but I intended to include a medical orderly in each team. I made no pretence of forecasting the sequence of events in detail. Once the teams were set up they would have to seize such opportunities as presented themselves. By this time I had made a careful study of the country, its people and the terrain over which the operation would take place and I was absolutely convinced that the plan would work, providing the right people were chosen for the job. That was the key to everything.

My idea did not carry immediate conviction in the War Office, but in view of the worsening situation and the rejection of the first plan even the possibility of a complete and economic victory was attractive. Soon after putting my plan forward I accompanied the Director of Military Operations to the Foreign Office to try and get their support: without it we would get nowhere. After some discussion, it was decided that a committee should be set up to examine the plan. It would be called the Muscat Working Party and would include representatives of all interested Whitehall departments. The first meeting would be held on October 8th and the plan was to be presented in the form of a 'Note by the War Office'. The plan might be unconventional, but the procedure for dealing with it was strictly in accordance with the normal workings of Whitehall.

The Foreign Office was a peculiar place which combined the squalor of the War Office with a sort of 'Emett' atmosphere. A caller such as myself would be conducted by an aged man in a frock-coat down long, dimly lit corridors which seemed to be full of junk such as disused lockers or chairs with missing legs. On arrival outside the office of the person being visited, the caller would be invited to take a seat on a large leather sofa, while the man in the frock-coat knocked on the door. Perhaps it was the row of leather sofas which gave the corridors their cluttered look. On October 8th the room to which I was escorted belonged to a moderately distinguished diplomat, who had recently returned from being ambassador to some second-rate country and who had become the chairman of the Muscat Working Party. He turned out to be practical, friendly and efficient. The meeting lasted for some time and a surprising number of views were expressed. One suggestion, put forward by a person who had taken part in skirmishes along the North West Frontier before the War, was that we should avoid operating against the rebels at all. He maintained that there was nothing they liked more

than a game of hide-and-seek among the rocks. He held the opinion
that if we ignored them, their morale would sag and they would soon
give up altogether. Unfortunately experience indicated that this
view was over-optimistic. In the end it was decided that I should be
sent to Aden. If, as a result of my visit, the Commander of the
British Forces in the Arabian Peninsula and the Political Resident in
the Persian Gulf and the Commander of the Sultan of Muscat's
armed forces all backed my plan, then the Working Party thought
that they might be prepared to recommend it to the Government.

The subject uppermost in my mind during the two weeks before
my departure for Aden was the question of where to get the right
officers to make the plan work. It was essential to get at least one
good man with experience of special operations to run the project
and a few others with a background of anti-terrorist work to organize the teams. There was no unit in existence such as the one I had
recommended in my Staff College paper which could supply such
people, so it meant selecting individuals. I prepared a list of likely
officers and the manning department set to work to see whether they
were obtainable. Up to the last moment I hoped that at least some
of them would be nominated before I left, so that work could start
on selecting teams while I was away. But as the last few days went
by, each of my nominations was ruled out for one reason or another.
One man had to sit for the Staff College Exam, another was ear-
marked for the job of adjutant of his battalion and it was said that
his career would suffer if he was sent off on a wild-goose chase to the
Middle East. Yet a third was turned down because his commanding
officer said that he was wanted to run the battalion boxing team!
The War Office accepted these reasons and set about looking for
other people.

Just before I left, the Director of Military Operations had an idea.
Some years earlier a unit had been raised in the Far East to carry
out patrols in deep jungle. It was in effect a descendant of the old
wartime Special Air Service and in due course it became known as
22 SAS. By the summer of 1958 the Malayan Emergency was nearly
over and it was decided that 22 SAS should move to England and
hold itself in readiness to carry out patrol tasks in other parts of the
world if necessary. General Hamilton reckoned that 22 SAS might
provide most of the soldiers needed in our teams, which would be a
quicker and more efficient way of getting individuals than collecting
them from the army as a whole. If this idea worked out all right, the

manning branches in the War Office would only have to find a few
officers with the knowledge necessary for mounting a special operation. The General sent a signal to the Headquarters of our forces in
the Far East asking that the Commanding Officer of 22 SAS should
meet me in Aden to examine the situation.

I left England on October 23rd and had a thoroughly unpleasant
flight in an aeroplane which seemed to be full of women and
children. As the ancient aircraft roared and rattled through the
heavens I tried to take stock of the position. It was difficult to know
where to start. Certainly when I first suggested a special operation,
no one would have offered much for my chances of getting it
seriously examined. Indeed my plan would undoubtedly have been
rejected had it not been for the fact that it offered a chance of
success at the very moment when the only other plan had been
turned down by the Government. Furthermore it could be implemented within the limitations set by the Government.

I suppose that I should have been extremely pleased with the
progress of events, but misgivings were crowding in thick and fast.
By far the worst aspect of the business was that the War Office was
obviously not going to be able to get hold of the best men to run the
teams. Another odd thing was that my status was not clearly defined.
I had the feeling that I was being sent to Aden as an individual who
had thought up some hare-brained scheme, parts of which might
merit examination, rather than as the accredited representative of
the General Staff bearing official Whitehall proposals for ending the
rebellion. But amidst all the uncertainty, one thing was certain and
that was that I would be away from the War Office for a week or
two, which was consolation enough for all my difficulties. In fact the
Colonel told me that if the operation was agreed I might have to
direct it for a while until some other suitable officer could be found.
With this interesting thought for company I settled down to get
what sleep I could.

———— ✳ ————

Chapter 15

Approval for the Plan

On arrival in Aden I was met by my opposite number, a major in the operations department. He said that a meeting had been arranged for the following morning with the Commander of the British Forces in the Arabian Peninsula, who was an air vice marshal and with his deputy, who was a brigadier. I explained the Whitehall plan in outline and asked him to ensure that the two Commanders were briefed so that the meeting would at least start by my explaining why the original plan had been rejected and outlining the political limitations which must form the background to any alternative one. Next morning I arrived at the Headquarters for the meeting, prepared to give a concise summary of the situation and the proposed plan. As we entered the Commander's office, my friend of the previous evening told me that he had been unable to make my points to anyone in authority and that I must play it 'off the cuff'.

It was a good office by Aden standards: it was air-conditioned and there was a nice view of the sea. As I shook hands with the Air Marshal, he asked me why some aircraft carrier was suddenly being withdrawn from his command without consultation. I had been given to understand that brevity and clarity were the qualities most required of a staff officer, so I told him that aircraft carriers were the business of the Admiralty and that as no aircraft carrier featured in our plan, I knew nothing about it. Evidently it did feature in one of his plans because he turned abruptly to the Colonel of the Special Air Service Regiment from Malaya, who had just arrived and asked him for his views on the use of SAS in Muscat.

After a short time the conference started, but instead of my being asked to give the background to the proposed plan, we were treated to a forty-minute briefing on the situation in Muscat, all of which was well-known to me already. At the end of the briefing, the Air Marshal turned to the Colonel of the Special Air Service Regiment and asked him to outline a plan for dealing with the situation. This the Colonel duly did. Only then and almost as an afterthought was I asked whether I had any comments. I explained, as briefly as I could, that the plans which they had been discussing might well be sound from a military point of view, but would not stand a chance of being accepted by the Government. At this point I was at last able to outline the Whitehall proposals. They were received with considerable reservations, but although I was not able to convince anyone of their usefulness, I had at least rubbed in the limitations which would be imposed from London. As a result, it was agreed that our proposals should be examined in the Persian Gulf and in Muscat. It was arranged that the Colonel of the SAS and I should do a trip round the area taking with us a staff officer from the Headquarters in Aden. We were to start next morning.

So far as I was concerned the aim of the meeting had been achieved, but we had taken a mighty long time about it. My dislike of meetings became greater than ever. After it was over we had luncheon with the Brigadier. I sat next to the Captain of a cruiser who had been a midshipman in HMS *Rodney* when my father had been the Captain. I spent the afternoon with the Colonel of the SAS whose name was Deane-Drummond.

It cannot be denied that my first impressions of Lieutenant-Colonel Deane-Drummond were unfavourable. He had marched into the Muscat venture that morning without knowing the first thing about it and had immediately set about explaining just how the SAS would deal with the enemy. He had a prominent nose, a clipped moustache and something of a Monty look. There was a hint of ginger in his neatly trimmed hair which I felt might well be reflected in his temperament. Looking across the table at him during the morning's meeting, I remembered hearing about his adventures after Arnhem when he had remained hidden in a cupboard for some days. More recently he had been badly knocked around by the Cypriots. Neither of these experiences appeared to have affected him, but despite his evident vitality I wished that the Director of Military Operations had left him in Malaya because I felt sure that he was not going to be much help with regard to the plan. It is not

unlikely that Colonel Deane-Drummond was having equally un-
charitable thoughts about me and wishing that he could be left alone
to get on with the job without interference from London.

But during the course of the afternoon we reached an understanding which held together throughout our visit to the Persian
Gulf and Muscat. For his part Colonel Deane-Drummond realized
that the introduction of SAS into the project in any shape or form
was dependent on my being able to sell the idea in London. Although he had no intention of having his men used as suggested in
the plan, the first thing was somehow to get them to the theatre of
operations. For my part, I had come to realize that the plan in its
original form would have to be adapted to the fact that the right
officers to run it were obviously not going to turn up in time. I was
therefore quite ready to compromise on details. I also realized that,
with the rather sketchy backing which I had got from London, I
would be lucky to get approval for the project in Aden, Bahrein and
Muscat. The chances would be greatly improved if Colonel Deane-
Drummond supported it and virtually nil if he opposed it. There
were therefore good practical reasons for us to pull together during
our forthcoming journey. I soon discovered that practical considerations carried great weight with Colonel Deane-Drummond.

The sun was just poking up over the edge of Khormackser airfield
when the three of us reported to the Air Movements Office early
next morning. We discovered that we would be going as far as
Sharjah in a Shackleton bomber and that we would change there
into a light aircraft for the last leg of the journey into Muscat. In
accordance with the time-honoured tradition of travel in RAF aircraft, we were kept hanging around for a good long time before the
crew of the Shackleton appeared. In the early morning light the
tarmac of the airfield seemed to stretch away for miles so that the
barren rocks of the Crater looked as though they were rising out of
the end of the runway. Yesterday they were hot, harsh and brown.
Now they were pink-tinged and reasonably friendly.

After we had been waiting for twenty minutes or so, a long-legged
youth appeared with some tea. His skin was nearly as brown as an
Arab's and he wore the shortest of shorts, a khaki shirt and some
sandals. Only a faded RAF beret thrust well back on his head
showed that he was in fact a serviceman. Colonel Deane-Drummond
looked at him with such evident distaste that I thought he might
refuse the tea, but practical considerations dictated otherwise.

When they ultimately appeared, the crew turned out to be a friendly bunch. They were working to nothing more definite in the way of a schedule than a rather vague intention of reaching Sharjah in time for a late lunch. They were going to Sharjah in order to spend a few weeks dropping bombs on the Jebal Akhdar.

By the time we became airborne the sun was up and all the early colour had fled from the bare, bleached landscape. We flew along the coast for a while, but at such a height that the undulations in the desert appeared as waves in the sand. By contrast the sea looked very blue and flat. It was beautifully cool in the aircraft and after a while I fell asleep. When I woke up, we were circling around the airfield at Sharjah. There was an imposing building some distance from one end of the runway which I later learnt was the Sheikh's palace. At the other end was the usual cluster of huts and hangars which was obviously the RAF base. The town itself was spread out along the sea-shore and from the air it all looked very picturesque.

At Sharjah we had some food and transferred into a Pembroke for the flight to Muscat. Soon after taking off, the ground below us started to rise into range upon range of small hills. Gradually the hills became bigger until in the distance far ahead of us we saw the Jebal Akhdar, a monstrous rock-like projection which seemed to hang on the horizon for miles. Before leaving Sharjah we had asked the pilot to fly us over the Jebal so that we could have a good look. He had not been very enthusiastic about the idea because he had had one of his engines put out of action by rebel machine-gun fire a few weeks earlier. Despite this fact, he kindly took whatever risk there was in order that we should get a good view of the land. With its sides rising almost vertically for thousands of feet, the Jebal was certainly impressive, but I had heard it described so often that the impact of seeing it was lessened.

The afternoon was well advanced when our aircraft touched down on the airstrip at Beit El Falaj about five miles outside the town of Muscat. Enclosed on three sides by low hills, Beit El Falaj in the summer is one of the hottest places in the world. When we arrived it was hot, but not unbearably so. We were greeted by a retired army officer called Colonel Waterfield, who was employed by the Sultan of Muscat as his Minister of Defence. Later this title was changed and he became known as the Military Secretary, but the job remained the same. He acted as the Sultan's link with the out-side world for all matters connected with the procurement of officers, men and supplies and he was also involved in the financial affairs of the force.

The Headquarters of the Sultan's Armed Forces was situated in a white fort which had a large red banner flying from one of the turrets. The fort stood a short distance beyond the end of the runway and dominated the whole scene because of its size and its whiteness. Tents and huts were clustered around it. Colonel Waterfield took the Staff Officer from Aden to his house. Colonel Deane-Drummond and I were taken to the officers' mess which stood a short distance away from the fort.

That evening I had a long talk with the operations staff officer of the Sultan's army and learned a good deal about it. Like me, he was doing his first staff job since leaving the Staff College and he was finding it rather different from anything he had ever experienced in his previous career as a soldier. A night spent in the officers' mess was also instructive. It is generally a fairly safe bet that if the officers' mess of a unit is bad, the unit will be bad also. This mess fully reflected the fact that the Sultan's army was being built up at a great rate: *ad hoc* arrangements were inevitable under the circumstances. At the same time it need not have been nearly so dirty. The washing arrangements, which consisted of a shower made from an old oil-drum, did just work after a fashion, but the lavatories were indescribably revolting.

We arrived in the Sultanate on a Sunday and we left again on the following Wednesday. The intervening hours were packed with discovery. Our job in Muscat consisted of two parts. In the first place we had to discover whether the plan – or something like it – could be put into effect. Then we had to persuade the officer commanding the Sultan's Armed Forces to back it.

The officer concerned was a man of medium height and very fair hair called Colonel Smiley. He had taken over the job somewhat reluctantly four or five months earlier, having previously been Military Attaché in Stockholm. Before that he had commanded the Royal Horse Guards at Windsor. It was perhaps a bit surprising to find such a person in a place like Muscat, but Colonel Smiley had a record of unorthodox soldiering and in the War he had worked with partisans in the Balkans. Julian Amery, who was Under Secretary of State at the War Office, had also operated with partisans in the War and knew Colonel Smiley. The latter's appointment to Muscat resulted from this acquaintanceship and although the combination of guerrilla leader and courtier was unusual, it was quite well suited to the Sultan of Muscat's army at that time.

Colonel Smiley had found the Sultan's forces in rather poor shape when he first arrived. Quite apart from the obvious material deficiencies, the morale of his men was low and virtually no efforts were being made to stop the rebels from reinforcing their position. Convoys carrying men and equipment were arriving in the country and were getting through to the Jebal without hindrance. Colonel Smiley set about restoring the situation by mounting a series of small operations designed to clear the rebels out of positions which they were holding at the foot of the mountains. In this way he reckoned to give his men confidence and at the same time to make life more difficult for the rebels on the plateau by cutting off their line of supplies to the outside world which meant, in effect, Saudi Arabia. He was greatly assisted in this part of his plan by the Royal Marine NCOs who had been lent to the Sultan's Forces to cover the gap until seconded officers could arrive.

Despite the success of his immediate measures, Colonel Smiley was soon convinced that victory over the rebels required help from outside and he had been anxious for the brigade operation to take place. When approval for this course of action was withheld he decided to strengthen his positions in the foot-hills and patrol up the tracks leading to the plateau in order to give his men experience and at the same time to collect information that would be useful later on should an assault by the Sultan's army become possible. All the time his forces were becoming stronger and better trained and at the same time the blockade of the Jebal and action by the RAF was slowly weakening Talib's position. The only trouble was that without help the weakening process might drag on for years.

Colonel Smiley therefore had a plan, which offered a good chance of success in the long term. Whether or not he backed our plan would depend on how well it fitted in with his own. Colonel Smiley soon made it clear that he would welcome help providing that there were no extra demands on his administrative resources which were already grossly overstretched as the result of the rapid build-up of the Sultan's army. He was also adamant that anyone operating in Muscat must be unreservedly under his command. Finally he had always maintained that the Jebal Akhdar was no place for National Service soldiers because he did not consider that they could be well enough trained to operate successfully in the very difficult conditions prevailing there. When the brigade operation was being discussed he had asked that at least one of the units should be a Parachute Battalion or a Royal Marine Commando.

At our first meeting with Colonel Smiley on the Monday morning it was clear that we would have little difficulty in getting him to back our plan because all of his essential requirements could be met. In the first place, nothing could be tougher or less like National Servicemen than the SAS who were all regulars and all volunteers. In the second place, the plan would obviously have to be put into effect under the overall command of Colonel Smiley: there would be no point in it being directed from outside Muscat. In the third place, the teams could be made self-supporting from an administrative point of view. They would not need much support and this could all be provided from the Aden base. It was obvious that the plan would have to be bent in any case to take account of the fact that the right officers would not be forthcoming from England and to meet Colonel Deane-Drummond's requirements. My only concern was to make sure that it could still be presented as the same plan when I got back to England. Fortunately both Colonel Smiley and Colonel Deane-Drummond well understood this problem.

After our meeting with Colonel Smiley we went by air to Nizwa. The Headquarters of one of the two battalions of the Sultan's army was stationed there, but more important from my point of view was the fact that the Sultan's half-brother, Said Tariq, lived in Nizwa castle. From all accounts Said Tariq controlled the only sources of information and would be the best man from whom to get guides, interpreters and other useful people. He seemed to be the equivalent of the Provincial Commissioner, Chief of Police and Special Branch Officer all in one. Soon after our arrival at Nizwa, Colonel Deane-Drummond went off to have another look at the Jebal Akhdar and I made my way to the castle with one of the officers of the Sultan's army.

We approached the castle along the bed of a river which only contained water during the wettest months of the year. There was no water to be seen as we drove across the sand and shingle, but there must have been moisture below the surface because the banks were lined with trees in the shade of which a variety of men and animals rested. This world had nothing in common with the hills and plains of Kenya or the steaming green jungles of Malaya. It was quite new to me and the herds of scraggy camels which we passed seemed to symbolize the very essence of Arabia. The whole scene could have come out of the Old Testament, but for the fact that every male over the age of about eight seemed to be carrying an immense and ancient rifle. The timelessness of the scene was not altogether an illusion. The way of life in Muscat and Oman had probably altered less since biblical times than that of any other country and it was the Sultan's intention that his people should continue to live without the corroding influences of alien civilizations.

Nizwa castle was in keeping with its surroundings. From the outside it gave an impression of impregnable solidity, its great stone keep and battlements dwarfing the buildings of the town. Inside it was a veritable rabbit-warren of stairways and passages and little rooms. Said Tariq was sleeping when we arrived, so we had a look round. From the tower there was a fine view out over Nizwa and the surrounding countryside to the great sweep of the Jebal Akhdar, which rose out of the plateau a few miles away. We also saw a dungeon in which the Prophet Jeremiah would have felt thoroughly at home. It consisted of a deep hole in the ground and to leave it a prisoner would have had to be drawn up in the traditional manner by a rope slung under his armpits. Two prisoners were incarcerated in this pit and were dimly visible through the gloom. I could not see whether they were embedded in mire, but it is not unlikely that they were. The prisoners were men accused of contacting rebels from the mountain. They would be interrogated eventually by Said Tariq's henchmen, but no doubt a lot of their value would be lost because no professional intelligence organization was available to make use of them.

Said Tariq was a most impressive man: four-square, aquiline and vigorous. After twenty minutes of discussion, I was confident that the necessary Arab backing could be obtained for the teams, providing that the officer running the project was able to get on with Said Tariq. I was also reasonably certain that prisoners from the Bani Riyam would not be too difficult to collect.

We returned to Beit El Falaj in the evening and had dinner with Colonel Smiley. He intended to go next morning to watch a load of donkeys being disembarked from a large ship which was lying some distance off shore. The donkeys had been bought in Somaliland to act as pack-animals for the big operation and they had been despatched before the plan had been turned down. Colonel Smiley was very much opposed to the arrival of the donkeys because they

G

were not administratively self-supporting and although they were coming unreservedly under his command, he had no idea what to do with them. All the same he felt that it was his duty to see that they were properly put ashore and he invited us to go with him to watch this unusual performance.

Next morning we got up early and drove with Colonel Smiley into Muscat. It was a picturesque port with one or two impressive buildings such as the British Consulate, a castle similar to that at Nizwa and the Sultan's palace. The Sultan himself seldom visited Muscat, but lived in Salalah several hundred miles along the coast towards Aden. The donkeys had come from Somaliland in a ship owned by the War Department and designed to carry tanks in an amphibious operation. A motor-boat took us out to this ship and soon after we arrived on board unloading commenced. The donkeys were tethered on the tank deck and from there they were hoisted over the side in nets and lowered into waiting Arab craft which took them to the shore. When we had seen enough, we too descended into an Arab boat and together with a load of donkeys, got ourselves deposited in the surf a few yards from the beach.

A short way from the disembarkation point some Arab fishermen were selling the morning's catch. I went to have a look and found thousands of little fish, like whitebait, wriggling around in the nets where the sand and the sea met. The sun flashed on their silver bodies as they splashed in the edge of the tide. Above them the Arab fishermen squatted on their haunches, long robes tucked into their belts and bare, brown toes hooked into the moist sand. My interest in the fish was as nothing compared to their interest in the donkeys. They doubtless thought it strange that we should be bringing the animals in by sea when a strong resident population already existed in the country. A further cause for surprise was that the incoming donkeys were small and weedy compared to the local brand.

In due course we returned to Beit El Falaj and spent the rest of the day finalizing our plan. Next morning we had a talk to Colonel Smiley before leaving for Bahrein. The decision, which we reached, was that, in theory at any rate, the plan would be very like the one we had set out to examine. The main difference was that the SAS would start patrolling in the normal way under their own troop commanders, if the officers to lead the teams had not arrived ahead of them. Obviously the SAS could not sit around doing nothing in such circumstances. If officers from England arrived subsequently they would start working from selected centres in close touch with the SAS troops, providing them with intelligence or using them to get intelligence, according to the situation. The later stages of the operation were purposely left a bit vague. In other words we arranged things so that the plan as agreed in London could be put into operation within the context of Colonel Smiley's overall arrangements for the campaign. At the same time an alternative plan of deep patrolling backed by such intelligence resources as were forthcoming would be put into operation if the officers from the UK did not turn up in time. If the plan agreed in London was to be abandoned, it would be because the resources required from England were slow in arriving and no one in Arabia could be blamed for that. With my knowledge of the Whitehall machine on the one hand and of Colonel Deane-Drummond on the other, I had little doubt as to which of the alternatives would be adopted.

Before we left Beit El Falaj I had a final interview with Colonel Smiley. He gave me letters to be delivered in Whitehall in which he expressed his approval for the plan as modified in our discussions. In the afternoon I flew to Bahrein with Colonel Deane-Drummond.

As we touched down on the airfield, I was very conscious of being back in a British-run area. Muscat was a foreign country and Colonel Smiley was the commander of a foreign army owing allegiance to a foreign sovereign. In Bahrein the military commander, who was a brigadier, was a straightforward subordinate of the military commander in Aden. Entering the Headquarters there made me feel that I was already half-way back to the War Office.

The Brigadier together with the naval and air force commanders formed a committee under the chairmanship of the Political Resident for the Persian Gulf, an officer of the Diplomatic Service of ambassadorial rank. This was called the Military Co-ordinating Committee (Persian Gulf) better known as the MCC(PG). It was now necessary for us to get the approval of this committee for our plan. The MCC(PG) met next day with us in attendance and speedily agreed to our proposals, backed as they were by Colonel Smiley. A signal to the Foreign Office was duly drafted and despatched next day.

That concluded the first part of our enterprise, in that we had got agreement for the plan from Aden, Muscat and Bahrein. Colonel Deane-Drummond departed during the night by air for Malaya and the Staff Officer from Aden returned there to start making arrangements for the reception of the SAS. He had a big job on his hands in collecting together all the necessary stores and equipment and arranging for them to be shipped into Muscat.

There was no aircraft available to take me back to London until the next afternoon so I busied myself around the Headquarters finding out how the intelligence organization worked in the Persian Gulf as a whole. It was quite clear that events on the Jebal had their roots in Saudi Arabia and I wanted to know what information would be available about Talib's base there and his lines of communication into the Oman. I took off for England on Friday, October 31st and arrived in London in the early hours of the following morning. The whole trip had taken only eight days.

Soon after my return from the Persian Gulf, it was decided that the Government should be asked to approve the plan for a Special Operation. On November 13th I was told that I would have to explain the plan to the Prime Minister but this was later changed and the Director of Military Operations said that I was to report to the Chief of the Defence Staff instead. He added that if Sir Winston Churchill had been Prime Minister I would certainly have been required to report to him in person. The Chief of the Defence Staff was Marshal of the Royal Air Force, Sir William Dickson and my interview with him must have been satisfactory because next day the Government approved the plan. It was then decided that I should return to Muscat on Sunday to help get the operation going. So far, only one officer had been nominated to take part and he would not be ready to leave England for about two weeks. I met him briefly on the Friday afternoon and took off again for the Gulf on November 16th.

Chapter 16

❋

Mounting the Operation

The journey to Beit El Falaj took two days because I had to spend a night in Bahrein on the way. I arrived in Muscat on Tuesday, an hour or two ahead of D Squadron 22 SAS who flew in from Malaya. Colonel Deane-Drummond was with them. It was no surprise to find that the SAS had arrived ahead of the officers who were supposed to be running the teams and I had already decided that the most useful task which I could do would be to set up an intelligence organization designed to support the SAS and at the same time keep a direct link with Whitehall in order to hasten the supply of anything found to be urgently necessary. An important aspect of the intelligence work would be to try and get a line on the supply route between the Jebal Akhdar and Saudi Arabia.

The arrangements made for the SAS were that the whole squadron should spend four days settling in at Beit El Falaj and then on the following Sunday the four troops of the squadron would move into base camps around the Jebal Akhdar. There was something to be said for my basing myself at Nizwa because of its proximity to the rebels and because so much of the information on them came through Said Tariq or his henchmen. On the other hand the reasons for remaining at Beit El Falaj were greater. Colonel Smiley was based there and so was my link with the Foreign Office which ran through the British Consulate in Muscat. Nizwa was also cut off from the north side of the Jebal and it seemed probable that the rebel line of communications ran in that direction. Furthermore intelligence on this subject would not come from Nizwa: a lot of it would come direct from British sources in Bahrein and the rest from the villages along the coast. Finally I had no vehicle of my own and if I went to Nizwa I should probably be stuck there for good.

On Wednesday I tried to get hold of the £15,000 which the Foreign Office told me would be made available through the British Consulate in Muscat. Despite their assurance, I found that it had not arrived. My first reaction was to send for some money of my own on the assumption that I should be able to reimburse myself, as I had done in Kenya a few years earlier, but on reflection I decided that this course was too risky because I might be withdrawn to England before I had time to conclude the necessary financial adjustments.

During the next four days I made several trips to Nizwa by air and provided the SAS Squadron Commander with such background information as I could pick up. Two interesting developments had taken place since my previous visit. The first was that a major of the Sultan's army had discovered an unguarded track which led into the Jebal plateau from the Awabi side of the mountain. The second was that Talib had offered to call off the rebellion, subject to certain conditions being met by the Sultan. Whereas the first of these developments was of great significance with regard to the future pattern of operations, the second made it questionable whether any further operations would be required at all.

There were varying views regarding the offer of surrender. The feeling in Bahrein was that Talib's men could not stand the bombing, but in Beit El Falaj it was put down to the effects of the blockade. In Nizwa the Commander of the Northern Frontier Regiment and Said Tariq thought that it was no more than a trick, designed to make the Government forces relax their vigilance, so that further reinforcements and supplies could be got through to the Jebal. The Commanding Officer at Nizwa was busy working out a plan for assaulting the Jebal without outside assistance and he considered that it stood a good chance of success.

By the end of the week it was known that the Sultan would not accept Talib's terms. The SAS squadron deployed so that two of its troops could start patrolling from the Nizwa side of the Jebal and the other two troops from the Awabi side. Colonel Deane-Drummond returned to Malaya and news came through that the officer, whom I had met in London, would arrive on the following Tuesday.

Of the many loose ends remaining, one required urgent attention. This concerned the provision of trackers. It had never occurred to me that there would be any difficulty in finding good trackers from amongst the Arab population of a country like Muscat and Oman. I had raised the matter on our earlier visit and Colonel Smiley had said that he would try and find some suitable men. On my return he said that trackers were not available in the country. He suggested that it might be worth trying to get some Africans from the Northern Frontier Province of Kenya where the terrain was somewhat similar to the Omani Desert. Colonel Smiley's wife came from Kenya and he owned land there. Getting trackers from Kenya was easier said than done and there would obviously be some tricky problems involved in their selection, collection and movement into Muscat. As I had experience of tracking, a working knowledge of Kenya and direct access to the Ministries concerned in Whitehall, it was decided that I should go and get them, as soon as the officer from England arrived.

On Monday there was a conference at Beit El Falaj to discuss the attack on the Jebal proposed by the Commanding Officer of the battalion in Nizwa. It was attended by the Brigadier from Bahrein and his RAF opposite number. The general feeling of the meeting was that it might work. The officer from England arrived on Tuesday, as arranged, and we had a good talk about the situation. He had no news about the £15,000 so we sent a very angry signal back to Whitehall. Later in the day I flew to Bahrein and on the following morning set off in another aircraft on the first stage of the journey to Kenya. Unfortunately engine trouble resulted in a twenty-four hour delay at Sharjah, but there was nothing very surprising about that. Considering the immense demands made on the few aircraft available in the Arabian Peninsula it was amazing that they managed to fly at all.

There was a further delay in Aden and I took the opportunity of visiting the Brigadier. I also called on the Commissioner of Police. During August and September I had been instrumental in getting Whitehall's agreement to the setting up of an Internal Security Headquarters in Aden, designed to co-ordinate anti-terrorist operations in the Colony. I had been particularly anxious to get this Headquarters established before the situation deteriorated too far. A military intelligence officer to help the Special Branch was also included in the arrangement. The Commissioner took me around the new Headquarters and for once I had the feeling that something we had done in London had borne fruit.

I arrived in Nairobi shortly before midnight on Friday, November 28th and went to bed in an hotel a short distance from the cathedral.

Next morning when I woke up I found the sun shining on a rain-washed garden. Everything was sparkling and fresh as I remembered it from the days at Kamiti: red earth in the flower beds, a mass of purple bougainvillia clinging to a trellis beyond the lawn and a group of tall clear blue gum trees behind. It was all a wonderful change from the arid atmosphere of Arabia. Later in the morning I arrived at the military Headquarters and found it exactly as I had last seen it three years before. It was familiar, friendly and compact and my business, which would have taken a month in Whitehall or a week in Arabia, was completed in about an hour. By lunch-time I had seen the General, his Chief of Staff, the Minister of Defence and the Chief Game Warden. He, it seemed, was in the best position to help over the provision of trackers.

My visit to the Minister of Defence was necessary because he would have to give permission for the trackers to leave the country. This he did, subject to the proviso that they should be accompanied by a European to look after them. Under these circumstances it seemed sensible to find the European first. That afternoon I set off to see Eric Holyoak hoping that he might perhaps be able to take the trackers to Muscat. For old time's sake I took the road through Limuru and Uplands and thence along the forest edge to Njabini. As the Landrover, which had been lent to me by the Royal Army Service Corps, bumped in and out of the potholes it was easy to imagine myself back chasing Mau Mau. Every turn in the road, every new vista and each changing smell was familiar. In a journey, which took well under two hours, we passed through Kiambu coffee farms, Kikuyu Reserve, the forest and then the open grain-growing lands of the Kinangop. Soon we were driving along the track leading to Holyoak's Saw Mills Limited, where we were met by Eric and his dog.

Unfortunately Eric could not leave the mill and our conversation turned to a discussion of possible alternatives. After a time it seemed that Stan Bleazard would be the best choice and we thought of one or two other people who might do if he was not available. The next question was how to find Bleazard. Eric told me that there would be a party at the Headquarters of the Kenya Regiment in Nairobi that evening to say goodbye to the second in command, who was leaving. Stan might well be there, but if not, someone else would be sure to know where he was.

The sun was already well down over the Rift Valley when I left the Kinangop and started on the forty-mile journey back to Nairobi. It was dark by the time I got there. Outside the Kenya Regiment Headquarters cars of all descriptions were parked in profusion. I walked in and was immediately surrounded by a number of men whom I knew. Luckily Bleazard was at the party. His first reaction to the suggestion that he should take a party of trackers to Muscat was favourable, but he asked to be allowed to think about it overnight. After all, as he pointed out, he was in a steady and pensionable job, he had no idea where Muscat was or who we were fighting or why. Also there was no means of knowing how long he would be away. All things considered his request was reasonable and we agreed to meet for lunch on the following day.

Next morning I moved from the hotel into the officers' mess of the Kenya Regiment and then met Stan Bleazard as arranged. He agreed to take the trackers to Muscat, provided that I could organize things so that he could return to his present job with the Post Office when he got back, preferably without loss of pension rights. As it was Sunday, we had to wait until the following day in order to fix up the details. It was important to get Stan's position in relation to the Post Office cleared up as soon as possible because there was no time to be wasted in collecting the trackers. But the matter was fairly complicated because the Post Office was not an agency of the Kenya Government but came under the East African High Commission. I therefore started by calling on the High Commissioner himself, who passed me on to the Postmaster General. They were both incredibly helpful and soon everything was arranged.

The next snag to develop was totally unexpected and came in the form of a signal from Colonel Smiley. In it he said that he was having second thoughts about trackers and only wanted two instead of the ten which I had been asked to collect. He also said that he did not want a European to accompany them. Consideration of this signal led me to believe that Colonel Smiley had not fully realized the difficulties involved in selecting trackers, or the time it would take to find them and get them to Muscat. To collect two and try them, then get more, would mean that a useful number would not be working on the ground for some weeks. Also, as the Kenya Minister of Defence had pointed out, we could hardly maintain a small number of very primitive Africans in a totally foreign environment without someone to look after them, who understood their background and knew their ways. In the end I decided to go ahead with our plans on the grounds that the Colonel would undoubtedly wish me to do so, if he knew the full circumstances.

Stan Bleazard and I left Nairobi in search of trackers at 2 a.m. on Tuesday morning and drove north through the darkness. On the advice of the Chief Game Warden we were heading for Isiolo where the Game Warden was George Adamson, a man who had an un-rivalled knowledge of the Northern Frontier Province and its peoples. It had been a hot evening when we left Nairobi and we were in our shirt sleeves. An hour before dawn we crossed the high ridge of land which joins Mount Kenya and the Aberdares above Nyeri and the cold cut through us like a knife. It was raining and the Landrover slid around on the red mud of the road. Although we could not see the great forested mountains, their presence was evident in every breath we took. By the time we reached Timau it was getting light. Although we were right alongside Mount Kenya, there was no breathtaking view of the snow-capped peak. Instead there was a uniformly damp greyness about the scene. Heavy cloud obscured the mountain itself. Soon afterwards we turned left off the road from Nairobi and started to drop down into the Northern Frontier Province. Our descent was so steep that the windows and windscreen of the Landrover misted up. About half-way down we stopped where a stream ran under the road and we washed and cooked some breakfast. Behind us the escarpment rose up sharply into the grey dampness which hung like a shawl around Mount Kenya. Below and ahead for mile after mile lay the Northern Frontier Province. Far away the sun was shining and it was easy to visualize herds of buck and wildebeeste feeding on the seemingly endless plains.

It was nearly 8 a.m. when we drove up the last bit of track and stopped outside George Adamson's house. We were anxious to start interviewing trackers and hoped that some would be waiting, as a result of a telegram which the Chief Game Warden had sent on Saturday. But a disappointment was in store for us because Adamson and his wife were both away on safari and the Assistant Game Warden was keeping the telegram until he returned. He was expected back any time in the next few days. The Assistant Game Warden was Julian McKean and he had been in the same National Service intake as Eric and Stan during the Emergency so we had at least fallen in with a friend. He made no pretence of being an expert on the subject of trackers, but he said that he had passed the word round and could get us some men to interview later in the morning. I filled in the time by calling on the Provincial Commissioner, which it was my duty to do in any case, and on the Superintendent of Police. We had an interesting discussion on the subject of Somali ambitions and incursions. Later on we tested Julian's trackers, but they were no good. There was nothing to be done but to await the return of the Adamsons so Julian took us out to look at game. In this way we spent a most enjoyable afternoon.

We passed the evening talking to Julian in his tent and he told us some amusing stories about a lioness which Mrs Adamson used to keep around the place. Apparently it had become too difficult to keep her any longer so she had set her free some sixty miles away. The Adamsons were in fact visiting her at the time which accounted for their absence. If I had known how famous the lioness Elsa was to become, I should have paid more careful attention to Julian's stories.

Bleazard and I were administratively self-supporting in a way which would have delighted the heart of Colonel Smiley, so we were able to bed down in a shed near Julian's tent. The Adamsons arrived back in the early hours of the morning, but it was nearly midday by the time we broached the subject of trackers. George Adamson was optimistic and helpful, but said that it would take him about a week to get men of the quality we required and he could not guarantee getting as many as ten. He suggested that Stan should come back a week later and that in the meantime we should visit Rodney Eliot who was the Game Warden at Maralal and who might also be able to find some suitable men for us. We arrived at Maralal just as it was getting dark. Rodney Eliot knew all about tracking and had been responsible for getting and training trackers during the Emergency. His advice was the same as George Adamson's. Come back in a week's time and he would see what he could do. In the morning we returned to Nairobi.

The next day, which was Friday, was taken up with making arrangements for equipping and moving Bleazard and his trackers to Muscat. There seemed to be a lot of detail involved, such as the provision of pay, clothes, food, arms, passports and an aircraft. As always, administration is an inescapable prelude to military achievement. On Saturday I left Kenya and got as far as Aden. There were no aircraft going to the Persian Gulf on Sunday, but on Monday I became airborne again, this time in a Beverley transport which contained a mass of heavy equipment and the Senior Chaplain for the Arabian Peninsula who was making a visit to Bahrein. Some years earlier we had both been in the same battalion. He was a first-rate padre by any standards; the only drawback being that he could not bring himself to conclude his sermons at the end of ten minutes.

At Aden we had been told that Sharjah would be the first stop, but in fact the Beverley put down at Firq, a village about four miles from Nizwa. I decided to take the opportunity of visiting the two SAS troops operating on that side of the Jebal so I made my way to the Headquarters of the battalion stationed there. The Commanding Officer received me with a great deal more enthusiasm than that extended to guests at Beit El Falaj, but he was not optimistic about getting an aircraft to take me to Muscat because both the Pioneers of the Sultan's Air Force had broken down.

After a cup of tea I set off to find the SAS and ran them to earth just as it was getting dark in a little camp which they had made out in the desert.

In the half-light the Jebal hung over us like the wall of a cathedral. They talked in the hushed voices of men accustomed to life in the jungle. Peter de La Billière was the troop Commander and as he spoke a number of incidents which had taken place among the rocks of that formidable escarpment sprang to life. He and his men had already taken part in several engagements and it was obvious that they had established their supremacy in an unmistakable way. To begin with, they had tended to underrate the skill of Talib's men, but in one of their earliest encounters they had lost a soldier as the result of a well-placed shot at long range which had made them revise their opinions. Their greatest success so far had been an attack on a cave in which one of Talib's piquets was based. They had identified it at long range and then crawled up under cover of darkness to within 150 yards. At dawn the piquet Commander paraded his men in front of the cave and the patrol opened fire with devastating effect and then discharged a rocket into the mouth of the cave itself. It was obvious that the SAS were enjoying themselves and achieving considerable success. As usual they were right on top of their job. I returned to Nizwa very heartened by their account of events.

Next morning I met an officer called Hywell-Jones, who had just arrived from England to run one of the teams. It only needed a few minutes conversation for me to discover that he had an intuitive understanding of anti-terrorist warfare and a certain amount of experience of normal operations against such people. He had no first-hand knowledge of special operations, but he was unquestionably the right sort of man for the job. But by now things had gone too far for the original concept to be revived and he would have to concentrate on providing whatever information he could lay his hands on for the benefit of the SAS. He would have plenty of scope.

Also living at Nizwa with the battalion of the Sultan's army was the tactical Headquarters of a squadron of the Life Guards. The squadron was normally stationed at Sharja, but it had been sent to Muscat to replace the two armoured car troops which had been left behind after the 1957 operations. The squadron had its main Headquarters at Beit El Falaj and its job was to keep open the roads leading from Muscat to Nizwa and to Awabi. Troops were based at various strategic points along these routes.

After seeing Hywell-Jones I went to have a talk to the Squadron Commander and discovered that one of his troops was driving from Nizwa to Muscat that afternoon. He kindly said that I could travel with it.

The mining campaign was at its height and the Life Guards were having their scout cars blown up regularly. Fortunately the mines were small ones and seldom caused casualties or such serious damage as to render the vehicles incapable of repair. Just before we left news came through that a vehicle had been blown up near Awabi: earlier in the day another one had struck a mine on the road to Muscat. The troop with which I was to travel was moving in two halves about ten minutes apart and I was firmly made to sit in the second vehicle of the second half.

We left Nizwa in the afternoon and set off on the eighty-odd miles to Beit El Falaj. By the time we reached Izki the sun was already low in the sky. On our left-hand side the Jebal loomed above us all the way. There were a few villages built round the oasis and passing through them the road wound between walled orchards of date-palms. At other times it was no more than a track through the empty desert. Only when it crossed the many wadis was it canalized into a set area and these were the favourite places for laying mines.

After a time the ferocious face of the Jebal mellowed, as we left the main mass of the mountain behind. The sun sank down until it was like a huge red football perched on the crest of the ridge. In a surprisingly short time it was half a football and soon afterwards it was no more than an orange rim. Throughout the drive I had been very conscious of mines and I wondered how my nerves would stand up to regular travel of this sort. Every minute of the time, even when admiring the view or thinking about the operations or the trackers, something inside me was waiting for the bang. And then it happened. A scout car in the leading group went up. A few minutes later we were on the scene. Fortunately no one was hurt. The incident had taken place where the track wound its way between two small hills. By the time we arrived the crews of both the leading scout cars had dismounted and a Cornet was leaning languidly against the wreckage of the blown-up vehicle while his Corporal of Horse was issuing orders. Thinking that the Cornet might be feeling a bit out of things I entered into a discussion with him about the general situation. He said that he had only recently joined the regiment, but that he enjoyed the life. The mine incident did not seem to worry him or even interest him very much, and he was quite happy to let his Corporal of Horse deal with what he evidently regarded as a pure matter of routine. Meanwhile the Corporal of Horse having deployed the members of the troop in a suitable manner, got back into his scout car to contact the Squadron Corporal Major on the wireless and get further instructions. He was told to send me on at once with half the troop while the other half waited for the recovery vehicle to reach them. It was late in the evening when I reached Beit El Falaj.

On the morning after my return to Beit El Falaj I had a long talk to the commander of the SAS squadron who described in detail the events which had taken place since his men had started to operate on the Jebal. I had already heard about the engagements above Nizwa, but this was the first I had heard of the actions which had been fought by the two troops on the Awabi side of the mountain. It was little short of amazing to find out how much had been achieved. The Squadron Commander explained his plan and it seemed to me that every one of his decisions had been dead right. In addition his men had obviously killed a lot of rebels in a number of separate engagements. It is always difficult to estimate casualties inflicted in such circumstances, but at the very least the squadron must have killed twenty or thirty of the enemy for the loss of one of their own men. If events were to continue in this way, it seemed unlikely that the rebels would be able to keep going for more than two or three months, bearing in mind the added effects of the blockade and the bombing. The only unsatisfactory aspect of the business was that the Squadron Commander was in a bad frame of mind. He was thoroughly depressed and he felt that he was likely to lose more of his men to no purpose. It is of course a fact that in every operation there comes a time when progress appears to be arrested and when there is no immediate prospect of further success. I had suffered from just such a period of frustration and depression in Malaya during August of the previous year, although in retrospect it is clear that it was the fruitless patrols and ambushes, then being carried out, which laid the foundation for the successes of September. Colonel Smiley was also rather less satisfied with the situation than he had been when I last saw him, but his dissatisfaction resulted from a difference of opinion which he was having with the Commander in Aden.

Unfortunately the officer from England who had been sent out to run the Special Operation was away visiting various posts around the Jebal and he did not return until Thursday. When he got back he was bursting with optimism and enthusiasm.

He and I spent most of Thursday morning discussing the position between ourselves and came to the conclusion that the measures so far taken would be likely to bring the campaign to a successful conclusion in due course. We saw this coming about as a result of the casualties which were being inflicted on the enemy. We felt that as Talib's hard core were killed off there would be an increasing likelihood of an SAS patrol killing Talib himself because he would be obliged to take a more personal part in the operations of the survivors. Alternatively, we thought that the enemy leaders might surrender if their chances of ultimate survival were sufficiently reduced. An important part of the operation would be to tighten up the blockade to such an extent that the rebel leaders could be intercepted if they tried to escape. This was entirely a matter of straightforward intelligence and there seemed a reasonable chance that the necessary measures could be taken over a period of two or three months. We did not see any likelihood of the operation developing on the lines of the original plan.

During the afternoon we saw Colonel Smiley who expressed the opinion that the campaign was unlikely to be brought to a successful conclusion using our present methods by the onset of the hot weather in April. He was also concerned about the mining campaign. He said that he had discussed the matter thoroughly with the SAS

Squadron Commander and that he had decided to ask for a second SAS squadron.

I must admit that I did not like this idea at all from a personal point of view. For one thing I wanted to demonstrate that the old-fashioned military method of saturating the enemy with a vastly excessive force of one's own was uneconomical, unnecessary and un-desirable. Even if the original plan for a Special Operation had been bent out of all recognition, my point would have been made if the campaign could have been brought to a successful conclusion by the use of seventy members of the SAS as opposed to the original plan of using a brigade. If more SAS were used, my point would be cor-respondingly weakened. Another reason for my disliking the idea was that the job of 'selling it' to the Foreign Office would undoubt-edly be given to me. My associates on the Muscat Working Party had doubtless already heard how the operation had developed from the original conception under which a few individuals were to be introduced into the country, into one involving the use of a formed unit and they probably considered that my first plan had been solely designed to obtain their agreement by trickery. If I now appeared asking for another squadron, their worst suspicions would seem to be confirmed. On the other hand there were several good reasons for supporting the proposal. For one thing my superiors in the War Office would be strongly in favour of sending a second squadron of the SAS. For another, the concept of the operation had changed and the aim was now to wear down the enemy by causing casualties. For this purpose two squadrons would obviously be better and quicker than one. The matter of speed was not altogether unim-portant because so long as the rebellion continued people would go on getting killed. On balance there could be no denying that Colonel Smiley was right. Next day the Political Resident for the Persian Gulf arrived in Muscat and the idea was discussed with him. He said that he would support the proposal.

I left Muscat for England on Saturday December 13th, but did not arrive until the following Wednesday after a journey which in-cluded every known form of discomfort and delay. In the end the aircraft was diverted to an airfield in Cornwall because of fog and I spent the best part of a day in a very slow and steamy train, which arrived in London late in the evening. Colin James, my good-natured landlord and flat-mate, had not seen or heard of me for many weeks and my return was not very tactfully timed from his point of view. All the same, he made me as welcome as the circumstances permitted.

The Foreign Office members of the Muscat Working Party were every bit as annoyed about the request for a second squadron as I had feared, but the Chiefs of Staff supported the idea and the Government eventually agreed. With the despatch of this squadron from Malaya shortly afterwards my connection with the steps taken to quell the rebellion came to an end.

The subsequent course of events is worth recording in outline. Colonel Deane-Drummond arrived with the second squadron early in the New Year and quickly saw that the combined effect of air action, the blockade and the patrolling done by the SAS squadron had gravely weakened the enemy position. Soon after his arrival Colonel Smiley delegated to him the tactical control of all forces operating against Talib and Colonel Deane-Drummond made a plan to assault the Jebal using both of his own squadrons, the Life Guards squadron, elements of both battalions of the Sultan's Armed Forces and the RAF. This plan was brilliantly conceived and on January 26th 1959 it was executed with immense skill and energy. As a result the Jebal was captured and the rebellion came to an abrupt end. Unfortunately the rebel leaders made good their escape to Saudi Arabia.

Chapter 17

❋

Repercussions and Developments

The British Government's decision in September 1958 not to authorize a brigade operation in Muscat had been taken for reasons of world politics, with particular reference to the damage which such intervention might do to our standing in the United Nations. The decision was greeted with dismay by senior officers in London and Arabia because they could not see how the situation could be brought under control without such a large-scale assault. But despite the Government's refusal to permit it, the rebellion collapsed within five months, the rebel leaders fled the country and the Sultan regained control over the whole of central Oman and thereafter maintained it for the rest of his reign.

It would be reasonable to suppose that this all happened as the result of a brilliantly conceived plan put into effect with precision and efficiency, but nothing could be further from the truth. What actually happened was that I produced an unconventional and hazardous plan which only received serious consideration because it met the stringent political limitations of the moment. What started as a plan to establish an intelligence organization and exploit its information by the use of a force composed of a few specialist officers and captured enemy tribesmen, was put into effect as a series of deep patrols by a squadron of the Special Air Service using such odd bits of intelligence as could be scraped up at short notice by one or two officers sent out from England. This operation in turn, although showing good prospects of success, was succeeded by a different one in which two squadrons of the SAS assisted by the Life Guards squadron and elements of the Sultan's army, made a straight-forward assault on the Jebal Akhdar.

Undoubtedly the final operation was highly effective: Colonels Smiley and Deane-Drummond deserve great credit for it. But they were only able to act as they did because the political restrictions which had precluded an overt military operation in the summer had been relaxed by the New Year. Had this not been the case, the ending of the rebellion would have been delayed until the patrolling of the Special Air Service had worn the enemy down, as it almost certainly would have done judging by the rate of attrition which was being achieved when the concept changed. But even the patrolling of one Special Air Service squadron went beyond the initial political restrictions which limited extra assistance to the Sultan's forces to forty individuals. Had this rule been rigidly applied, we would have been obliged to implement the original Special Operation or something like it.

It is difficult to say whether the original idea would have worked had the right people and the money been made available. Admittedly when I first made the plan I had no first-hand knowledge of Oman, but later having seen the country and having studied more fully the background of inter-tribal rivalry, I believe that there was nothing wrong with the idea in so far as events on the ground were concerned. The part of the plan which was impracticable concerned getting the right people and the money to the scene in a reasonable time. I have described in some detail how the various bits of the force were collected together. What in practice we tried to do, was to extract a number of individual officers from jobs all over the world, get hold of some trackers from Africa and some money from the Treasury, move a small unit from Malaya and marry the whole lot up, together with some vehicles and equipment, in a remote part of Arabia, doing the whole thing under a cloak of deep secrecy. We succeeded in doing most of this, but we were unable to get the key officers or the money within the time required to make the plan work. In my opinion we could only have done this if some organization had existed in advance, capable of moving into a country at short notice for the purpose of collecting intelligence and developing it into contact information, as this was in effect what we were trying to do. Because no such unit existed we had to try and set one up by *ad hoc* methods and this we failed to do.

Although the campaign had been successful, the shortcomings of our arrangements for mounting the operation in its original form had been seen in the War Office and it seemed to be a good moment for me to resurrect my idea of raising a unit designed to go to any part of the world at short notice, reinforce or set up an intelligence organization and run a Special Operation if necessary. I therefore returned to the plan which I had put forward at the Staff College three years earlier, but realizing that there was little chance of getting a new unit raised from scratch I based my approach on giving the role to the Special Air Service. I wrote a new paper on this basis.

One advantage of being in the War Office was that I was able to circulate my paper as an official document and it received rather more attention than had been accorded to my earlier work. In due course Colonel Deane-Drummond was called on for his opinion, but although he had been vaguely encouraging when we had discussed the matter in Muscat, he came out firmly against the idea as expressed in my paper. His reason for opposing it was perfectly sensible. He maintained that if the Special Air Service could be enlarged to include an element for the job which I had in mind and at the same time retain squadrons organized for deep patrolling, then there might be some merit in my proposal. But if the regiment had to be organized for one job or the other, then their present role was the more important. In fact there was no question of enlarging the Special Air Service at that time. On the contrary there was a move afoot to have it disbanded or reduced so that as few resources as possible in terms of men and money should be diverted to it from the rest of the army. Colonel Deane-Drummond was therefore obliged to oppose my plan.

There was also opposition within the War Office on the grounds that the Muscat rebellion was a freak situation which would not recur and that the unit, if formed, would prove to be a waste of high-quality manpower. The events of the next fifteen years were to prove that Colonel Deane-Drummond was right in wanting to retain the deep patrolling capability. They were equally to show that the other part of the force could have been usefully employed throughout the period. At the time the opponents of the proposal prevailed and my paper was shelved.

If it had done nothing else, the Muscat campaign had opened my eyes to some of the problems concerned with providing the framework within which counter-insurgency operations could successfully take place. In Kenya and Malaya such a framework had existed by the time I got there and I had been able to take it very

much for granted. In Muscat I had been more involved in manipulating the framework than in taking part in operations, so I had
gained valuable experience of a new sort.

MO4 seemed a pretty dull place after my return from Muscat and
when the paper which I had written in order to streamline the procedure for introducing or reinforcing an intelligence organization
and for providing the nucleus of a Special Force foundered, I looked
elsewhere. At this point I decided to see whether the general interest
in counter-insurgency, which the Muscat operations had sparked
off, could be exploited in terms of teaching ordinary tactical commanders how to collect background information and develop it into
contact information, as I had been doing in Malaya. In practical
terms the only way of doing this was to ensure that company and
platoon commanders knew as much as possible about the business.
The subject was not taught at any of the army schools and although
some officers picked it up by trial and error, most of them remained
in almost total ignorance of the part which they could play in this
vitally important matter. By dint of a good deal of agitation on my
part it was eventually agreed that courses should be run for captains
and majors, designed to teach them how information is collected by
intelligence organizations and how they, as company and platoon
commanders, should set about getting hold of it and developing it.

From a company commander's point of view the business of
getting hold of contact information represents the major part of
tactics so far as counter-insurgency is concerned so, in theory at any
rate, the course should have been run at the School of Infantry. On
the other hand the Intelligence Centre at Maresfield was much
closer to London and it would be easier to get the right sort of guest
lecturers to go there than it would be to get them to travel down to
the far end of Salisbury Plain. It was therefore decided to hold the
courses at Maresfield. I was consulted during the preparation of the
syllabus and on several occasions I went to Maresfield to give lectures. For a time it seemed that all was well and I was very pleased
to think that at long last one of my projects had been accepted for
use by the army. But after a time it was found that commanding
officers were not sending people to attend the courses, probably because they associated them with intelligence rather than tactics. In
the end they were abandoned through lack of support.

But although my idea for establishing a Special Unit and my
efforts at getting the business of collecting and developing informa-

tion taught to normal regimental officers petered out, the Muscat campaign had at least made my name known to a wider section of the army. I was now recognized as someone who had ideas on dealing with insurgents and I was frequently asked to speak at brigade and divisional Study Periods, and at places like the Staff College and the School of Infantry. The publication in 1960 of a book which I wrote about my experiences in Kenya called *Gangs and Counter Gangs* also helped in this respect.

In 1962 I was sent on a six months' course to the Armed Forces Staff College in the United States of America. The main value of the course was the insight which it gave into the mentality, characteristics and methods of working of middle-piece American officers. At the time there was an immense surge of interest in anti-terrorist operations because of the Vietnam campaign and the emphasis laid by President Kennedy on the study of the subject. As a result, I was invited to give a number of lectures at service establishments outside the college and I thereby saw more of the American forces than I would have seen in the normal course of events. On these occasions I was surprised to find how genuine was the interest taken. Attendance was not limited to junior officers and once no less than seven generals sat through the performance, much to my astonishment.

Shortly before I returned to England, President Kennedy asked the Vice President to set up a symposium to study in detail every known aspect of counter-insurgency operations. The task was handled by the Rand Corporation who decided to get representatives from as many different counter-insurgency campaigns as possible to come and give evidence. I was asked to talk about the Emergency in Kenya. When I arrived the symposium had already been in progress for several days and the conference room was full of an extraordinary variety of people. Not only were there representatives from most of the world's armies, which had fought against guerrillas, but also in a few cases there were representatives of the guerrillas themselves. Very soon after arriving I became aware of an interesting fact. Although we came from such widely divergent backgrounds, it was as if we had all been brought up together from youth. We all spoke the same language. Probably all of us had worked out theories of counter-insurgency procedures at one time or another which we thought were unique and original. But when we came to air them, all our ideas were essentially the same. We had another thing in common. Although we had no difficulty in making our views understood to each other, we had mostly been unable to get our respective armies to hoist in the message. Only the Americans seemed to be prepared to spend money and use up men to find the right answer, but of course there is more involved than money and men when it comes to changing attitudes.

I have strayed some way in this chapter from the arid wastes of Arabia. In retrospect Oman was not as significant in terms of the development of my ideas as either Kenya or Malaya, but it had played a part in weaving together the various threads of my thoughts. From the point of view of the army as a whole the most important effect of the campaign was that it ensured the continued existence of the Special Air Service. The regiment had been formed in Malaya for operations deep in the jungle and might well have been disbanded at the end of that campaign had it not been able to demonstrate that it had a use outside the jungle as well.

A final matter of interest relates to the fate of the Somali donkeys which I had seen unloaded across the beach from the tank landing ship. Colonel Smiley had been right in supposing that they would cause extra work to little purpose, but he found a use for them in the end. When the Jebal Akhdar fell to the Special Air Service it was discovered that the blockade had been more effective than had been thought and that many of the Bani Riyam tribesmen were on the verge of starvation. It was then decided that as a gesture of the Sultan's forgiveness and goodwill, the donkeys should be driven onto the plateau and slaughtered for meat, which all goes to show that even the most surprising administrative decisions can be turned to good account in the end.

Part IV

※

Cyprus

Chapter 18

※

The Cyprus Problem

Cyprus is an island which is about 140 miles long and 60 miles across. Blue sea and white clouds driven on the wind are basic to its character and for a few months of the year at least it compares favourably with the most beautiful parts of the earth. Every square inch capable of cultivation is sown and in March when the young corn can still be measured in inches its vivid green is interlaced by veins of poppies and charlock. There are also orange groves and vineyards, olive trees and carobs. There are stony areas ablaze with the yellow rock-rose and in the mountainous regions of Troodos and of the Kyrenia Range, peaks and valleys, rocks and streams, are thrown together in a changing pattern of grey, green and brown. The mountains too are alive with wild flowers to such an extent that the air is heavily scented. Narcissi, anemones and cyclamens can be gathered by the armful.

But the Cyprus problem has less to do with the beauties of nature than with the division of its people into two groups. In 1960 the population numbered just over half a million, split between Greek Cypriots and Turkish Cypriots in a ratio of roughly four to one. In order to understand the nature of the problem correctly it is necessary to understand why over the years Greek Cypriots have been so anxious for the island to be united with Greece and why this has not so far been possible.

The feeling that the term Greek should apply primarily to the descendants of the inhabitants of the ancient city states, such as Athens or Sparta, is one of the crudest misapprehensions of the present day. It is as if the term British were to be reserved for the descendants of the Ancient Britons. In fact the first political entity which can reasonably be described as Greek was the Empire set up by the successors of Alexander the Great to administer his conquests. It was based on Alexandria and covered a large part of South-East Europe, Asia Minor and North Africa. The Romans inherited this Empire and incorporated it into their own from a political point of view, although much of it retained its Greek culture. When the Roman Empire split into two in A.D. 395, the eastern part which had its capital in Constantinople was, to all intents and purposes, a second Greek Empire. It long outlived the western part of the Roman Empire and continued politically until it was finally overthrown by Moslems in 1453. This Byzantine Empire, like the earlier Greek Empire and like the Roman Empire for that matter, was not a state in the modern sense, but a grouping of peoples bound together by a political link reinforced by cultural ties. When the Empire was overthrown politically the Greek Orthodox Church, whose patriarch remained in Constantinople, became the repository of the Greek national consciousness until a new political entity started to emerge some 370 years later in the wake of the Napoleonic Wars.

Islam was born in Arabia when the Byzantine Empire was at the height of its powers and the impetus which the new religion gave to its followers led to many raids and incursions against the Empire's outlying provinces. From the tenth century onwards the Empire was also subjected to attack from the potentates of Western Europe who were not above taking advantage of the opportunities afforded by a crusade to plunder the riches of Byzantium. But it was neither the Arabs, nor the crusaders, who finally toppled the Empire, but Moslems of a different race altogether. For centuries Turkish tribes from central Asia had been drifting south to settle in or near Arab lands. They adopted the Moslem religion and many joined in attacks on the Byzantine Empire. On the other hand, some took service with the Byzantine rulers in the defence of that part of the Empire which was being threatened from the west. But from the middle of the eleventh century onwards it was the Ottoman Turks who posed the main threat and they were the people who finally inherited and extended the Empire. By the middle of the seventeenth century the Ottoman Empire had spread across the Balkans up to the gates of Vienna and included Greece, a large slice of what is now Iran and Southern Russia, together with most of the Arab world. It also included Cyprus.

Modern Greek Cypriots are descended from people who came to Cyprus from many different quarters. Very early settlers are thought to have come from Anatolia and they may have been followed by men from mainland Greece and by Phoenicians. But irrespective of their racial origins, the Greekness of the Cypriots derives from the fact that Cyprus was fully incorporated into the first Greek Empire based on Alexandria, retained its Greek culture throughout the days of the Roman Empire and remained part of the Byzantine Empire until shorn from it by the English crusader, King Richard, in 1191. It was not until 1571 that Cyprus became incorporated into the Ottoman Empire, at which time the Turks took it from the Venetians, who had captured it from a dynasty of Norman rulers, who in turn had bought it from King Richard.

From a western viewpoint it would be reasonable to assume that incorporation into the Moslem Empire of the Ottomans represented an unmitigated disaster for the Christian Greek Cypriots and there were certainly some grave disadvantages, including the arrival of some 20,000 Turks who were forcibly settled on the island. But there were also compensations arising out of the fact that the rulers of the Ottoman Empire were in many ways more experienced and more tolerant in their handling of members of the Orthodox Churches than had been the Western rulers of Cyprus over the past 350 years. The Roman Catholic administration of the Norman Kings of Cyprus and of the Venetian Republic had tried hard to stamp out Greek culture and in the process they had suppressed the Orthodox Church. The Ottomans restored it and recognized its Archbishop as the leader or ethnarch of the Greek Cypriot community. They needed him to keep the people contented so that revenue could flow uninterrupted into Ottoman coffers. But when it came to extracting wealth from the island, they were completely ruthless and the Cypriots groaned under the burden of taxation.

And so for several centuries Cyprus, together with the rest of the Greek world, lived as part of a religious and cultural entity inside the Ottoman Empire. Mainland Greece was in exactly the same position as Cyprus, having been captured from its former owners the Venetians and incorporated into the Ottoman Empire. From a geographical point of view the centre of the Greek-thinking world was still Constantinople where the patriarch of the Greek Orthodox Church officiated in the capital of the Ottoman Empire.

It is not necessary to discuss the reason for the break-up of the

Ottoman Empire, but the form of its dissolution is directly relevant to the contemporary problem of Cyprus. In a sense what happened was that in the century 1823–1923 the old Greek Empire which had been drowsing inside the Ottoman Empire, became conscious of its captor's declining power and fought its way out. In the process it changed its nature and emerged as a modern nation state called Greece, part of which, by chance, occupied the land in which the original city states of Athens and Sparta existed. In the process also, the old Ottoman Empire collapsed, although a small part of it turned itself into another modern nation state called Turkey, which geographically covered the heartland of the second Greek Empire, that is to say Constantinople and Anatolia. Not all of the races and nations which had been incorporated in the Ottoman Empire joined up with one or other of these two new states. The Arab peoples, for the most part, detested the Turks and after thirteen centuries of Islam they equally had nothing in common with the Greeks, even if they had been in one of the earlier Greek Empires. They therefore went their own way. Likewise many of the European parts of the Ottoman Empire had been incorporated into it directly and had never been in either of the two Greek Empires, so they too went their own way. The Greek Cypriots were passionately aware of their Greekness and very much wanted to join up with the new Greek nation. The reasons which have so far prevented them from doing so must now be examined with some care.

Great Britain, France and Russia all supported Greece in her war of independence during the 1820s, but when the success of this venture gave rise to the possibility of further dissolution within the Ottoman Empire, Russia found herself at odds with her former allies. The British had no wish to see Russia enlarge her influence where she could threaten India or the route to India and the French were interested in obtaining a foothold in certain parts of the Ottoman Empire. At one stage the French and British were so concerned about the increase of Russia's influence that they fought her in the Crimea, but later the interests of Britain and France diverged and a further war was only averted by a general settlement reached at the Congress of Berlin. This was concerned mainly with controlling Russian expansion, but it also established a number of independent states in the Balkans at the expense of the Ottoman Empire whilst restoring Macedonia to it. At this time France was to all intents and purposes given a free hand to pursue her interests in parts of North

Africa, and Cyprus was leased to Britain. This happened in 1878. Ostensibly the Cyprus lease was designed to give Britain a base from which to defend the Ottoman Empire from Russia. In practice Britain wanted it to guard her communications with India and for financial reasons. Later, when Britain gained control of Egypt, she obtained a better base, but she saw no point in relinquishing her hold on Cyprus which she governed by a constitution designed to ensure that the Administration's officials and the Turkish Cypriots together could always outvote the Greek Cypriots in the Legislative Council.

During the First World War the Ottoman Empire allied itself with Germany which gave Britain an excuse for terminating the Cyprus lease and annexing the island instead. Soon afterwards in 1915 Britain offered Cyprus to Greece, if Greece would enter the War on the side of the allies, but this she would not do. Later the allies forcibly used Greece as a base for their operations and eventually in 1917 Greece entered the War on the allied side. As a result the post-war peace treaty would have been very favourable to the Greeks, if it could have been enforced because it gave them a foothold on the Turkish mainland at Smyrna, as well as giving them the northern shore of the Bosphorous and therefore part of Constantinople. It is possible that at this stage the Greeks had visions of a restored Greek Empire, based as the old one had been, on this city. However at this moment the dissolving Ottoman Empire gave birth to the new state of Turkey which, under the dynamic leadership of Ataturk, engaged the Greeks in a new war and threw them headlong from the Turkish mainland. The 1923 Treaty of Lausanne which ended this war left Turkey in a far stronger position than the earlier treaty had done. Before the war there had been many Turks in Greece and very many Greeks in Turkey; possibly as many as two and a half millions. At the end of the war all the surviving Greeks in Turkey were moved to Greece except for about 100,000 who were allowed to remain in Constantinople as compensation for a slightly larger number of Turks left in Thrace. At the same time nearly half a million Turks were moved from Greece to Turkey. All this resettlement effectively killed any possibility of a revival of the old Greek Empire and sorted the Greeks from the Turks throughout most of the Eastern Mediterranean. In all this turmoil and bloodshed however, Cyprus remained British and unscathed.

Although Cyprus had escaped the bloodbath, Greek Cypriots

were naturally anxious that the island should join up with the rest of the Greek nation: the Turkish Cypriots were equally anxious that this should not happen. In any case Britain had by now become even more powerful in the Eastern Mediterranean, having gained control of large areas formerly administered by the Ottoman Empire and Greece was in no position to challenge her. In 1931 there were riots in Cyprus in support of union with Greece, known as *enosis*, but these were quickly suppressed with very little bloodshed. Afterwards Britain revoked the constitution, banned political parties and took some relatively mild steps to discourage Greek culture, apparently in the hope that the Greek Cypriots would forget two thousand years of their national heritage and transfer their allegiance body and soul to the King Emperor. There followed twenty years of comparative serenity which included the Second World War, during which gallant little Greece fought as Britain's ally. This circumstance made it embarrassing to implement the anti-Greek measures with the vigour displayed by earlier Western rulers of Cyprus, such as the Venetians. Indeed at the end of the War a certain amount of political activity was again permitted, but when Greece asked Britain for Cyprus she received a firm refusal. At this time Greece was in no position to press her claim because she was involved in a civil war and was heavily reliant on Britain for support.

Despite the fact that Britain originally obtained Cyprus as a base to safeguard the route to India, the island was never of much strategic use to her because a better base in the form of Egypt had soon become available. It is probably true to say that the only reason why Britain still held Cyprus at the end of the Second War was that Greece had not made a sufficiently good offer for it during the time that Turkey was weak or aligned with Britain's enemies. The fact that Britain offered Cyprus to Greece in 1915 is an indication that she was prepared to sell at the right price. But from the early 1950s a new situation prevailed. Despite the fact that India was gone, Britain still wanted a base in the Eastern Mediterranean to prop up her influence in such countries as Iraq and at this time she was obliged to evacuate Egypt. Britain therefore found herself with a genuine strategic need for Cyprus. At the same time Turkey, which had been neutral during the War, was becoming valuable as a potential ally against Russia. Turkey was most anxious that Cyprus should not fall into the hands of Greece because of the possible domestic political reaction and because Turkey had an important strategic interest in ensuring that the island, lying a mere forty miles from her coast, did not fall into the hands of a potentially hostile country. Britain therefore had two good reasons for resisting *enosis* and she set herself against the idea in so resolute and tactless a manner that both Greece and the Greek Cypriots felt that no further progress was likely to be achieved by normal diplomatic means.

In March 1955 Greek Cypriot insurgents started a campaign of violence against the British colonial Government of the island. The insurgents were led by Colonel Grivas, who was a retired Greek officer, although a native of Cyprus. His campaign was backed by Archbishop Makarios, the leader of the Greek Cypriot Orthodox Church and *de facto* leader, or ethnarch of the Greek Cypriot community. The campaign also had some backing from the Greek Government, the most important aspect of which was the heavy and sustained propaganda offensive aimed at rallying world support for the insurgents. The campaign lasted for four years and was very poorly handled from the British point of view. Although Grivas seldom disposed of more than about 150 full-time insurgents, he managed to tie down on occasions as many as 19 regular army units, comprising about 25,000 men. His campaign was not designed to beat the British army in battle, but to bring about *enosis* through a process of attrition by harassing, confusing and finally exasperating the British.

From the British angle the campaign took the form of operational measures to contain the insurgents, combined with a series of offers to the Greek Cypriots designed to reach a settlement. Each new offer naturally reflected the overall political and strategic situation in which Britain found herself at the time when the offer was made. Thus, although in 1955 Britain felt obliged to hang on to the whole of Cyprus in order to back the newly-formed Baghdad Pact and to safeguard her position in the Near and Middle East, by 1959 her requirements were rather less demanding, since the Baghdad Pact had collapsed, together with most of Britain's influence in the area. She was thus prepared to consider settling for a small part of the island to serve as a base for the safeguarding of her residual interests in Libya and the Persian Gulf and this enabled her to move closer to the Greek position. However, the closer Britain came to satisying the Greeks, the more opposition was aroused amongst the Turks. They had been quiescent when they considered that Britain was determined to retain control of Cyprus, but started to put forward

H

claims of their own as soon as they saw that Britain might be considering surrendering to the Greeks. The basis of the Turkish claim was some form of partition and they started to build up an underground force called VOLKAN for use should they ever find it necessary to bring pressure to bear on the Government in support of their claim. The Turks remained throughout totally opposed to *enosis*.

In the end, the main impetus for a settlement came from American determination that Greece and Turkey should not renew their ancient feud and so jeopardize the security of NATOs South Eastern flank. At the end of 1958 the American Government made it clear to these two countries that her continued support for their respective economies depended on them sorting out their differences over Cyprus without further delay. They, taking advantage of the fact that Britain was prepared to relinquish her hold on most of the island and realizing that Britain was not prepared to continue expending so much effort on containing insurgency once she had decided that Cyprus was not essential to her as a Colony, rapidly put forward a plan for ending the trouble. Early in 1959 Britain agreed to this plan and together with Greece and Turkey forced it upon Archbishop Makarios and the Greek Cypriot community.

There were basically four main parts to the London and Zurich agreements of 1959. Firstly, Britain granted Cyprus her freedom as an independent state, retaining only two small areas near the towns of Limassol and Larnaca as Sovereign Base Areas. This was formalized in a Treaty of Establishment between Britain and Cyprus. Secondly, Britain, Turkey and Greece guaranteed Cyprus's independence in a Treaty of Guarantee, signed by each of the four countries concerned. This Treaty explicitly forbade *enosis* or partition and all activities which might lead to them. Furthermore it gave each of the signatories the right to act unilaterally, if necessary, to maintain the Treaty. Thirdly, under a Treaty of Alliance, Greece, Cyprus and Turkey established a joint Headquarters in Cyprus to command contingents of the Greek and Turkish armies who would be stationed in the island. Fourthly, Cyprus was given a constitution which laid down the way in which the country was to be governed.

Although it is not necessary to go into detail regarding the provisions of the constitution, some description of it is required because subsequent unrest in the island has resulted from its imperfections. In outline the constitution provided for an executive, consisting of a

Greek Cypriot President, a Turkish Cypriot Vice President and a Cabinet, consisting of seven Greek Cypriots and three Turkish Cypriots. Cabinet decisions were to be by a simple majority of votes, but both the President and Vice President had the power to veto decisions. The legislature consisted of a House of Representatives in which 70 per cent of the members would be Greek Cypriots and 30 per cent Turkish Cypriots. Laws would be passed by a simple majority in the House, unless they concerned the running of municipalities, the making of electoral laws, or the raising of taxes. In these cases a majority of the Greek Cypriot members and a majority of the Turkish Cypriot members was required. Under the constitution separate Greek Cypriot and Turkish Cypriot Communal Chambers were set up to legislate on religious and cultural matters concerning their own communities and separate Greek and Turkish municipalities were to be set up in the main towns. Finally, the Civil Service was to be manned in the proportion 70 per cent Greek Cypriot and 30 per cent Turkish Cypriot while the country's small regular army was to be comprised of members of the two communities in the ratio of 60 per cent and 40 per cent.

Under the circumstances any constitution acceptable to both Greece and Turkey was bound to represent a precarious balancing act, so that trying to make it work would involve some very delicate steps on the tightrope. But in Cyprus a further hazard was bequeathed to the new country by Britain. Grivas had conducted a campaign designed to expel the British and bring about the union of Cyprus with Greece. In the event he indirectly achieved the first part of his design in that he made Britain realize that the price she would have to pay in order to stay in control was greater than the benefits that would accrue from doing so and this largely contributed to the final agreement. But this agreement, which Archbishop Makarios had reluctantly accepted, had specifically ruled out the second part of Grivas's aim, that is to say *enosis*. However, in conducting the campaign Grivas had naturally made full use of the emotional longing of the Greek Cypriots for *enosis*. He had also shown what could be achieved by violence. Furthermore although it was Britain, Greece and Turkey who set up the new country of Cyprus, it was the members of Grivas's undefeated organization EOKA who claimed the credit and who lived on in the new country as heroes, sustained by the patriotic impulses of the people and armed with immense prestige and a considerable number of

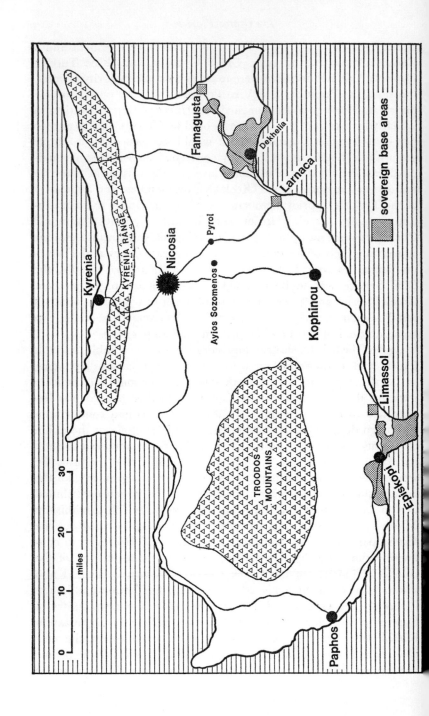

sovereign base areas

Kyrenia

KYRENIA RANGE

Nicosia

Famagusta

Pyrol

Larnaca

Aylos Sozomenos

Dekhelia

Kophinou

TROODOS MOUNTAINS

Limassol

Episkopi

Paphos

0   10   20   30

miles

weapons. Had Britain succeeded in bringing EOKA to its knees before leaving Cyprus, Archbishop Makarios, its new President, would not have been obliged to walk the constitutional tightrope with terrorist guns sticking in his back. In other words, the pressures he was under from a powerful section of his own people left him with insufficient room for manoeuvre in terms of getting the new country to work.

In the end, the constitution held together for four years and nine months. From the start the Greek Cypriots considered that the Turkish Cypriots had altogether too much influence in relation to their numbers, with particular reference to their ability to veto changes. It was also apparent that the Turkish Cypriots were unable to find enough adequately qualified civil servants to fill their quota of appointments. The Turks, on the other hand, felt that the Greek Cypriots were trying to undermine the state in the interests of *enosis* and stubbornly resisted any changes in the constitution, however sensible, in purely Cypriot terms, which might strengthen the Greek position. Finally in 1963 Archbishop Makarios submitted a number of ways in which the constitution might be amended with advantage, but the Turks rejected them lock, stock and barrel. Shortly afterwards fighting broke out between the two communities.

Chapter 19

————————— ✻ —————————

Christmas 1963

After leaving my job in the War Office I spent one year as an instructor at the Royal Naval College Greenwich, followed by a further six months as a student at the American Armed Forces Staff College. I also got married. Then, bursting with knowledge about the Royal Navy and the United States army, I returned in November 1962 to become second in command of my old battalion which had been renamed 3rd Green Jackets, The Rifle Brigade. The battalion formed part of the garrison of the Sovereign Base Areas which Britain had kept when Cyprus became independent in 1959. It was stationed at Dekhelia, but being so recently married, we did not qualify for a quarter there and had to rent a house in the nearby Cypriot town of Larnaca about nine miles away.

The Rifle Brigade was very much as I had left it four and a half years earlier, although most of the soldiers had changed their jobs or gone somewhere else. Jonathan Peel, now a captain, was the adjutant and Sergeant Bagley had become a colour sergeant. The battalion did not have a very exacting task; its main responsibility was to guard the Sovereign Base Areas, but as far as could be seen, no one was likely to attack them. For a full year after my return the battalion followed a peace-time routine in which training alternated with sport. Amongst the sporting facilities available was a pack of drag-hounds: I became the master and huntsman and my wife, Elizabeth, became the whipper-in. In October 1963 Elizabeth gave birth to a daughter and three weeks later the Dekhelia Drag had its opening meet. We seemed set fair for a good winter's sport.

It was at about this time that we began to get indications of increased tension arising between the Greek and Turkish communities on the island. Although there was no reason to suppose that either side would be hostile to the British, widespread disturbances would undoubtedly pose a problem regarding the security of those of our families who were living outside the Sovereign Base Areas in such places as Larnaca and Famagusta. The Commanding Officer of the battalion, Hew Butler, went on leave in early December, so I attended the conferences run by General Young, who was the officer commanding the British soldiers in Cyprus. We dusted off the various plans which had been made for safeguarding our families and other British nationals and settled down to await events.

As Christmas approached, we prepared the usual round of festivities. We arranged to give a party for the children in the barracks on Friday, December 20th and on the following Monday there would be a carol service. The programme for Christmas Day included a vehicle obstacle race, a comic hockey match between the officers and the sergeants, an immense dinner and finally a concert. Only the children's party went according to plan.

On the day after the children's party, Elizabeth and I took our hounds to Akrotiri in the other Sovereign Base Area, so that the Royal Air Force Saddle Club could have a Christmas hunt. The Station Commander had invited us to stay for the night so that we could go to a party in Episkopi during the evening given by the Commander-in-Chief and Lady Barnett. Hounds picked up the line soon after leaving the Saddle Club and went off in full cry and for the next hour or so I was concentrating fully on the business in hand. We galloped and scrambled along tracks, up and down shingle slopes and through little plantations of pine-trees. We had an interesting hunt and several empty saddles bore witness to the fact that some at least of the field had found it quite exciting. After the last line we headed for home, tired and happy. On our right lay the deep-blue Mediterranean, docile beneath the cliffs. On our left was the Akrotiri salt lake with the heavy mass of the Troodos Mountains rising up behind. The sky was unusually blue and as we rode by, a pink cloud of flamingoes circled over the water. There may not have been much of the traditional English Christmas about the scene, but it was certainly peaceful enough on the surface.

To start with, nothing unusual happened at the Barnetts' party, but it had not been going on for very long before it became apparent that something was in the wind. There was a certain amount of coming and going by senior officers and ADCs and soon it became known that fighting had broken out between the Greek and Turkish Cypriots in Nicosia. On hearing the news, I wondered whether I ought to rush back to Dekhelia, but I had arranged with one of the Company Commanders to carry out the family protection plan, if it was required, so it seemed unnecessary for me to go tearing off through the night. All the same we returned in good time next morning. Back in Dekhelia we pieced together such reports as were available of the happenings in Nicosia. There had been a sharp clash, but it had died down and from what we could tell there seemed to be a chance that events could be prevented from deteriorating any further. Nothing had happened in Larnaca or Famagusta.

On Sunday evening Hew Butler was due to arrive back at Nicosia airport and I decided to go and collect him so that I could brief him with regard to the situation on the way home. Taking my batman, Rifleman Rogers, as escort, I left Dekhelia after supper and headed for Nicosia. A bright moon lit up the ploughed fields as we drove along deserted roads towards the capital. The villages through which we passed were white and silent. It all seemed peaceful, but rather strange. Nicosia was the same; silent and deserted streets, white buildings and bold shadows. We came down the hill towards the walled city and stopped at the traffic lights before turning left for the airport. On the corner was a police station with a low wall in front of it. Three or four policemen, one of whom was wearing a steel helmet, were lining the wall. They were armed and looked expectant and a little frightened.

We got to the airport and picked up Hew Butler. He found it hard to believe that the peaceful Cyprus, which he had left three weeks earlier, could be on the brink of civil war and he obviously thought that my account of the situation was exaggerated. He was a big, calm man, who was by nature suspicious of sensation. The policemen were still behind their wall when we drove back, but even this did not seem to convince him. He took one look at them and laughed. Later that night, at home in Larnaca, I heard two or three shots. The firing came from the direction of the Old Turkish Quarter to the north of the town. It was not much, but it showed that Larnaca might easily follow Nicosia's example.

Next morning in Dekhelia we learned that fighting on a large scale had broken out again in Nicosia. Everyone held their breath, wondering what would happen next. No doubt the younger soldiers were hoping for a real battle with all the excitement which would go with it. But men with families in Larnaca felt rather differently. They were apprehensive and wondered what would happen if the town burst into flames while their wives were out shopping. That is more or less what did happen. During the morning, firing broke out at a number of places along the dividing line between the Greek and Turkish Quarters. We cancelled the carol service and sent the married men home to reassure their wives. We also opened up our operations room, got wireless sets into vehicles and organized family protection columns in accordance with our plans.

Soon after lunch, we asked Cyprus District Headquarters for permission to send patrols into Larnaca to protect our families, but we were told that the responsibility for maintaining law and order in the Republic of Cyprus still lay with the Cypriot police. Unfortunately the Cypriot police consisted of Greeks and Turks and they were too heavily involved in fighting each other to have time to spare for looking after our families. We cursed the Headquarters, but could do nothing but hope for the best. It was a very difficult time.

Later in the afternoon, Hew Butler sent me into Larnaca to try and find out what was going on. I went first to the house of one of the officers which was on some high ground overlooking the main Turkish Quarter and from there I was able to see Turks preparing defences and making ready to repel attack. Odd shots could be heard from time to time, but nothing which could be described as heavy firing. And then, whilst I was still watching, there was a sustained burst from a machine-gun a short distance away. It came from the direction of a street which had Greek houses down one side and Turkish houses down the other and which ran at right angles out of the road in which my Landrover was parked. A moment later an ancient car driven by one of our riflemen appeared with a shattered windscreen. The driver had been taking another rifleman home and had been fired on whilst parked outside his passenger's house. Neither of our men had been hit, but it was evident that the contestants were not even capable of distinguishing our men from the enemy in broad daylight which was a fair indication of their nervous condition.

Altogether I spent about an hour in Larnaca and the story was the same wherever I went. The families who were living on the border between the two communities were having great difficulty in getting in or out of their houses. Families who were living elsewhere were all right. Luckily my own house was in the Greek Quarter about equidistant from the Old Turkish Quarter and the main Turkish Quarter. I paid a quick visit to see if Elizabeth and the baby were all right, but could not stop; they seemed to be in fine fettle.

Back in the operations room at Dekhelia Hew Butler was trying to piece together the events of the day. In addition to my reports, he had received several telephone calls from men who had got back to their houses to find that their wives were missing. We assumed that they had been out shopping when the trouble started and that they had been unable to get back home. We told the men not to worry because their wives were almost certainly taking refuge with friends in more settled parts of the town. As always in a crisis the men concerned were terrific. They mostly rang off with some pathetic little joke about what they would say to their in-laws and we promised to sort out the situation as soon as we could.

Soon it got dark. We again asked for permission to send family protection patrols into Larnaca and again permission was refused. It seemed incredible that we should be obliged to sit around doing nothing while our soldiers and families were in such peril, but the orders were clear.

The fighting in Larnaca continued throughout the evening. At about 8 p.m. we heard that one of our men had been shot. Somehow he was pulled away from the place where he lay in a street on the border between the two communities, but although he was sent straight back to the military hospital in Dekhelia, he died soon afterwards. Later in the evening we were given permission to send a patrol into Larnaca, but it was to consist of not more than two Landrovers and we were not allowed to use our armoured scout cars. An officer went in, but found that he could do nothing in the troubled area because conditions were too bad for him to operate in a soft-skin vehicle. He was shot at on several occasions and there were two bullet holes in the bonnet when he got back.

At about midnight we were told that the Cyprus Government were being urged to allow us to take over the job of protecting our own families and that we should make plans on the assumption that we would be able to use the full scale of our resources next day. We had managed to gather a good deal of information about the whereabouts of men and wives who had got mislaid during the day and we spent the night arranging for their relief once daylight returned to the scene. We also made arrangements to evacuate those people whose houses were closest to the disputed areas. They would have to be billeted on families who were living in quarters in Dekhelia until new accommodation could be hired in the quieter parts of Larnaca or in Famagusta. Our plans were not confined to the families of men in the regiment.

Next morning the plan was put into operation and as the day wore on, wives and children started to appear in the reception centre which we had set up in the barracks. It was a depressing sight seeing these people arrive. Tired wives, with mystified or frightened children, stepped off the lorries clutching a suitcase or a few necessary articles of clothing tied up in a bit of brown paper. They would sit around trying to be cheerful until fetched to their temporary accommodation in Dekhelia. It was Christmas Eve. By that Tuesday evening about half of our evacuation programme had been completed and all but four of the missing wives had been located and reunited with their husbands. The remaining four had caused us a certain amount of anxiety, but we ultimately discovered that they had taken refuge together in the back room of a restaurant at the junction of the Greek and Turkish Quarters. It would have been too risky to try and rescue them in the dark, but we anticipated no great difficulty in doing so the next day.

I had to spend the night in the battalion operations room in Dekhelia, but I arranged to meet Elizabeth early next day so that we could go to church. On Christmas morning the situation in Larnaca seemed rather easier and most of the wives who were not actually besieged put on their finery to attend morning service. Afterwards we went back to our house in Larnaca for lunch, taking two unmarried officers as our guests. In spite of the disturbances, Elizabeth had managed to produce the traditional meal at the end of which she picked up the baby to give her a Christmas suckle. At that moment all hell was let loose outside.

Running out into the garden, we saw lines of armed Greek Cypriots moving down the street towards the Old Turkish Quarter. Men were blowing whistles and shouting and then firing broke out. We were obviously standing in the line of approach of the Greek forces, but we could see nothing of the battle itself so we moved to a vantage point on the by-pass which looked across a couple of fields to a school on the edge of the Turkish Quarter. This was the objective for the Greek forces and we watched as the attack was launched. From a professional point of view the operation was

clumsily planned and executed, but of course few of the contestants on either side had received any formal military training. In
the end the Greeks prevailed because of their superior numbers and
fire power and their blue-and-white flag was hoisted over the
building.

After this great attack, Larnaca became a bit more peaceful, but
in Nicosia the situation remained grave. Under the provisions of the
London and Zurich agreement which had governed the setting up
of Cyprus as an independent state, a Turkish battalion and a Greek
battalion were stationed in the island to safeguard the constitution.
Soon after Christmas proposals were put forward to the effect that
these two battalions together with the two British battalions in the
Sovereign Base Areas should move in and separate the two sides. If
accepted, the proposals would mean that we would no longer restrict our activities to looking after our families, but that we would
have to take on the far more formidable task of restoring law and
order throughout the Republic of Cyprus. During the next few days
while negotiations were in progress certain preliminary moves took
place. To start with, a joint force Headquarters was set up on the
outskirts of Nicosia and the Gloucesters, who were the resident
battalion in the Episkopi/Akrotiri Sovereign Base, moved into an
assembly area near the city. It was agreed that General Young
would command the joint force.

Because of the disturbance in Larnaca it was not possible for the
Rifle Brigade to move to Nicosia in the first instance. One of our
three companies was fully involved in looking after families and another one was deployed around Dekhelia itself guarding vital installations. Only one company was available for Nicosia and it
moved there during the weekend. It was understood that the other
two companies would follow as soon as a reinforcing battalion from
England could take over their duties in Larnaca and Dekhelia. Hew
Butler was naturally very deeply involved in making the arrangements for the move to Nicosia, so he left me to command the detachment which was left behind in Larnaca and which consisted of
'C' Company and the reconnaissance platoon. This arrangement
lasted for about a week during which time we changed our role from
family protection to Peace Keeping Force, in time with events in
Nicosia.

In order to control the activities of the so-called Larnaca Peace
Force, I set up a Headquarters in my house. From there I was able

to contact by telephone the official Greek leadership which operated from the central police station and the head of the Turkish community who had set up his Headquarters in a cinema in the main Turkish Quarter.

For the next few days we worked at high pressure rescuing individuals of either community who were lying wounded in the no man's land between the outposts or bringing help to the sick and aged. We had no clear-cut status and our orders were to use our weapons only in self-defence. It was therefore obvious that we could not forcibly prevent organized attacks between the two sides. What we aimed to do, was to prevent incidents building up into large-scale engagements by persuading individual Greeks or Turks in forward posts to 'hold hard' until their own leaders could give them proper orders. We would then help them to contact their leaders using our vehicle-borne wireless sets if necessary, once we had made sure that the orders would be of the right sort. For the platoon commanders and riflemen the work was often very exciting, because both sides were suspicious of any movement in front of their positions. It was only possible to go between them after warning both sides of our intentions. Even then it was difficult to make sure that the word would get down to the individual Greek or Turk behind the forward weapon and each of our detachments carried smoke-grenades to provide them with a screen behind which to make good their escape if the worst came to the worst.

In Larnaca, the leaders of both communities were friendly, polite and apparently grateful for our efforts on their behalf, but the same feelings were not always held by the young fighters. In particular, some of the Greeks, with recollections of the EOKA campaign fresh in their mind, were impatient with us for keeping them from killing Turks. It therefore came as no surprise when one of our men was shot. It happened on the morning of Friday, December 27th. Hew Butler had been visiting Nicosia and had called at my Headquarters on the way back. We were talking together on the bit of waste-land outside my house when a signaller came up with a message from one of the platoon commanders to say that Rifleman Kidney had been shot through the shoulder whilst patrolling the border. A few moments later Rifleman Kidney appeared in a Landrover supported by two of his mates. We sent for the Medical Officer and Elizabeth made a cup of tea and administered first aid. Kidney was suffering slightly from shock, but despite his pallor he kept up a steady flow of conversation, liberally punctuated with the sort of jokes which soldiers make, but which publishers do not publish.

Hew and I immediately went to the spot where the incident had taken place and talked to other members of the patrol. It was quite clear that Kidney had been shot deliberately from a little bit of woodland on the edge of the town which was about seventy yards away. There could be no question of mistaken identity and the shot came from the Greek side of the line. Hew Butler got very angry and drove straight to the administrative offices where he summoned the Greek Police Superintendent and the District Officer. He was red in the face when they arrived and he delivered himself of a strongly worded protest. His great fist kept banging the table around which we were sitting so that the coffee which had been provided as a peace-offering flooded the saucers. The two Greeks were very apologetic. They were unshaven and seemed to be tired out. They promised to execute the culprit, if he could be found, but pointed out that it would have been perfectly possible for a Turk to have crept round into the wood and shot our man in the hope of creating bad blood between us and the Greek community. Although un-likely, this was possible, but Hew would not listen to them. He stalked out looking furious. No more of our men were shot at deliberately in Larnaca.

For the next few days Elizabeth and I did not get much sleep at night because of the telephone, which was on the table by our bed. Either I was trying to ring up the Greek or Turkish leaders to sort out incidents reported by our patrols, or one of them was ringing me up to see whether I could stop the other from doing something which he regarded as being aggressive or provocative.

On the Monday after Christmas, one of our patrols came in at about four in the morning to say that the leader in the Old Turkish Quarter was concerned that some young children there were dying from a shortage of milk. The Turks had of course been blockaded into their enclave since the start of the trouble. He asked whether the Peace Keeping Force could escort a lorry-load of dried milk, which was available in the Main Turkish Quarter, through the Greek part of the town. On the face of it this seemed a reasonable job for a Peace Keeping Force to undertake, so I contacted the main police station to see whether the Greek leadership had any objec-tions. The Greeks refused on the grounds that it was well within the powers of the 'legal Government of Cyprus under Archbishop

Makarios' to relieve suffering of this sort. If only I could persuade
the Turks to stop shooting at any Greek approaching their area,
they, the Greeks, would bring in all the supplies needed. They
pointed out that if matters were as serious as I had reported, then it
was urgent for me to get the Turks to see sense and accept their
assistance.

I sat on the bed in my dressing-gown. It was very cold in the
house and a bitter wind from the Troodos Mountains rattled the
windows. Clearly, the problem was not one which could be settled
in half an hour so I abandoned any idea of going back to sleep and
got dressed. I went outside and discussed the situation with the
officer commanding the reconnaissance platoon. He was leaning up
against the scout car of the Section Commander who had made the
report on returning from the Old Turkish Quarter. We arranged
that he should go back and see whether the Turks would accept the
Greek offer. He could communicate the result of his discussions to
me by wireless.

The Platoon Commander went off and I settled down to wait with
the Section Commander. We chatted quietly to pass the time. The
red light on the wireless set cast a dim glow inside the scout car so
that it was just possible to distinguish the driver, who was dozing in
the driving seat, cocooned in an army blanket. Outside it was very
dark and I only saw the Section Commander when he drew on his
cigarette. He was a young man and he must have been tired after
operating flat out for a week, but the face that came and went in the
light of the cigarette was hard and alert.

Some time later the Platoon Commander came through on the
wireless. His message was to the effect that the Turks would not
accept help from the Greeks, who were no better than a gang of
cut-throats. Furthermore it was nonsense for the Greeks to pretend
that Archbishop Makarios and his associates represented the legal
Government because with the withdrawal of the Turkish Cypriot
Vice President and other Government members, the constitution
had become invalid. There was a lot more on the same lines, but my
concern was to see that the children got milk and not to pronounce
on the legality or otherwise of the various parts of the Cyprus
Government.

We seemed to have reached an impasse and I reported the situation by telephone to the garrison operations room in Dekhelia. Since
our battalion Headquarters had moved to Nicosia, I dealt with this

operations room direct. Some time later they rang back and said that, under the circumstances, I should see whether both sides would accept relief supplies from the Red Cross because there was a Red Cross representative available in Dekhelia, who had been given funds to spend in helping the population, should the need arise.

This led to another round of negotiation. This time the Turks in the Old Quarter said that they would agree, provided that the overall leader in the Main Turkish Quarter gave permission. But they pointed out that I would have to ask him because the Greeks who manned the Larnaca telephone exchange were – illegally – refusing to put through any calls between the two Quarters. By this time it was daylight and, having rung up the Turkish leader's Headquarters to make an appointment, I drove off to discuss the situation with him. He was full of indignation about the inhuman behaviour of the Greeks in denying him the opportunity of bringing help to his own people, but eventually agreed to the Red Cross doing so. We discussed a number of other points and I then drove back through his heavily sand-bagged line of outposts into the Greek part of the town.

My next call was to the police station to try and persuade the Greek leadership to allow the Red Cross to carry out the job. The same two men saw me as had dealt with the situation when Rifleman Kidney had been shot. They considered that it was shameful to think of the Turks denying their children the necessities of life, which the legal Government of Cyprus, under Archbishop Makarios, was anxious to provide. They pointed out that it was particularly unfortunate that the Turks were sacrificing the well-being of their own children just to score a political point. They asked me to thank the Red Cross on behalf of the legal Government of Cyprus for offering to help the Cypriot people in this way, even though there was no shortage of milk in the island. They finished up by saying that, in view of the serious nature of the situation and of the humanitarian principles involved, they would allow the Red Cross to deliver the supplies, providing that the Red Cross lorry was escorted into the Turkish Quarter by the legal (Greek) police. They were sorry to impose any provisos, but pointed out that they could not afford to take risks with regard to the safety of the Red Cross lady and that times were troubled thanks to the inexcusable behaviour of a small number of their fellow Cypriots (the Turks).

Although I knew that the Turks would never agree to a Greek escort accompanying the Red Cross lady through their lines, I felt that we were within negotiating distance of a solution. I therefore explained the situation to the operations room in Dekhelia and suggested that the Red Cross lady should appear with her supplies at my Headquarters, which she duly did. The Turks did not agree to the idea of an escort of Greek police passing through their lines, so I suggested to the Greeks that they should escort the Red Cross lady up to the edge of the Turkish Quarter, but that the British should have the responsibility of actually taking her through the outposts. I felt that this idea might find favour with the Greek policemen, who were perhaps a little bit apprehensive of carrying out the escort duty in the way which they themselves had laid down. After a great deal of argument they agreed. My next job was to persuade the Turks to accept the idea and to undertake not to shoot at the Greek escort when it arrived in front of their position. The Turkish leader in the Old Turkish Quarter agreed, but we had great difficulty with his superior in the Main Turkish Quarter. At one moment we had a three-cornered conversation going on between the two of them and myself using the telephone and two wireless sets. It was absolutely chaotic.

At last everything was fixed up. I went with the Red Cross lady as far as the main police station where her escort of Greek police were waiting, together with a photographer or two. The procession left with sirens sounding and drove down the main street of Larnaca. I followed at a discreet distance. As I suspected, honour was satisfied soon after we left the main road and the police inspector, who had been detailed to command the escort, stopped when we were still some distance from the Turkish lines and suggested that to avoid any disturbance it would be prudent for us to take over the escort duties. I accepted at once and we all shook hands.

Just before 3 p.m. the Red Cross lady drove into the Old Turkish Quarter with her tins of milk. There was a motley collection of individuals in a little square, who cheered and ran up to shake hands, so that for a moment I felt as if I had personally relieved Mafeking. This one situation had taken eleven hours of hard bargaining to sort out. It was typical of many.

A few days later the Sherwood Foresters, who had arrived from England, took over responsibility for Larnaca and I went off to join the rest of the battalion in Nicosia. It was a sad moment when I said goodbye to Elizabeth and the baby, but Nicosia was not very far away and I promised to come back and see them whenever I could. Also, with me out of the house, the telephone might stop ringing at night which would allow Elizabeth to get some sleep.

Chapter 20

※

Umpiring

It was a great deal colder than usual in Nicosia during the first half of January. Ice formed on the puddles at night and snow hung low on the Troodos Mountains. Our companies and platoons were tucked away in public buildings or in abandoned houses, but the men, manning the posts which we set up to keep the Greeks and Turks apart, had to crouch for shelter from the wind behind walls or sand-bags and warm themselves over little fires which they made at the street corners.

After the initial excitement, the soldiers had settled down to an arduous, uncomfortable and tiring routine which was usually boring. Occasionally some inconspicuous incident would threaten to flare up and then a lot would depend on the individual Rifleman or NCO who happened to be nearby because by the time an officer arrived it might be too late to prevent the matter from spreading.

Underneath their thick combat kit and heavy woollen pullovers the Riflemen were very much the same as the men who had sweated through the jungle from Bukit Serampang six years earlier. They made the same sort of jokes and looked forward to the same sort of things. Only their songs seemed different. Instead of little cockney ditties, they whistled Beatle tunes, or repeated *ad nauseam* the same few words that they had been able to decipher from the latest hit on the wireless.

Within the walls of the old city there was a clear division between the Greek and Turkish Quarters and the General had enough troops to keep the line between them permanently manned. But outside the walls in the sector allotted to the Rifle Brigade there was a suburb which had been shared between the two communities. A lot of the fighting during the Christmas period had taken place there and the Turkish population had either sought refuge with their compatriots in the old city, or had moved out to a large refugee camp about four miles to the north. Many of the houses had been ransacked and the wind whistled through the shells of gutted buildings and fluttered the debris left behind by the fleeing population. Starving dogs and cats hung shivering around the ruins until we sent for the Royal Army Veterinary Corps to round them up.

The actual fighting was over by the time that the battalion moved into Nicosia, but for days afterwards the soldiers kept turning up bloated corpses in back rooms. Sometimes they were the bodies of men who had been killed in combat, but there were others, old men and children, who had obviously been massacred in cold blood as the Greeks swept through the area. Civil war is not an attractive business.

As the first wave of violence died down, we were able to take stock of the situation. As explained earlier, the independent Republic of Cyprus had been in difficulties from the start because of the imperfections of the constitution and the existence of armed groups of former EOKA fighters, who were always on the look-out for an opportunity of promoting *enosis*. Whether the first shot was fired by a Greek Cypriot or a Turkish Cypriot is of little importance. The Greeks had some reason for firing it because the Turks had been systematically blocking all efforts by the Archbishop to amend the constitution peacefully and they may have felt that nothing short of a show of force would achieve anything at all. The Turks also had a reason for firing first, which was to bring on the apparently inevitable conflict before the Greeks were ready and before the disparity in strength between the two sides got any worse. The one indisputable fact was that, right from the start of the fighting, there was no chance of the status quo being restored.

If the two communities had been allowed to pursue their divergent aims in isolation, it is clear that the Greek Cypriots would have won. But, although Britain had nothing to gain from interfering, the same could not be said of Turkey. Irrespective of her material interest in Cyprus, it would have been political suicide for any Turkish Government to sit in idleness while the Turkish Cypriots were subdued. Turkey prepared to invade. But if Turkey came in on the side of the Turkish Cypriots, Greece might feel obliged to fight Turkey and in the two or three days immediately before Christmas there was a very real danger of major war breaking out in the Eastern Mediterranean. Greece and Turkey together formed the southern flank of NATO, so the only winner in a war between them would be Russia. The British Government therefore decided to try and get the agreement of Greece, Turkey and both of the Cypriot communities to break up the fight.

None of this was known to us in the two days before Christmas, but it had an important bearing on our lives. The British Commander did not press our demands to rush into Larnaca with all our troops to protect the families because at that time he was trying to get the Archbishop's agreement to use our soldiers as a peace force. A false move might have prejudiced this arrangement, brought in the Turks and led to a major war. It is not without cause that soldiers are taught to do what they are told, even when their orders seem senseless, but it only works if they trust their superiors. In this case we were required to risk our families for the sake of world peace and this is what we did. In fact, the risk was relatively slight.

The threat of war between Greece and Turkey not only brought us into the conflict, it also affected our subsequent actions. Within Cyprus the balance between the two sides was such that most of the fighting was caused by Greek Cypriots attacking Turkish Cypriots. By trying to stop this happening, we automatically found ourselves strengthening the Turkish position. In the wider context this meant that we were helping to bring about a crude form of partition under which the Turkish Cypriots occupied and administered certain parts of the island. The Greek Cypriots always suspected that partition was the ultimate aim of the Turkish Cypriots and were violently opposed to it. As a result, we rapidly became unpopular with the Greek Cypriots. Looked at objectively, our activities did favour the Turkish Cypriots, but the alternative was a Turkish invasion and a major war which would have been far worse for everyone, including the Greek Cypriots. But this fact was not apparent to them and in a very short time we became the target for an intensely hostile propaganda campaign, which made us even more nervous about the safety of our families.

Gradually the conduct of operations became more and more complicated. The man who bore the brunt of it all was the Commander of the Peace Keeping Force, General Young. He was doing for the whole of Cyprus the job which I had been doing in Larnaca during the first week and I knew only too well that it was a job which lasted twenty-four hours a day.

To begin with, General Young concentrated almost entirely on Nicosia because it was in Nicosia that events were most likely to blow up rapidly to the extent that would provide the Turks with an excuse for invasion. He divided the city into sectors which were controlled by the Commanding Officers of the Rifle Brigade, the Gloucestershire Regiment and of a detachment of the RAF Regiment. During January a brigade Headquarters arrived from England, together with other reinforcing units. General Young made the Brigadier directly responsible for the units in Nicosia, which enabled him to stand back slightly from the hour-by-hour control of events and take a wider interest in the country as a whole.

The key to controlling events within battalion sectors undoubtedly lay in establishing good relations with the local leaders of both communities. The battalion area was too big for the Commanding Officer to do this himself, so the task fell mainly on the Company Commanders. Experience soon showed that most of the incidents, which were beyond the powers of the Rifleman on the spot to control, required the intervention of the General himself unless the Company Commander could settle it with the local Commanders.

We had not been in Nicosia for more than a few days before we discovered that one of the biggest problems lay in getting to know who the local leaders were. In fact, finding out anything at all about the opposing sides proved to be very difficult. As soon as we arrived, we asked General Young's staff for full information, but nothing seemed to be known. General Young had brought an intelligence officer with him when he moved to Nicosia, but this man was fully occupied in arranging contacts and meetings for the General. Furthermore we were told that as Cyprus was a member of the Commonwealth no steps had been taken to build up an intelligence picture before the outbreak of trouble. Both sides had built up their forces in secret and secrecy had become a habit. We complained bitterly about the lack of intelligence, but there was nothing to be done about it. We could only piece together the order of battle for both sides, as best we could, by direct observation and by discussion with the fighters on both sides. Perhaps our greatest difficulty lay in the fact that we could not establish good relations with their commanders until we knew who they were, but any, except the most tactful enquiries, tended to cause an immediate loss of goodwill.

One evening early in February I was standing in an observation post on the roof of the school which housed battalion Headquarters. Rumour, based on a considerable amount of evidence, had it that the Turks were likely to launch an invasion within two or three days. I looked north-east across the plains towards the Kyrenia Range, half-expecting to see Turkish aircraft flying in towards Nicosia. It had been a bright day, but the sun was well down in the sky. The outskirts of Nicosia spread out towards the open country and it was easy to pick out our sand-bagged posts, many of which were built at the top of tall buildings. They were known by such names as 'The Flying Bedstead' or 'Jim's Inn' and through my binoculars I was able to see the sentries looking first towards the Greek positions and then towards the Turks'. It was important to site positions so that they did not appear to be directed against one of the communities and not the other.

I turned round and walked to the other side of the roof. The walls of the old city rose up from an empty moat a short distance away. Behind them stood the domes and towers of churches and mosques. In the distance were the Troodos Mountains. Snow still lay on the tops, but the weather had recently become warmer and the lower slopes were already clear.

Immediately across the road from our Headquarters was a large girls' school which had become a source of embarrassment to us. When we first arrived, the schoolgirls had been friendly and had smiled at our sentries, but as the anti-British campaign gained momentum they became sullen. Next we started to get complaints that the men were leering and being objectionable. We refuted these allegations and refused to move our sentries from vantage points about the building. A few days later, reporters and press photographers arrived, so we guessed that a 'spontaneous demonstration' was about to take place. Sure enough, girls assembled in front of the building and started shouting and waving banners with 'Go Home British' and 'Down with NATO' written across them. Some of the soldiers leant against the railings and sang 'We Want to Go Home' until the Regimental Sergeant Major chased them inside. The head-mistress made a little speech saying that she understood the girls' feelings, but that they must control their righteous anger and behave with modesty, decency and nobleness of soul, as befitted Hellenic youth. They should remember that no power on earth could, in the end, prevent the union of Cyprus with Greece, a union ordained by God and hallowed by the blood of their national heroes. The demonstration passed off peacefully.

But now, being evening, all the girls had gone. As it got dark, the school faded into the gloom. I noticed a light in one of the class-rooms and assumed that it was a night watchman. Right underneath my vantage point I could hear the roaring of petrol cookers in the courtyard. The smell of cooking reached me together with the voices of the cooks. I thought that it was time to return to earth.

My camp-bed was in a small room, used by the school to store exercise-books and pencils. On my way downstairs I went there for a moment to take off my coat and brush my hair. Soldiers were living in the class-rooms on either side of me and the smell of their cigarettes and Brylcreem mingled strangely with that of chalk and disinfectant. The sound of nailed boots echoed down a stone passage. Somewhere in the building a tape recorder was making a ghastly racket, which was punctuated from time to time by someone yelling 'I wanna hold your hand'. I went down to the ground floor and looked into the operations room. There was no news of the Turks and all seemed to be peaceful. I wanted to speak to the Intelligence Officer, but he had gone to Dekhelia for the day and was not back yet. We tried to give everyone in the battalion one day off a week so that he could return to the barracks and have a bath, or go home to his family. Next door to the operations room was a class-room which we used as the officers' mess. A picture of Archbishop Makarios beamed down from one of the walls, while on the other side of the room there was a portrait of General Grivas gazing heroically into the future. Jonathan Peel and I played darts to pass the time while waiting for dinner.

Later on the conversation turned to a discussion of recent events in Larnaca. Apparently the staff were getting concerned about the possibility of having to evacuate the British families living there in the event of a Turkish invasion. They were circulating instructions to the wives telling them what they should do and what they should take, if the worst occurred. It was doubtless necessary to take these precautions, but they had the effect of causing a certain amount of alarm. I wondered how Elizabeth viewed the prospect of being ready to move within an hour or two, taking nothing but the baby and a suitcase and flying out of one end of Cyprus while the Turks were flying in at the other end. It was not a cheerful prospect and it must have seemed truly terrifying to some of the teenage wives. They would have little idea as to what was happening to themselves, let alone to their husbands in Nicosia. Life would have been a lot easier if our wives had been quartered in Dekhelia and if the accommodation in Larnaca had been reserved for the wives of the garrison administrative units because in this case the husbands would have been available to help with the evacuation of their own families.

After dinner I drove to one of our company Headquarters to exchange some scraps of information, which we had picked up during the day. Soon after 10 p.m. there was a report on the battalion wireless set that one of our patrols had been shot at, so I returned to see what was going on. It turned out that the shot had come from the girls' school opposite our Headquarters. Our patrol immediately broke in and discovered a little nest of Greek fighters who had established themselves there in order to observe the Turkish positions along the walls of the city. They said that the shot was the result of an accidental discharge, but in any case the school was in an area which was supposed to be out of bounds to both sides, so the Patrol Commander brought them back to battalion Headquarters. Hew Butler had rung up the senior Greek police officer in Nicosia and had asked him to come round and deal with the situation.

When I arrived, the Greek fighters and the patrol were all in the mess together with several of our officers. Hew Butler was trying to establish exactly what had happened, but whenever he asked the Patrol Commander a question all the Greeks answered at once with a great display of rhetoric and gesticulation. They were very excited and completely incomprehensible. It was a typical Cyprus argument.

The Senior Superintendent of Police arrived in a surprisingly short time and took over the conduct of the investigation, but the shouting and excitement continued. The atmosphere was thick with smoke, so I walked outside to get a breath of fresh air. I found that the sentry on the gate was involved in a spirited argument with a very tall man who was demanding to be admitted. He produced a card which showed that he was a plain clothes police inspector so I let him in.

Once inside, he let it be known that he commanded all the Greek fighters in Nicosia and he dealt with the trigger-happy youths from the girls' school, who were marched off to their base in a sport's club about half a mile away. The tall man's name was Petros and he was soon joined by several of his friends. They had been to the funeral of one of the Greek fighters who had been killed in a shooting accident and had been passing our Headquarters by chance when the incident had occurred. We invited them all to have a drink with us and the party continued for some hours.

The ensuing conversation was very interesting. During the time we had spent in Nicosia, we had managed to identify a number of the junior Greek Cypriot leaders in the course of our daily business and Petros was very helpful in sorting out who was who in our area. But he was also careful to reveal no more than it was necessary for us to know, if we were to do our job properly. Quite apart from the secrecy habit, which had been handed down from EOKA days, the Greek Cypriots were anxious to prevent the Turkish Cypriots from finding out about their organization. For all they knew, we might pass information to the Turks by accident, or on purpose, and in fact we had to be constantly on our guard to avoid discussing the affairs of one side with the other.

I met Petros on one or two occasions subsequently and always found him to be a charming and entertaining person. Like nearly all the Greek Cypriot leaders, he had been a member of EOKA during Grivas's campaign against us; he had also made a thorough study of underground warfare. He was particularly well aware of the interplay between the use of force and the application of political pressures to achieve a given aim and, although in common with nearly all his countrymen he was capable of becoming passionately worked-up over some particular incident, he was unusually level-headed and objective when viewing the situation as a whole. He was well capable of seeing the broader issues and remained throughout uninfluenced by Greek Cypriot propaganda. He was also very conscious of the military shortcomings of his own side.

Inevitably, in dealing with Petros and his friends, I was brought face to face with the problem of how to regard men who had carried out the actions associated with Grivas's campaign. In many ways the deliberate assassinations, which formed the basis of EOKA terrorism, were more difficult to stomach than the blind blood lust of the Mau Mau, or the more military actions of the Communist Terrorists in Malaya. But the inescapable fact remains, that if EOKA was to fight us at all, then the methods which they adopted were the ones which offered the best chance of success. Also, although EOKA murders were essentially repulsive in their cold bloodedness, they were considerably more selective than many other forms of warfare, such as the massed bombing used by both sides in the Second World

War, between 1939 and 1945, to say nothing of the use of atomic weapons in Japan. Furthermore, the assassin was obliged to take risks in carrying out his task and many were shot or subsequently caught and hanged. Inevitably EOKA attracted some thoroughly unpleasant people, but it also attracted others, who were high-minded, courageous and patriotic according to their lights. The only logical course was to condemn the war, but to take the people who fought it on their merits.

For some days after our visitors had gone, nothing very important happened and the immediate threat of a Turkish invasion receded. Although the anti-British campaign intensified, the weather improved so that, on balance, life became more pleasant, especially for the soldiers who were manning posts out in the open. Things seemed to be settling down into a sort of a routine and an observer arrived from the United Nations in the form of an Indian officer called General Gyani, whose job it was to send objective reports to New York about the situation in Cyprus.

But as incidents became less frequent in Nicosia itself, there was a gradual increase in tension in other parts of the island. In an attempt to ease this situation each of the battalions in Nicosia was made responsible for a large area of the surrounding countryside. We were not supposed to deploy soldiers in these outlying regions because to have done so would have resulted in weakening our position in Nicosia to an unacceptable extent. What we were required to do, was to send vehicle patrols through the villages to make contact with the local communities and to give advance warning of unrest.

One morning, while sitting in the operations room, we intercepted a message between one of the other units in Nicosia and brigade Headquarters. The message had originated from a vehicle patrol and stated that two Greek Cypriots had been ambushed and killed near a village about twelve miles south of Nicosia. The incident had taken place outside our area, but quite close to our boundary so we listened to subsequent reports with interest. During the next hour further reports were made which showed that Greek Cypriot forces were closing in on a Turkish village which lay close to where the ambush had taken place. Hew Butler was away in Dekhelia, so I warned one of our companies to be ready to move at short notice, should the need arise.

As the morning wore on, it became clear that the situation was rapidly becoming worse. The officer in charge of the patrol was trying to contact the leaders of both sides to dissuade them from fighting, but he was having difficulty in finding anyone in authority. At about 12.40 p.m. we heard that shots had been exchanged between the Turks in the village and the Greeks outside. By this time Brigadier Gibbs had warned me that the Rifle Brigade would be called on for troops if any were required, because we could spare men from Nicosia with the least amount of difficulty. Soon after hearing the report that fire had broken out, I was told to take a company to the scene of the disturbance as quickly as possible.

Rifleman Rogers had been keeping in touch with the operations room during the morning, so everything was organized for me by the time the Brigadier ordered us to move. The Landrover was outside the front door of the school with its wireless sets netted-in and its engine running. In a very short time we were off. The name of the threatened village was Ayios Sozomenos and during the drive from Nicosia I thought about how our men could best be used to bring about an end to the fighting there. It was difficult to know precisely what to do because we were only supposed to fire in self-defence and there could be no question of using force to impose a cease fire. An opportunity might present itself for interposing our men between the two sides, but the possibility could only be assessed on the ground.

Before leaving battalion Headquarters I had sent a message to our reconnaissance platoon, which was carrying out patrols in the country to the south of Nicosia, to move towards Ayios Sozomenos. From the time of their arrival they were able to give a first-hand account of the situation over the wireless, which enabled us to approach the battle from the right direction. We turned off the main road at Pyroi and bounced along a heavily pitted track which ran beside the bed of a dried-up river. At one place the track crossed the river bed: a car which had been carrying some journalists was stuck there in the shingle. The men had climbed to the top of a small ridge about twenty yards away and it was from there that we got our first glimpse of the scene.

The village lay about a mile away at a point where the track, which we had been following across the plain, disappeared into a steep re-entrant. Between us and Ayios Sozomenos the land was ploughed and flat, but immediately behind it was an almost vertical cliff face, which stretched for several miles in both directions. The cliffs looked hard and brown in the sunlight and contrasted strongly

with the freshness of the young corn. A light breeze carried the sound
of firing to us which made us push on with increased impetus.

We next stopped in a field where a lot more reporters were
clustered around the vehicle of the patrol commander who had
made the original reports. He had been told to explain the situation
to me and then to take a Greek Cypriot, who had been badly
wounded in the fighting, to the nearest hospital. He told me what he
could and left soon afterwards.

The Greek Cypriots had surrounded the village. Beyond it, their
men could be seen through binoculars along the top of the cliffs. On
our side, the line ran only about two hundred yards ahead of us.
Spasmodic firing continued from a position to our left, but that particular part of the battlefield was out of sight in a fold of the ground.
In order to use our men to the best advantage, it was important that
they should not get involved until their intervention could be put to
good effect. It would have been particularly stupid to have got them
into a position from which they could not move, if the battle developed in any particular way. The field in which we were standing
seemed to be a good place for the company to assemble, so I left
my Landrover and Rogers there to meet them and tell them to wait
until I returned. I then set off down the track to try and find the
commander of the Greek forces.

I soon reached the forward part of the Greek position. On either
side of the track policemen were lying on their stomachs in the green
corn. The Cyprus police were dressed in exactly the same way as
their opposite numbers in England and it was strange to see the
familiar blue uniforms in such surroundings. In front of the Greek
line the ground fell away gradually towards the village; the nearest
buildings were less than two hundred yards away. It looked as if the
Greeks had been fired on as they came over the crest because two
dead policemen were lying by the side of the track at this point. I
made sure that nothing could be done for them before starting my
search for an officer.

I walked down the line and eventually discovered a Superintendent wearing a steel helmet. He only had a vague idea about what
was happening, but said that his men and the men on the cliffs
behind the village were supposed to be holding the ring while some
Greek Cypriot fighters prepared to assault the village from our left.
The village was pretty well shrouded in smoke, but looking in the
direction which he indicated I was able to see some men darting up

the line of some trees and they were obviously the assaulting party trying to close in on their objective. It was obvious that I would have to make contact with the leader of the assault party, but at that moment a helicopter appeared from the direction of Nicosia and started to descend near my Landrover. I guessed that it contained the Brigadier and decided to go back and see him before setting off to the village. I would have to go back in any case to give some in-structions to the company who would have arrived by this time. Al-though Brigadier Gibbs was a very good man, I was rather annoyed about his arrival because I had been looking forward to handling the situation by myself.

The Brigadier had sized up the situation very accurately from his helicopter and as soon as he got out I filled in the details. He had brought one of his staff officers with him and the three of us im-mediately set off across the fields to contact the Commander of the assault party. We passed through the line of the cordon, making a special request to the Superintendent that his men should not fire at us. We then made a circuit round the edge of the village and eventually came up with the assault force.

The Greek fighters were a motley collection of individuals and wore a wide selection of uniforms. Some had steel helmets, some had khaki overalls, some were dressed as policemen and some wore leather jackets and grey flannel trousers. They were armed with rifles, light automatics, shot-guns and grenades and were festooned with bandoliers of assorted ammunition.

The assault force had reached the edge of the village and had set fire to a thick thorn hedge which was blazing furiously, filling the air with smoke. Some men were running around under cover of the smoke trying to improve their position, whilst others fired at random into windows and doorways. The din was continuous and chaos reigned, apparently unchecked by human guidance. We asked one of the Greeks to tell us who was in charge, but he did not know for certain. He told us that it might be a police inspector, whom we could dimly see crouching down behind a nearby tree, or it might be a sergeant whom he had last seen some minutes before. The fact that an inspector is a senior rank to a sergeant in the police was not relevant because the Greek fighters had their own rank structure and were men from all sorts of occupations.

The sergeant had been wounded, but the inspector had not realized it. When we told him, he reluctantly accepted the fact that he was in command of the operation. The Brigadier immediately suggested a cease fire, but the inspector said that his orders were to arrest the men who had killed the two Greeks in the ambush earlier in the day and that he could not cease fire while the Turkish population of the village continued to obstruct him from doing his duty. The Brigadier then pointed out that the Turks probably felt themselves to be engaged in beating off an attack on their village, rather than obstructing a policeman from carrying out an arrest. He also pointed out that the Greeks would in any case be unable to achieve their aim using their present methods unless they captured the village and that to do such a thing in the face of determined opposition and without the support of artillery would be sure to result in heavy casualties. He suggested that a more sensible approach would be for us to go into the village to discover whether the Turks were in fact harbouring the murderers, and if so, whether they would give them up. He pointed out that the Greeks would lose nothing by agreeing to this idea because they would retain their positions on the cordon and could resume the battle later if we failed.

In making this proposal the Brigadier knew perfectly well that the Turks would refuse to give up their ambush party, but the important thing was to prevent the Greek assault from taking place at all costs. Not only would it result in casualties to the Greeks, but it would inevitably result in a massacre of the Turkish inhabitants of the village. The Greeks were already worked up about the ambush and they would be even more so by the time they had fought their way through Ayios Sozomenos. In fact, the inspector seemed quite glad of an excuse for not pressing on with the attack. Waves of passion had carried his men into their present positions, but they were rapidly sobering down, as they realized what the next phase would involve. Although they cried 'on, on', they were secretly happy at being made to stand fast, provided they could go on firing their weapons. I sympathized with them.

The Brigadier decided that the best arrangement would be for me to go back across the fields and then drive down the track into the village with the scout cars. I was to keep one with me in the centre of the village and send the other one through to where we were now standing on the outskirts to report to the Brigadier. We would then talk to each other on the wireless. I ran back through the ploughed field with the mud clinging to my boots, only stopping when I reached the Greek cordon. I explained the situation to the

Superintendent and warned him that we would be going out through his lines again in a few minutes. I then went back to where the men were waiting, boarded a scout car and set off down the track towards the village.

As we came to the place where the track passed over the crest, we were held up by some policemen who had recovered the bodies of their two colleagues. They were loading them into a vehicle, which was parked on the track, but we edged past and set off across the open ground between the rival parties. The cease fire was not working very well and bullets were still cracking around, hitting rocks or buildings and whining away through the air. We were quite safe, as we banged up and down within our armoured vehicles and shortly afterwards we pulled up on a bit of grass in the centre of the village.

We seemed to be well screened by buildings from the effects of the Greek fire, so I thought that we were in a good place to discuss matters with the Turks. I got out and found two men who were sheltering in the doorway of a house nearby, but they did not speak English. We smiled and shook hands, but could get no further. Soon, other men arrived, but none of them could speak English. This situation continued until somebody sent for the schoolmaster. Whereas most of the men were middle-aged and friendly, this man, when he arrived, turned out to be young and touchy. Before I had a chance to say anything at all, he started saying that the British should have prevented the Greeks from attacking the village, that we were responsible for the death of the Turks who had been killed defending it and that, unless we did something quickly to stop the fighting, there would be a massacre. I explained that I had come with the sole purpose of stopping the fight.

By this time one of our scout cars had worked its way through the village and reached the Brigadier. I spoke to him on the wireless and asked him to get the Greeks to cease firing in accordance with our plan. A few minutes later he said that the Greeks had stopped.

Meanwhile I asked to see the village headman and an older man, who had just arrived, was pointed out. He could not speak much English, so I asked the schoolmaster to translate and through him explained that we had arranged for a cease fire with the Greeks and asked him to order his men to stop as well. He said that he would, but at that moment some more shots came from the direction of the

Greek line. The schoolmaster gave me a very nasty look. I got on the wireless again and the shooting died down.

Next I tried to discuss the question of the ambush with a view to working out a way of satisfying the Greeks so that they would go away. But when I told the schoolmaster to translate, he merely said that there was a boy in the next-door house who had been shot and that the first thing for me to do was to go and see how barbarous the Greeks were in killing children. I said that I was very sorry, but that if the boy was dead I would be better employed in trying to prevent further loss of life than in examining a corpse. I told him to get on and translate my previous remarks to the headman. Instead, the schoolmaster pointed out that shots were still being fired and as this was in fact the case I got on the wireless to try and get them stopped. Brigadier Gibbs said that they were coming from a Greek who had taken up a position some distance away from the main group, but that a message had been sent to him and that all firing would stop in a few moments.

I passed this news on to the Turks via the schoolmaster, but the words were hardly out of my mouth before heavy firing broke out once more. Some bullets even hit the wall of the house by which we were standing, showering us with plaster and stones. I burst out laughing and so did several of the Turks, but the schoolmaster started screeching at me and accusing me of heartless indifference to the fate of women and children. He was a little man with light brown eyes, sandy hair and a nasty, sour face.

In fact, there was not much to laugh about because my prestige as a negotiator was heavily jeopardized by the constant infringement of the cease fire agreement. Once more I got on the wireless to the Brigadier and protested that my job was being made very difficult by the irresponsible behaviour of 'his' Greeks. He replied, rather huffily, that the fault lay entirely with 'my' Turks who had sparked off the latest outburst by shooting a Greek who had been lying on the ground a few yards from where the Brigadier was standing. The schoolmaster actually smiled when he heard what had happened.

In fact, this incident nearly upset our whole plan for ending the fighting because the Greeks, who were just beginning to cool down from the passions aroused by their earlier casualties, became enraged at their further loss and renewed their preparations for the assault. Realizing that there was no time to lose, I told the schoolmaster that he was to translate my remarks to the headman in future and that he was not to concern himself with the negotiations. I then asked whether the headman was prepared to surrender the men responsible for the ambush of the Greeks, but he assured me that his people had not been involved in the business in any way and that the murderers were not in the village.

In an attempt to play for time I asked him whether he would come with me in a scout car to meet the Greek inspector. The firing was growing more intense and after some persuasion he agreed to do so. He was a courageous and dignified man. In this case the balance was redressed to some extent by the schoolmaster. My last impression of the village centre was of this man shaking his fist and cursing the British for not doing more. I privately hoped that if, through some mischance, we failed to prevent a massacre, he at least would not escape unscathed.

We soon got through the village and reached the place where the Brigadier and the police inspector were standing. Although there was little chance of the headman being able to reach any agreement with the Greeks, we had at least staved off the assault for a bit longer. Already the sun was beginning to drop and in another hour it would be getting dark.

The end came suddenly and in rather an unexpected way. While we had been active on the battlefield, the General had been persuading the Minister of the Interior to call off the Greek fighters and the police. At last word reached the Superintendent on the cordon, who told one of our officers. The inspector would not believe us at first because he thought that we had made up the story in order to delay him further. He ordered his men to prepare to attack, but he agreed to talk to the Superintendent over the wireless before giving the final order for assault. To start with, they both tried to talk at once which resulted in the usual series of squeaks and whistles in the ear-phones. Eventually they made sense and the inspector was convinced.

The Brigadier gave a sigh of relief and started the return journey to his helicopter. The position in Nicosia was too tricky for him to be away for longer than necessary. I was left in charge to clear up the mess. I had been sorry to see him arrive, but there was no denying that he had done a magnificent job. He had been calm and decisive and he had always managed to see the humorous aspect, when there was one.

Our company had spent a frustrating afternoon watching events from behind the Greek cordon, but now they were able to move in closer and take up positions to discourage any renewal of the assault. Teams also entered the village to care for casualties. There had been a number of Greeks wounded during the engagement, but it had been possible to get them away while the battle was in progress. Now we started getting out the Turks. Helicopters arrived through the dusk to evacuate the seriously wounded. A light mist came in with the night and soon the only thing that could be seen were the headlights of the vehicles and the torches of our men, as they poked around the houses to see what help was necessary. When the dust had settled, I handed over to the Company Commander and returned to Nicosia in case disturbances should break out there during the night.

Altogether five Greek Cypriots and seven Turkish Cypriots were killed in the engagement and a lot more on both sides had been wounded. Perhaps the Peace Keeping Force had been at fault in allowing the battle to start, but it is hard to know how we could have stopped it. Undoubtedly we had been responsible for preventing the village from being overrun and if that had happened the death roll would have been very much higher. Under the circumstances prevailing at the time it is quite possible that a massacre at Ayios Sozomenos would have resulted in a Turkish invasion of Cyprus. I have often wondered whether this was in some Turkish mind when the two Greeks were ambushed so close to the village in the morning. After all, it was not very difficult to forecast the Greek reaction to this happening and the villagers had no adequate means of defending themselves.

Chapter 21

Keeping the Peace

By the middle of February 1964 I had spent six weeks as a peace-keeper and most of that time had been taken up in trying to discover what was going on. Once again, as in Oman, we had been operating without the backing of an intelligence organization, and we had therefore been obliged to get what we could for ourselves. In Larnaca there had not been time for us to piece together a picture before being relieved by the Sherwood Foresters, but in Nicosia the fact that we had succeeded to a large extent in containing trouble within our sector mainly resulted from discovering who was influential and working out what they might be planning to do. Similarly, when trouble did break out, as it did at Ayios Sozomenos, it was largely due to the fact that the unit in whose area it was did not know what was happening until it was too late. This was not their fault because, like us, they had been told to concentrate their resources in Nicosia, but it was true none the less.

Having no intelligence organization, we started to build up our picture in Nicosia by collecting every scrap of information which any of the officers or men in the battalion happened to pick up as they went about their task. Initially we concentrated on collecting the names of all those who appeared to be taking any active part in the affairs of either of the two communities, even if it was only a Christian name or nickname. Using telephone directories and trade directories we discovered where some of them lived and where they worked, and then we examined the background of people living nearby, or working in the same business, in the hope that a connection in ordinary civil life would lead to a connection in one or other of the fighting organizations. Every detail we discovered was recorded in files and on card indexes, so that we soon had a mass of names, addresses, telephone numbers and car numbers. Gradually by staring for hours at this conglomeration of facts and figures we began to discern the outline of the opposing organizations, and it sometimes happened that when a particular leader realized that we knew who he was, and what his position was in the hierarchy, he would be happy to put us right about minor errors which we had made, especially if he thought that we had underestimated his importance.

Once we had made a start, the information began to snowball. Stage one had been to work on the many scraps of information given to us by our companies and once we had added it all together and built up an idea of some part of the picture, we sent it back to them to examine and test. Company Commanders might do this by conversing with the people concerned, or by putting soldiers into observation posts to watch the comings and goings of particular groups, or individuals. They might also send out patrols to follow new telephone cables, which had perhaps been laid for the purpose of linking one group of fighters to another, and this could lead to more addresses and more names. The whole thing was a very interesting and enjoyable game which kept everyone usefully occupied and greatly increased our potential as peace-keepers.

One of the results of the fighting in Cyprus was that many journalists descended on the island. They mostly lived in the largest and most luxurious hotel in Nicosia waiting eagerly for incidents to report. In the early days, when we were so desperately short of information, it occurred to us that these men, whose job was to know what was going on, might be able to help. Jonathan Peel knew several of them, having met them a few years earlier when he was working with the United Nations Force in the Congo, so once or twice a week he and I would go to the hotel for a drink. We felt rather out of place wearing our combat kit, sitting on red plush stools in the heavily-ornamented rooms, but the journalists were friendly, hospitable and interesting, so that our evenings there were usually productive and always pleasant. The value of these meetings was not entirely one-sided because we were able to help the journalists to some extent by talking to them about operations, and by helping them to meet and photograph the soldiers at work. We had to be careful not to cross wires with the army public relations organizations, but we encountered no real difficulties. We knew well enough what subjects to avoid and certainly the journalists with whom we talked understood our problems and took care not to embarrass us. Our two greatest allies were the reporters of the *Daily Express* and the *Daily Mirror*.

During February the conflict spread throughout the island, although the situation in Nicosia remained under control. By this time a large number of troops had arrived from England, mostly from the 3rd Division. A logical outcome of this development was that Major-General Carver, who commanded 3rd Division, arrived with his Headquarters and took over the direction of the Peace Keeping Force from Major-General Young. General Young was thus able to return to Episkopi and devote himself to the problems of the defence of the Sovereign Base Areas, the protection of the families, and the logistic support of the Peace Keeping Force which depended for its existence on the base installations in Dekhelia.

The change in the command arrangements for the Peace Keeping Force had no immediate implications for the Rifle Brigade, but it did have a marked effect on my own activities. Soon after the arrival in Cyprus of the new Headquarters, General Carver lost his intelligence Staff Officer, who was obliged to return to England unexpectedly. Having known me in Kenya and again in the War Office, the General decided to borrow me from the regiment until a new man could be supplied.

He appeared at our school with the news one morning, and I moved to his Headquarters the same evening. Rogers came with me. The change in my employment was accompanied by a noticeable lowering in my living standards. Instead of a comfortable little room in the school, I had to make do with a half-share in a tent, and my office was the partitioned corner of the divisional operations room which I shared with the Grade 2 Operations Staff Officer. But the worst privation was that I had no vehicle and as the Headquarters was established on the edge of Nicosia airfield, I had to borrow a Landrover from the pool every time I wanted to go anywhere. In fact these disadvantages did not worry me for long. I got used to the tent, spent little time in the office and managed to scrounge a Landrover which Rogers took over and drove for me. Under normal circumstances the job of an intelligence staff officer at a Divisional Headquarters is to put together and process information gathered by other people, and to feed it to the Commander and to superior and subordinate formations. But the circumstances under which 3rd Division was operating in Cyprus were not altogether normal. There was a grave shortage of information of any kind and my first job was to ensure that what little was known did at least reach us. From my own experience during the first six weeks, I knew that a lot could be collected by the men on the ground, so I went around all the units in the island suggesting ways of getting hold of it which we had been using in the Rifle Brigade.

On one or two occasions I tried to produce intelligence appreciations for the General, but he was only interested in the facts on which I based them. If I had no facts he did not want the theories, and if I had some facts he preferred to make his own assessment of them. This was sensible of him because he was in a much better position than I was to interpret what was going on. It was in any case obvious under the circumstances in which we were operating that the most important thing was for the General to get factual information in time for it to be of practical use. This often meant passing it on at top speed regardless of the way in which it was presented. Later on, after we had collected a worthwhile store of background facts he might become interested in our assessment of events.

My work at the Headquarters afforded me a good opportunity for seeing how General Carver handled the task of keeping the peace throughout the island as a whole. It was particularly interesting to be able to view his methods against the backcloth of experience which we had gained in Larnaca and Nicosia. On the face of it the General seemed to be doing no more than reacting to situations as they arose. He appeared in the operations room before breakfast to read signals and telegrams and worked in his office for a short time afterwards. He usually spent the morning in Nicosia and reappeared in the operations room at about lunchtime to tell his staff about the various meetings which he had been obliged to attend. On these occasions he was often in a hurry. In the afternoon he went visiting units or trouble spots around the island and then held a meeting of his own about 6 p.m. at which the events of the day were discussed by a wide circle of people. In the evenings he sometimes went out and had dinner with individuals who might be able to throw light on the situation in the island; alternatively he might invite such people to the Headquarters. In this way he was able to have informal discussions with the leaders of both communities, the Diplomatic Corps, United Nations officials, or anyone else who might be useful.

Gradually it became apparent that General Carver was not just reacting to events. In addition to stopping fights which had already started, he spent a lot of time trying to prevent incidents from arising at all. The business of keeping the peace concerned both of these activities and of the two, the second was probably the most important. Prevention involved identifying likely causes of trouble in advance and taking steps to avert it. Such steps varied greatly. For example, if one side looked as if it intended to occupy a building or a piece of ground which would cause a reaction from the other side, then members of the Peace Force might pre-empt the initial move and occupy the place themselves. If, as was more often the case, one side had already occupied an area which was provoking hostility from the other side, the General would try and arrange a withdrawal, possibly by negotiating a corresponding concession from the other side. Sometimes it merely looked as if tension was rising in a particular town or village, and on these occasions he could do little more than speak to the leaders on both sides and try to persuade them to prevent the situation from deteriorating. There was only one practical way of doing these things, which was to meet the people concerned, and the constant round of formal and informal meetings, which the General attended, was largely arranged with this end in view.

When it came to stopping fights which had already started General Carver usually left the Commander on the spot to get on with the job whilst he made contact with the leaders of the two communities in Nicosia in an effort to get them to call off their forces. If the disturbance was in any way prolonged, he would of course visit the scene of the action possibly taking some of the Nicosia leaders with him in order to convince them of the real situation. Accurate reporting was not a strong point with either the Greek or Turkish Cypriots, and the leaders in Nicosia invariably had distorted ideas about what was going on in the field.

A constant cause of concern to all our commanders was the question of when, if ever, we should use force. The position had never been clearly defined, but no one denied us the right to fire in self-defence. It was also clearly understood and tacitly agreed by both sides that we would use force if either community attacked the other across the dividing line in Nicosia. But this line had been negotiated with both sides during the Christmas fighting, was easily recognizable, and was fully manned by the Peace Keeping Force. It had no parallel anywhere else in the island and there were no other foreseeable circumstances in which both communities would

recognize our right to shoot. The next problem therefore was to decide how we could keep the peace if we were not going to use force.
On the face of it, the only possibility was to confine our activities to
persuasion in advance of an outburst, and negotiation thereafter
such as we had practised at Ayios Sozomenos. In many cases this
was in fact as far as we could go.

Some of the braver spirits were of the opinion that we should try
and push our men between the two sides in such a way that they
would automatically be shot at unless the contestants ceased firing.
We would then be entitled to shoot back in self-defence! Although
prepared to admit that such a course might be justified, if it was the
only way of averting a massacre, I felt that it should only be adopted
as a last resort. Quite apart from the risk that the men would run,
there were two other disadvantages. In the first place, if we did
return the fire, we might kill someone and in the prevailing circumstances the victim would almost certainly be a Greek. Passion and the
propaganda campaign would then be likely to spur other Greeks to
take revenge on one of our isolated posts or patrols or possibly on the
families. We would then be obliged to squander a large part of the
Peace Keeping Force in order to guard our own people. The other
disadvantage was that one of the opposing parties might be able to
go on firing at the other without putting shots close enough to our
troops to warrant a return of fire, but at the same time close enough
to prevent our men from moving. We would then be in an embarrassing position, and neutralized into the bargain. In practice
the only sensible answer was to avoid using force for as long as
possible. Neither of the two sides could be sure of our intentions and
consequently we were able to achieve more by a display of confidence, backed by the threat of action, than we would have achieved
by the use of force itself.

In addition to peace-keeping, General Carver had a certain
amount of work which was solely related to commanding the troops.
In mechanical terms his problem resolved itself into working out a
way whereby he could carry out all the tasks connected with preventing outbreaks and commanding his force, and at the same time
be immediately available to help should incidents look as if they
were getting out of control. The twin keys to solving this problem
were intelligence and a capability for receiving information and influencing action, that is to say communications.

Soon after my arrival in the Headquarters it was decided that the

British Peace Keeping Force should be replaced by troops of the United Nations at the end of March. The plan for the United Nations takeover was that General Carver should hand over command to General Gyani, but stay on as Deputy Commander and Chief of Staff of the United Nations Force. An important part of the plan was that the original two battalions of the Cyprus garrison would return to the Sovereign Base Areas when the United Nations Force came into being. Thus on the day when most of our units changed into light-blue berets, the Rifle Brigade returned to Dekhelia. A few days later an officer arrived to take over the job which I had been doing so I was able to rejoin the battalion.

Although I had only been away for a month, it seemed much longer. The winter had been unusually severe, and when I arrived in my tent that first night I had been well wrapped up against the cold. But spring came early and during March the temperature shot up rapidly. The corn ripened and a start was made with the harvest. Flowers burst into bloom and migrant birds came flocking into the island. When I got back to Dekhelia on Good Friday, people were paddling around in the sea, and boats from the yacht club were cutting through the waters of the bay under a bright blue sky. The reversion to a peace-time existence was so abrupt that I found it difficult to adjust myself. Outside the Sovereign Base Areas, units and Headquarters were continuing to live in schools, aircraft hangars or derelict buildings, while officers and men were working round the clock just as we had been doing for the past three months.

The battalion stayed in Cyprus until the end of the summer and then returned to England. I had been lucky to get such a good education into the military activity called peace-keeping in such a short time. Between Christmas and Easter I had been in command of a detachment in a small town in Larnaca; I had been second in command of a battalion deployed in a highly sensitive city, i.e., Nicosia; and I had been the principal intelligence Staff Officer to the Force Commander for the whole of Cyprus. There is no doubt that peace-keeping is a totally different business from fighting insurgents because the peace-keeper is an outsider, called in by both parties to a dispute, to help them settle their quarrel, whereas those active against insurgents are operating as agents of the government against a section of the people. On the other hand, peace-keeping has more in common with counter-insurgency than it has with any other form of military activity. In both cases units and sub-units are likely to be strung out over a large area and success depends more on finding out, or working out, what other people are trying to do, than it does in the actual action of one's own troops. Furthermore, political factors which tend to have a more direct bearing on those involved in countering insurgency than they do on soldiers involved in more conventional forms of war, have an even greater impact on peace-keeping. For these two reasons peace-keeping provides very good experience for counter-insurgency and *vice versa*.

When the battalion returned to England, I was promoted and sent to work in the Ministry of Defence for two and a half years. During that time the three separate Green Jacket regiments were merged to form a new regiment called the Royal Green Jackets and when I eventually escaped from London I found myself appointed to command the first battalion of this new regiment. One month later the battalion was sent to Cyprus as part of the United Nations Force. After the end of 1964 the situation had improved, but by the time of the battalion's arrival in October 1967 there were signs that further trouble was about to break out. That these portents were not fictitious was to be borne out in a way which affected us all most violently within a matter of weeks.

Chapter 22

***

Pitched Battle

The Commanding Officer of a battalion is always a person of some consequence in the British army. He has great authority over about six hundred and fifty men and he is responsible for a lot of expensive equipment. In October 1967 I was not only Commanding Officer of my battalion, but I also became the senior United Nations Officer for the whole of the south-west part of Cyprus, an area which stretched about seventy-five miles from west to east and about twenty-five miles from north to south. My zone, as it was called, included the towns of Limassol, Paphos and Polis, and I was directly responsible to the United Nations Force Commander, Lieutenant-General A. E. Martola of the Finnish army. General Martola exercised his functions in close conjunction with the Secretary General's Special Representative in Cyprus, Mr Osorio Tafall of Mexico. Brigadier Harbottle, a British officer, was General Martola's Chief of Staff.

From my previous experience of peace-keeping I realized that my job would consist of preventing trouble from arising where possible, restoring the situation where necessary, and exercising command over my battalion in the normal way. Because the island had remained relatively peaceful for a considerable time there seemed good reason to hope that neither of the first two of these functions would cause me overmuch difficulty, and I looked forward to getting to know my new battalion in a relatively leisurely manner as the weeks went by. My life would inevitably be punctuated by a series of social contacts with Greek and Turkish Cypriots, and with the officers of the other United Nations contingents on the island, and I guessed that exchanges of hospitality might put a considerable strain on my digestion. None the less, in the evening of our first day in Cyprus, as I looked out from my Headquarters over the rocky scrub towards the lights of Limassol, I felt well satisfied with the prospect ahead of me. I expected to be able to enjoy the responsibilities of my position without being subjected to the risks of conflict, or to the strain of working under operational conditions.

During our first few weeks the thing that struck me most was the way in which the balance of power between the two sides and the Peace Keeping Force had shifted since my last involvement in the struggle. On the Greek side, the various fighter groups of early 1964 had been incorporated into the National Guard, which was a properly uniformed and equipped army, officered by professional soldiers from mainland Greece. In addition, there were now a number of Greek army units in Cyprus amounting to well over 5,000 men and some of these units were equipped with tanks and artillery. George Grivas, who had been the terrorist leader in the old EOKA campaign, now a general in the Greek army, was supreme commander of all Greek and Greek Cypriot forces on the island. From a military point of view therefore the Greek and Greek Cypriot forces were far more numerous and better equipped than the small United Nations contingent, which no longer had the power to defend itself, nor the strength to dictate to the two sides in an Emergency, as had been the case with the original British Peace Force. At the time this did not strike me as being too serious a matter because peace-keepers are not expected to achieve their aims by the use of military strength, nor should they fear hostile action from either of the two contesting parties.

But although the Greek Cypriots had nothing to gain from undermining the position of the United Nations Force whose presence was largely designed to reassure the Turks and thereby avoid a Turkish invasion, Grivas lost no opportunity for reducing its influence by interfering with its freedom of movement and by dominating its activities whenever he could. His purpose in doing this was to weaken restraints on the action he wished to take against the Turkish community. It seems likely that the presence of the mainland Greek units with their tanks and their guns led him to feel that the Turks would be reluctant to invade, and thereby encouraged him to take risks in his dealings with both the Turkish community and with the United Nations Peace Force.

On the Turkish side, the position did not seem to be much

different from that which had existed in early 1964. Local fighter groups had been issued with uniforms and I subsequently learnt that a few officers of the Turkish army had been sent to organize and train the fighters in the more important places. But the Turks had neither artillery nor tanks, nor were there any units of the Turkish army in Cyprus, other than the one battalion which had been stationed there since 1959 under the Treaty of Alliance. The main difficulty in dealing with the Turks was that we always had to contact the official spokesmen of the various Turkish communities, and it was impossible to know whether these people had any power in their own right, or whether they were merely front men for the real leaders. Very little information on this subject was available.

In order to carry out its functions, our battalion was spread out so that there was one company commander, known as a United Nations District Commander in each of the main administrative centres within our zone. Thus one company commander was responsible for Limassol together with the country around it and he dealt with the Greek District Officer on the one hand, and with a man designated by the Turkish community to represent them, on the other. Another company commander was similarly employed in Paphos District and a third in Polis. Our fourth company commander, who was known as the Kophinou District Commander, looked after a small part of Larnaca District, the rest of this District being in the zone covered by the Swedish contingent. Although he had the smallest area, from a geographical point of view, he had the biggest problem. The officer who filled this post was called Bob Pascoe. He had been in Cyprus during the days of the EOKA campaign and he was well known for his composure in difficult circumstances.

The area around the Turkish village of Kophinou had been sensitive from the start of the troubles because of its strategic position at the junction of the Nicosia to Limassol road with the Limassol to Larnaca road. Craggy hills around the village made it easy for the Turkish inhabitants to impede movement along these roads which would have been extremely awkward for the Greeks had they wished to move troops in an emergency from the southern part of the island to Nicosia, or laterally along the southern coast. The National Guard might well have needed to do this in the event of a Turkish invasion or of widespread inter-communal fighting. Because of the sensitivity of the area the United Nations Force had always maintained a presence in the old village police station on the main road which was where Bob Pascoe had his Headquarters. By the time of our arrival the Turkish element of the police had moved to another house in the middle of the village, and a Greek Cypriot police post had been opened about one mile down the road towards Limassol, just beyond Skarinou Bridge.

Bob Pascoe's company, like the other companies of the battalion, was spread around the area in sections of six to eight men under a corporal. Each section manned an observation post in some prominent place. The post itself consisted of a blue tin hut with the letters UN painted on it in white, and in order to get the best view these huts often had to be sited on narrow rocky outcrops or ledges, greatly exposed to the weather. At some more spacious and sheltered spot nearby, preferably within a hundred yards or so, the section would have a tent or another hut where the men could sleep and cook. Neither the observation post, nor the living area, was prepared for defence in any way because this would imply a measure of hostility towards the two sides. It would also have been far beyond the financial resources of the United Nations Force to have carried out the work needed to do this. The positioning of all the posts had been the result of minute negotiation over the years between the two sides and United Nations Headquarters in Nicosia. No commander had discretion to move a post or to alter the number of men manning it without getting the alteration accepted by both sides in Nicosia, and the time taken to do this had usually to be reckoned in months rather than weeks. The purpose of the posts was to enable men to observe and thereby provide information which commanders at every level could use in negotiation. The men in them were not expected to manoeuvre or to fight.

Over the years the Turkish leadership had carefully built up their ability to exploit the strategic value of the Kophinou position should the need arise. A regular officer from mainland Turkey was in charge of the local fighters and he was responsible for training them and ensuring that they were filled with martial ardour when the great day arrived. A very aggressive young man had held this post for most of the year preceding our arrival, but he had recently been replaced as a result of a series of outrageous confrontations which he had arranged between his men and representatives of the United Nations Force. He had been carrying out on a small scale and in a crude way the same sort of harassing tactics which Grivas had been using over the island as a whole, and for the same reason, that is to say he had been trying to reduce the ability of the United Nations Force to interfere with such action as he might one day wish to take against the opposing community. In order to do this, he tried to restrict the freedom of movement which United Nations troops had in the area immediately around Kophinou so that they could not see, publicize, and therefore prevent the preparations which would be a necessary prelude to attacking the Greeks. He also tried to build up an ascendancy which he could use to inhibit the action of the United Nations District commander at a critical moment. Although the aggressive Turkish officer had been replaced by a less forceful character, the policy was still the same when Bob Pascoe arrived, and negotiations following incidents had led to agreements which debarred United Nations troops from a number of places in the area.

Although it is easy enough in retrospect to understand the game which the local Turkish commander was playing, it was not at all clear at the time, and even if it had been it would not have been easy to counter it. One of our main difficulties lay in the fact that the Kophinou District Commander was not supposed to have any direct dealings with the local Turks and was obliged to carry out all contact through the official Turkish spokesman in Larnaca which was about twelve miles away. The official Turkish reason for this was that there was no local leader at Kophinou, but merely a lot of simple farmers. Discipline was so strict amongst the villagers that none of them was prepared to talk direct to our men, but this was put down to the fact that the locals disliked the United Nations soldiers so much as a result of previous incidents that they would have nothing to do with us any more!

All matters concerning the area were therefore discussed at a weekly meeting which the District Commander had with the Turkish spokesman in Larnaca and which was attended by the Swedish District Commander who covered the rest of the Larnaca area. Normally I accompanied Bob Pascoe to these meetings which could be exceedingly stormy as the Turkish spokesman roared with anger and banged the table whenever he had what he judged to be some cause of complaint against the United Nations Force. He had a gleaming, bald head and piercing eyes and looked very fierce on these occasions. At other times he could be charming, amusing and immensely interesting. He was a consummate actor who usually contrived to be particularly nice to the Swedes when he was being beastly to the British and *vice versa*. These attainments, together with his immensely superior knowledge of local affairs and past events, gave him an advantage over the United Nations officers with whom he dealt, and negotiations were made even more hazardous by virtue of the fact that he usually insisted on working through an interpreter. As he had a fair knowledge of English this gave him a moment or two to work out his rejoinder to any point while it was being translated into Turkish, but he would sometimes burst violently into the conversation to contradict some remark which one of us had made with a sentence which started with the words 'As I believe. . . .'

The particular problem in Kophinou District when we took over concerned the right of the Greek Cypriot policeman at the Skarinou Bridge police post to travel along the small road to the village of Ayios Theodoros which lay about one and a half miles away. Ayios Theodoros was a village with a mixed population and the road from Skarinou Bridge passed through the area in which the Turks lived before it entered the Greek Quarter. Furthermore throughout most of its length the road was dominated by high ground along which Turkish fighters from Kophinou held fortified positions. Up until July the Turks did not interfere with the policeman's visits to Ayios Theodoros which had taken place at weekly intervals, but at that time there was a certain amount of unrest in the village largely as the result of the aggressive Turkish officer's activities, and the policeman voluntarily discontinued using the road in order to avoid giving the Turks an excuse for stirring up further trouble. When the policeman tried to resume his weekly visiting in September he found his return journey barred by the Turkish fighters and he had to make a long detour over rough tracks. The situation immediately escalated to the highest level because an important issue of principle was involved for the Greek Cypriot Government, that is to say the principle of freedom of movement along the roads of the country.

Soon negotiations were being conducted by the Secretary General of the United Nations in New York with the Governments of Greece, Turkey and Cyprus, and by the time we arrived both parties were playing for higher stakes than the mere settlement of the dispute. The Turks were undoubtedly totally in the wrong and it is probable that Archbishop Makarios and General Grivas were aiming to force them into an act of surrender which would damage their prestige and teach them a salutary lesson for the future. Certainly the Greek side had been very patient up to this point. The Turks, on the other hand, had many genuine grievances in other parts of the island and wanted to get some concessions from the Greeks as their price for reopening the road. More specifically, they wanted Grivas to withdraw the National Guard from a new position which it was occupying near to the Turkish Quarter in Larnaca. Although these negotiations were going on well above our heads, we knew about them, but we did not expect the outcome to be particularly dramatic. Many similar situations had built up over the previous three years and had dragged on for weeks before yielding eventually to United Nations mediation, to the slight advantage of one side and the corresponding detriment of the other.

Early in November the situation seemed to be easing and I was told that the Turks had more or less agreed to a United Nations plan for a gradual resumption of the policeman's visits to Ayios Theodoros. But the Turks never quite got round to implementing the agreement and on November 13th there was a meeting between Archbishop Makarios, General Martola and Mr Osorio Tafall which was attended by Grivas and the Greek Cypriot Minister of the Interior. At this meeting Makarios and his colleagues said that the Cyprus Government could not be expected to wait any longer for the resumption of the policeman's patrol. General Martola and Mr Osorio Tafall made a strong plea for a bit more time on the grounds that negotiations with the Turks appeared to have been successful, but they received no encouragement from Makarios.

Suddenly therefore, after many weeks of negotiation everyone realized that November 14th might become the day of destiny for Cyprus. Grivas had built up a powerful army capable of overrunning any of the Turkish positions in the island and capable also of resisting a Turkish invasion for a number of days at least. The Turks had established defences around the strategically sensitive Kophinou area and had gained a sufficiently tight grip over the fighters there to ensure that a battle with the Greeks could be arranged whenever the general Turkish interest demanded it, regardless of the effect which it might have on the local Turkish Cypriots. Both sides felt that they would gain from a clash, and both sides had systematically contrived to undermine the United Nations Forces' ability to gather the sort of information which they needed if they were to pre-empt action by the contestants. There was of course no question of the United Nations using physical force to stop a battle because by the very nature of the situation this would have meant fighting the Greeks in support of a Turkish line of action which the United Nations had consistently condemned. This was a major policy matter which had been made clear to me on several occasions and I had of course passed it on to Bob Pascoe.

During the morning of November 14th I called at our District Headquarters in the Kophinou compound. A Turkish shepherd had been reported missing and although no extra Greek troops could be seen Bob Pascoe reckoned that the shepherd might have bumped into some soldiers in an area hidden from our observation posts and had been taken prisoner to prevent him from carrying the news back to the Turks. We thought it best to assume that extra Greek forces were in that direction. We then decided that although we were not allowed to shadow the National Guard, there could be no objection to our sending a couple of vehicles down the road to Nicosia and a couple more towards Larnaca to see what they could see. This task was entrusted to Robin Laugher who was the officer in charge of the reconnaissance platoon. Bob and I walked up and down within the compound chatting to the soldiers while we waited for the patrols to reappear. As we did so, a number of Royal Air Force bombers from the Sovereign Base Area flew overhead on a routine flight.

Some time later Bob Pascoe received a telephone message to say that the local National Guard Officer would like to see him at the Skarinou Bridge police station. I decided to go along, so we set off together down the Limassol road in my car. Looking over the white plastered buildings of Kophinou to the sun-bleached hillside beyond, it seemed a very ordinary day. At this stage, although we knew that the situation was tense we were still not convinced that anything would happen. We spoke light-heartedly and laughed about the way in which the Turkish leader in Larnaca had shouted at our Swedish colleague a few days earlier. But when we got to the police station we were confronted by an efficient looking major of the Greek army instead of the easy-going captain who normally commanded the local National Guard company. The major had been told to warn us that it was dangerous for the Royal Air Force to fly around the area and that they should stay away. We pointed out that we were members of the United Nations Force and had nothing to do with the British in the Sovereign Base Areas. A second warning was politely but firmly given and we returned to Kophinou wondering whether the Greeks thought that the British were carrying out reconnaissance flights on behalf of the United Nations, or whether they merely wanted to impress us with the gravity of the situation.

Further evidence of the Greek build-up awaited us on our return in the form of Robin Laugher. Although he had not seen any large concentration of troops, he said that he had come across a group of officers not far from the Nicosia road about three miles away from Kophinou. His description of one of them seemed to fit Grivas except that Robin would not agree that he was particularly short. He kept pointing to me and saying that he was about my size, i.e., about five feet seven inches. I had been led to believe that Grivas was much smaller, but Grivas or no Grivas, it was becoming increasingly obvious that something was going to happen soon.

Soon after 12.45 p.m. Bob Pascoe as the United Nations District Commander was again summoned to see the National Guard Commander at Skarinou Bridge where he was asked to give protection to two police patrols which he was told would be moving into Ayios Theodoros at 1.15 p.m. One was going down the road from Skarinou Bridge and one would be entering the village from the south. He was also told that if he did not provide the protection required, the National Guard would escort the police themselves. The circumstances in which the request was made were clearly designed to ensure that it would be refused for two reasons. Firstly, by a long-standing arrangement with the Cyprus Government all requests for United Nations escorts had to be channelled through the Ministry of the Interior. Secondly, it was obviously impossible to organize protection of this sort in twenty to thirty minutes. I contacted United Nations Headquarters in Nicosia and was told that no protection was to be offered. In passing this on to the National Guard Commander Bob Pascoe strongly urged them to prevent the police from carrying out their patrols as negotiations were still going on at a high level.

At 1.30 p.m., despite many weeks of negotiation by the United Nations, the police set off with a National Guard escort of armoured cars and infantry. We had little doubt that a battle was imminent. I went into the operations room in the old police station and listened to the reports which were coming in from our observation posts overlooking the route. I wondered vaguely where the Turks would choose to carry out their frequently repeated threat to block the road. Much to our astonishment nothing happened and the policeman with his escort reached Ayios Theodoros and drove through the

Turkish Quarter, across the bridge into the Greek Quarter where he met up with the other patrol which had come into the village from the south. Shortly afterwards both patrols returned along their former routes. The lack of reaction from the Turks came as a great surprise to us all.

Bob Pascoe and I walked out of the operations room and up to the wire perimeter of the compound at the edge of the main road. Opposite us was the village clinic, blinding-white in the strong sun. A great load seemed suddenly to have been lifted from us. It looked as if Grivas had called the Turkish bluff and won. It had been a great gamble on his part, but it had paid off. Now perhaps the Turks would drop the whole wretched business of the road to Ayios Theodoros and we could all wind down. At that moment three large staff cars drove down the road from the direction of Nicosia, one of which was decorated with four stars and flew the flag of the supreme commander of all the Greek and Greek Cypriot forces on the island. General Grivas was evidently driving to the Skarinou Bridge police station to congratulate his people on the success of the patrol. As his car drew level, I saluted the old terrorist as I was obliged to do, since he was officially a general officer in an army recognized by the United Nations, but memories of his past activities imposed some mental reservations on my military duty. All the same, I admired his courage and determination even while deploring some of his other characteristics so I did not greatly grudge him the courtesy of a salute. If I had foreseen the daring of his next move I should have grudged it him even less.

As the cars passed out of sight, I felt that no more would happen that afternoon, but a moment or two later a signaller came up to Bob Pascoe with a report from the observation post overlooking Skarinou Bridge to say that Grivas with his three staff cars had turned off the main road and was heading for Ayios Theodoros. It seemed incredible and we ran back to the operations room to get confirmation. Much to our amazement our observation posts continued to report the progress of this small convoy as it drove all the way to the village, through the Turkish Quarter over the bridge, and into the Greek Quarter. There Grivas got out of his car and had himself photographed talking to a collection of villagers. He then returned the way he came. Next morning all the newspapers carried the pictures. The Turks had been humiliated to an extent which no one would have thought possible, while the Greeks had scored an

advantage which they would be able to use in negotiations for some
time to come.

Next morning the policeman from Skarinou Bridge together with
his escort again made the journey into Ayios Theodoros and back
despite the fact that the Turkish leadership in Nicosia had reiterated
their threat to prevent by force all future patrols from entering the
village. At about this time I was summoned to United Nations Headquarters in Nicosia where I was given precise instructions as to how
the situation should be handled. I received my orders from General
Martola in person in the presence of Mr Osorio Tafall. He told me
that he had again asked Archbishop Makarios to stop further patrols
on the grounds that the point about freedom of movement had been
amply demonstrated and that further forays into Ayios Theodoros
could only end in disaster. He also told me that if fighting broke out,
troops of the United Nations were not to become involved, but were
to report events as they happened in order to provide up-to-the-
minute information on which negotiations could be based, at a
higher level.

After receiving my orders, the Chief of Staff accompanied me to
the helicopter: he wanted to make sure that I thoroughly understood what I had to do. I tried to appear confident and adopted the
line that in my view there was not much chance of trouble now, the
Turks having already demonstrated on three occasions that they
were not prepared to provoke a major Greek attack on their positions. Brigadier Harbottle did not agree and warned me not to take
too much for granted. As I got into the helicopter, I looked back at
him. Wind from the rotor blades pressed his trousers against his legs
and he held his blue beret in place with one hand. He looked serious,
but I felt no foreboding as we lifted into the air and flew across
Nicosia airfield. It was a relief being cooled by the breeze inside the
aircraft and I leant back to enjoy the view of Nicosia and of the sun-
burnt plain below. Away to the south on the route to Limassol lay
the Troodos Mountains, but we would not be crossing them this
time: we were heading for Kophinou. Bob Pascoe met me on arrival
with the news that yet another police and National Guard patrol
was shortly due to leave for Ayios Theodoros. Referring to the repeated Turkish threats, he expressed doubts as to whether it would
get through unscathed. Disregarding Brigadier Harbottle's warning,
I told him to rustle up some food and stop worrying about the
Turks. Inverting the famous jingoist couplet I said of them, 'We do

want to fight, but by jingo, if we don't'. At that moment the Skarinou Bridge observation post reported that the patrol was heading off down the road.

By now the commentary from our observation posts covering the route into Ayios Theodoros was becoming familiar and nothing untoward occurred until the patrol arrived at the entrance to the village. At this point it found its way barred by a tractor and various bits of farm machinery. Some members of the patrol got out to move the obstruction and a second party moved north from the Greek part of the village to join up with them. The scene was being described by one of Bob Pascoe's platoon commanders, called Philip Ling, from the observation post known as Water Tower Hill about four or five hundred yards away.

At 2.10 p.m. Philip Ling reported hearing three shots followed by a burst of automatic fire. Although no one could see exactly who fired the fatal shots, it was almost certainly a Turk. As was to be expected, there was an immediate response from the Greek patrol. Within a few minutes of this exchange the Greeks launched a number of major assaults by infantry and armoured cars, supported by mortars and artillery onto the whole Turkish position around Kophinou and Ayios Theodoros. The Turks had evidently given Grivas such justification as he required to set in motion the large-scale, set-piece attack which he had been preparing with such care for the past few days.

On hearing that the police patrol had met an obstruction on the road, and before any firing had taken place, I got into my Landrover and set off towards Skarinou Bridge, intending to get into a position from which to see what was going on. The battalion Signals Officer, Nigel Mogg, came with me and together we listened to the reports coming over the wireless as we drove along. We were still on the main road when the first exchange of fire took place and, expecting that the action would be confined to the outskirts of Ayios Theodoros, we continued on our way. We were therefore somewhat surprised to see a force of National Guard led by armoured cars appear over the crest to our right, that is to say to the north of the road and about two miles from the scene of the action. We were even surprised when they opened up with their machine-guns straight over our heads into the side of the hill which rose up on the left of the road. Soon artillery and mortar fire began to land in this area as well.

For a time I did not understand what was happening and could only watch with interest and a certain amount of trepidation as the National Guard assault rolled down the hill towards us. As the armoured cars pitched up and down over rocks and into furrows the muzzles of their guns did likewise, and this was reflected on the other side of the road where squirts of dust kicked up by the arriving bullets traced a crazy pattern over hundreds of yards of sandy scrub. These armoured cars were of an antiquated make and were painted bright yellow as for desert warfare. Their commanders were standing up in the turrets wearing steel helmets and firing their guns at nothing in particular so far as we could see. I only hoped that they would notice our large blue United Nations flag and not mistake us for Turks.

From the scene before us and from what we could hear on the wireless, it was soon obvious that the original confrontation on the outskirts of Ayios Theodoros was no longer important. It had provided the excuse for the battle, but the major areas of fighting had now shifted elsewhere. I decided to return to the District Headquarters in the compound at Kophinou where I could be adequately informed of events as they developed and at the same time keep in touch with United Nations Headquarters in Nicosia. We therefore turned the Landrover and headed back up the road, stopping at one point to pick up two of our soldiers who had been sent out earlier on a foot patrol. As they were climbing on board I noticed that the Greek assault was crossing the road behind us and was pushing on up the slope towards our post on Tango Hill, still firing their weapons. A few minutes later as we reached the compound, we were able to see another Greek assault moving against the Turkish position on the high ground behind it. In this case fire was being returned by the Turks who seemed to have one or two recoilless weapons, judging by the clouds of smoke and orange flame which punctuated their discharge.

Inside the operations room Bob Pascoe was piecing together reports from our observation posts. Although it was some time before he was able to work out exactly what was happening, it eventually became clear that Grivas had launched three simultaneous assaults immediately after the initial exchange of fire. At this point it will be found convenient to refer to the map on the facing page. The southernmost assault had started from the feature known as National Guard Hill and was moving towards Ayios Theodoros. At the time

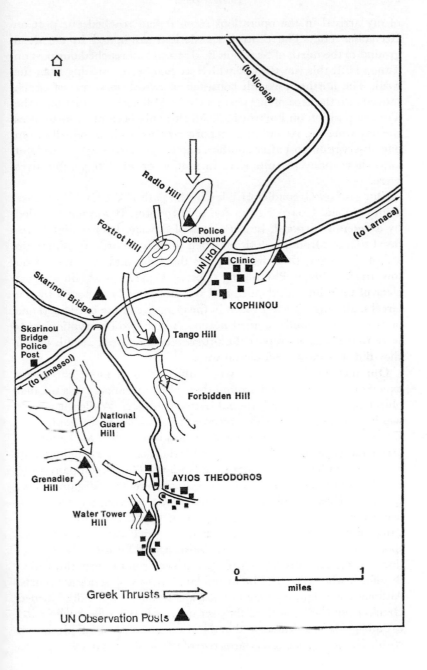

(to Nicosia)

(to Larnaca)

Radio Hill

Foxtrot Hill

Police
Compound

UN HQ

Clinic

KOPHINOU

Skarinou Bridge

Skarinou
Bridge
Police
Post

(to Limassol)

Tango Hill

Forbidden Hill

National
Guard
Hill

Grenadier
Hill

AYIOS THEODOROS

Water Tower
Hill

0   1
miles

Greek Thrusts

UN Observation Posts

of my arrival in the operations room it had reached our post on Grenadier Hill. The central assault had originated in the dead ground to the north of Skarinou Bridge and had reached our post on Tango Hill: this was the one which we had been watching from the road. The northern assault consisted of two thrusts, one of which moved into the area of our post on Radio Hill and the other onto the Turkish position on Foxtrot Hill. All this only became clear to us as the day wore on. At the time, reports reached us haphazardly from one observation post after another, and at this early stage we did not know how many assaults were in motion or what their objectives were.

Our post on Grenadier Hill lay in the path of the Greek advance from National Guard Hill to Ayios Theodoros. It was commanded by a veteran corporal, by the name of Savage, who resolutely refused to move from his position when the Greeks ordered him to do so. In the event, they did not press the point and soon moved on towards the village. Philip Ling's post on Water Tower Hill was just clear of their line of advance and was not directly molested by the Greeks, although it was caught in the cross-fire of the battle and one or two mortar bombs landed nearby. These two observation posts were well placed to report the progress of the Greek assault which they did in a most professional way.

Our men on Tango Hill were subjected to a more harrowing experience as the ground around their observation post was the first objective of a complete National Guard company. While the assault was in progress their position received a sprinkling of the haphazard Greek fire which I had witnessed earlier, but as soon as the Greeks arrived it naturally became a target for the Turks on Forbidden Hill across the valley. Furthermore the National Guard company were hostile to our men and badly disciplined into the bargain. Thus, whilst the Greek company commander was ordering our section to leave their trenches and stop reporting events over the wireless, gangs of his men were looting their tents which were in a sheltered spot about one hundred and fifty yards away. Fortunately the section was commanded by a young, but very robust corporal, called Bradford, who refused to be intimidated or to stop sending reports. Although our eight men could not expel well over a hundred armed Greeks from their position, they set upon a Greek officer who tried to damage the wireless set and in the ensuing scuffle cut off his thumb with a bayonet. Soon afterwards two of the National Guard platoons assaulted Forbidden Hill, leaving the remainder of the Greek force with our men on Tango Hill.

On Radio Hill our soldiers had an even worse time. When the attack started the section there stood to in their slit trenches, but because of the layout of the ground this meant that four men under the Section Commander were in one place and two others in another trench a short way away. Before the National Guard arrived on the position our men were caught in an exchange of fire between the assaulting force and the Turks on Foxtrot Hill. Several mortar bombs intended presumably for the Turkish position fell around the post, one scoring a direct hit on the hut used for cooking, whilst another hit a tree a yard or so beyond the trench from which our men were observing the battle. All this was reported on the field telephone which connected this section with the compound. Then the telephone went dead.

My first reaction, as I stood in the operations room watching the situation develop, was one of anger at the Greeks. Their operation was undoubtedly an over-reaction to the behaviour of the Turks, but more infuriating from my point of view was the callous disregard and even hostility which they were showing towards our men of the United Nations Force. This was not only inexcusable, but also pointless. Trying hard to prevent emotion from affecting my thoughts, I started to work out exactly what I personally should be doing. From the orders I had so recently received from General Martola it was obvious that the most important thing, for which we must be prepared to sacrifice lives if necessary, was to report exactly what was happening so that he and Mr Osorio Tafall could swing the whole weight of the United Nations negotiating machinery into action in the most effective way possible. In the normal way reports from the observation posts would be put together in Bob Pascoe's District Headquarters and sent to my Headquarters near Limassol for onward transmission to Nicosia. Being at Bob's Headquarters with my signals officer I decided that one of us would send all reports direct to Nicosia as this would not only save time, but enable me to make a more personal and immediate impact on events.

The next point to be considered was the effect which the fighting might have in other parts of my zone. A disturbance of such magnitude at Kophinou could easily spark off a reaction in Limassol or Paphos, so I telephoned to the battalion second in command and asked him to keep a careful watch on the situation in these places.

I also asked him to rake together all the spare men he could muster, form them into two *ad hoc* platoons and send them towards Kophinou together with the Medical Officer and some extra signallers.

The third main point to be considered was the extent to which I should try and direct events round Kophinou. Putting myself in Pascoe's shoes and realizing how much I should resent interference from above at such a time, I decided to leave him as free as possible to exercise his function both as District Commander and as Company Commander. This would mean restricting myself to laying down the bounds within which he should work, supporting him in moments of stress and keeping all pressure off him from United Nations Headquarters. I decided that any extra troops sent to operate in Kophinou District, such as the reinforcements which I had asked for, should also come under his command on arrival: he already had two troops of armoured cars belonging to 5th Inniskilling Dragoon Guards which had been allocated to him before the battle. Naturally the responsibility for what happened would remain mine, regardless of the extent to which I delegated it and this tempted me to take a more direct hand in events, but I was swayed by the fact that Bob knew the position around Kophinou better than I did and by the thought that I might get caught up in events elsewhere as the situation developed. In the event Pascoe did a magnificent job and I never had cause to regret my decision.

It might be supposed that the making of decisions on such simple matters posed few problems because from a purely intellectual point of view there was not a great deal involved. On the other hand making sensible decisions seldom seems so simple when viewed from the centre of a storm, such as the one which was raging around us. For several years a series of United Nations mediators, force commanders and special representatives together with ministers and ambassadors from many countries had laboured to prevent a war in the Eastern Mediterranean. Now the whole fragile edifice of checks and balances which they had built up, was cracked and swaying in the tempest. A bad decision from any of a relatively small number of people at this juncture would swiftly lead to disaster and I was one of the people most closely concerned. It was the speed with which grave consequences would follow bad decisions which made clear thinking difficult, rather than the distractions of the battle itself.

But it should not be imagined that the distractions of the battle could be ignored entirely. From the start of the fighting the odd shell had been directed at the village of Kophinou from National Guard artillery occupying a position about 4,000 yards to the north of us. The police compound in which we were working lay directly in the line of this fire and several shells fell around us. We had lifted the window frames off their hinges and lain them on the floor to prevent being showered by glass and a hot wind blew dust from a nearby stubble field into the operations room. I sat with a telephone in one hand connected to Brigadier Harbottle in Nicosia and a cup of tea in the other. Much to my annoyance I jumped every time a shell landed close to us and the tea slopped into the saucer. I envied the steadiness of Robin Laugher's hand as he sat opposite to me keeping the log of events. He was ruling neat lines under each entry and there were no kinks in them to mark the explosions.

At about this time Bob Pascoe discovered what had been happening at Radio Hill. He had sent out half a troop of armoured cars to find out why the telephone there had gone dead and this turned out to have been caused by it being struck by one of the many bullets which had landed in the section position. Soon afterwards a National Guard platoon arrived while our men were still shaken from the mortar bombs and cross-fire and the Greeks demanded that they should lay down their arms and leave their post. This the Section Commander and the four men with him refused to do, but the two men in the second position away from the others were forcibly relieved of their weapons by twenty or more National Guardsmen. The National Guard then turned their attention to the section's living area and systematically looted it, stealing money, cigarettes, clothing, photographs and even the rosary beads and religious medallions of one of our soldiers. There was also a weapon in one of the tents belonging to a man who was away for the day at the dentist and this too was stolen. By now other National Guard platoons had dislodged the Turks from Foxtrot Hill and the gang on Radio Hill moved off to join them. Our section received a new telephone and continued to report.

Bob Pascoe was naturally most upset by the treatment meted out to his men on Radio Hill. To a soldier, nothing is more shameful than to be forced into giving up a weapon to the enemy. I considered the desirability of telling the men to resist all such demands in future by opening fire, even if it meant certain destruction, and I also considered withdrawing the men from posts in the line of the National Guard advance. But both ideas were bad ones because they were not consistent with the achievement of our aim. Our task was to provide information about the battle between Greeks and Turks for the use of those who were trying to stop it: it did not include becoming involved as a third party in the battle itself. Despite their outrageous behaviour, we were not at war with the Greeks, nor were we at war with the Turks. For one or more of our sections to have laid down their lives in defence of their military honour would have added a glorious foot-note to the regimental history, but it would not have enabled us to know what was happening. Likewise to have withdrawn men from posts exposed to the National Guard advance would have saved them from danger and abuse, but it would also have prevented us from supplying the required information. There was no alternative but to stick things out and wait for the negotiators to have some success.

While Bob Pascoe and I were talking about these matters, we noticed that the racket around us had greatly increased. Shells were arriving more frequently and the showers of muck which they threw up kept rattling against the walls. One of the officers had just done a tour of the compound to see how the sentries and lookouts were faring in their slit trenches. He reported one man as saying that he was praying hard for the first time in his life. He also said that the tent in which the Pakistani charwallah worked had been torn by shrapnel in several places, and that one of the wireless aerials had come down. A lot of small-arms fire was now passing immediately over our heads and reports started to come in from the Larnaca Road observation post to the effect that a new assault was being launched onto Kophinou from the north-east. Other posts reported that the National Guard who had already moved onto Tango Hill and Foxtrot Hill were supporting this assault with fire.

It soon became clear that the Larnaca Road observation post was going to be subjected to the same sort of ordeal as the post on Radio Hill because it lay directly in the path of the new National Guard assault. Bob Pascoe had already sent a half troop of armoured cars to support this section and to ensure that there would not be another breakdown in communications. Soon heavy fire was falling around the soldiers and hitting the armoured cars, but the assaulting company did not misbehave towards our men as it passed through the post on the way to its objective. Indeed the officer in command even came back to discover whether the section was safe, once his company had established itself on the Turkish position.

At about this time hostility between the National Guard on Tango Hill and our section there came to a head. The Greek battalion commander had moved to this position and was ordering our men to leave the post at once. Bob Pascoe therefore drove through the battle and personally told him to get his men away from Tango Hill as it was legitimately occupied by men of the United Nations Force. Although the National Guard refused to go, it soon became apparent that they were not prepared to use force against the United Nations section in support of their demand. Instead they insisted that our men should neither observe their activities nor report them. Bob made it absolutely clear that we had every intention of doing both these things and once again the National Guard decided not to force the issue. Eventually a *modus vivendi* emerged and the National Guard started to prepare a fortified position all round our post, but without further molesting our soldiers.

Having dislodged the Turks from their defensive positions around the two villages, the National Guard set about moving into the houses themselves in search of Turkish fighters. Immediatcly across the road from our compound was the village clinic. The Greeks evidently thought that this was going to be used as a centre of Turkish resistance because they wheeled up one of their armoured cars which proceeded to blast it with its machine-gun and two-pounder cannon totally regardless of our position a road's-width away. Having spent the last two and a half hours as a marker for shells and small-arms fire, we were thus privileged to act as a stop-butt for this display of obsolescent ballistics.

By now darkness was closing in on us bringing with it a night of considerable suspense. It seemed that Grivas intended to continue his operation until he had rammed his conquest down the throat of every Turk he could find. This was to be the great lesson for the future and a release from the frustration of recent years. But it was becoming increasingly obvious that unless Grivas could be restrained, intervention from mainland Turkey would inevitably follow, and the first thing to be expected was attacks from Turkish aircraft onto Greek positions as soon as it got light. My immediate concern should this come about was for those of our observation posts now in close proximity to Greek troops. Of these the post on Tango Hill was in the greatest peril.

Throughout the battle we had been passing back every detail of the situation to United Nations Headquarters in Nicosia who in turn had been keeping the Secretary General's staff in New York acquainted with events. This steady stream of precise information ensured that the Governments of Greece, Turkey, the United States and of other interested countries knew exactly what was going on, which would not have been the case had they been obliged to rely on the garbled and edited reports sent back by the two contestants. We were thus providing United Nations officials in Nicosia and New York with the raw material which they needed in order to bring about a cease fire, and at about ten o'clock in the evening we heard that one had been agreed. In fact Grivas had no intention of implementing the cease fire until he was ready, and the National Guard continued clearing through the Turkish villages for several more hours. Our men on Water Tower Hill came under fire again during this phase of the operation.

Meanwhile the Turkish Government demanded a complete withdrawal of the National Guard from all the places they had captured during the day and it was clear to us that failure to comply would result in direct action from the air at first light. For me the suspense of the negotiations became almost unbearable, as I realized only too well what the result of such action would be. During the night reinforcements reached us in the form of a squadron of Canadian armoured cars, parts of an Austrian field hospital and the extra men who I had earlier ordered to be sent from our own battalion Headquarters. Reports of the negotiations therefore reached me against a background of arrivals and briefings, of headlights in the compound and of medical equipment laid out in the passages. The whole place was bulging at the seams with people crashing around trying to get organized. There was no confusion, but a great deal of bustle and noise in several different languages.

One gentleman, trying to be helpful, repeatedly reminded me of the likely plight of our men on Tango Hill should the negotiations have failed by the time it got light. Fearing that I might not have considered withdrawing this post he several times suggested that I should do so. I had to explain that although I had certainly thought about it, it was not a satisfactory course of action for several reasons, not least because I had been given clear orders to hang on to all our positions. I tried to make it clear that I was fully aware of the risk and had not rejected his suggestion lightly, but I also had to make

the point in such a way as to avoid adding to the worries of Bob
Pascoe and his officers. I even tried to be polite although frequent
mention of the subject was anything but soothing.

As the night wore on our hopes rose and fell. First we heard that
Greece had agreed to recommend a National Guard withdrawal to
the Greek Cypriot Government in Nicosia. Next we heard that
Archbishop Makarios was not prepared to give the necessary instructions to Grivas, although another version of this story was that
he had done so, but that Grivas had declined to obey them. Finally
it appeared that the Prime Minister of Greece, not wishing to go to
war with Turkey, had personally contacted Grivas and told him to
withdraw the National Guard. In the early hours of the morning
Brigadier Harbottle visited us and it seemed that a withdrawal
would definitely take place, but we were on tenterhooks until it
actually started at 5 a.m. By that time it had been agreed that
United Nations Forces would take over all the Turkish defensive
positions occupied by the National Guard, who would also hand
over any Turkish prisoners, and the inhabitants of the two villages
most of whom had been removed from their homes. In the end we
had little time to make a detailed plan and issue the necessary
orders, but as the National Guard withdrew, our detachments and
medical teams moved in and a start was made to the business of
restoring the villages and reviving the shocked and battered inhabitants.

As soon as it got light, I set off in my Landrover for a tour of the
area. I wanted to see how our men in the outposts were bearing up
and I wanted to get up-to-date, first-hand information regarding
the casualties and damage which had been suffered by the Turks. It
seemed likely that in the next few days exaggerated accounts of the
battle would circulate among the Turkish communities throughout
the island and I wanted to visit the leaders in my area as soon as
possible in order to kill rumour and avert the consequences.

For the most part our soldiers were revelling in the aftermath of
what to most of them had been their first taste of war. They had
been shot at and shelled, and they had survived. Some were indignant
about the behaviour of the National Guard, but they mostly had
some funny story to tell of the ill-disciplined youths who had been
wandering around their positions. If the term 'yobbo' had been
invented they would have used it to describe these people.

On the Turkish positions our men were collecting the dead and

K

preparing them for burial. Most of the Turks seemed very young with wispy moustaches and staring eyes, coated with grit blown around by the hot wind of the previous day. As I looked at their up-turned faces I was glad they had not heard me say 'We do want to fight, but by jingo, if we don't'. These men had not wanted to fight but there they lay, evidence of Turkish tenacity and of the heartless determination of their leaders who had calculated that a killing on this scale would give Turkey an excuse for invasion or alternatively the power to extract considerable concessions from the Greeks in return for not invading. Altogether twenty-seven Turks had died and many of the villagers had been wounded during the shelling of Kophinou.

Once satisfied that I had an accurate understanding of the situation, I set off to see the Turkish leader in Larnaca. Inevitably he would hold us responsible for what had happened and although we had carried out our orders to the letter, I could not rid myself of the feeling that somehow we should have averted the catastrophe. Rather to my surprise he was very kind when we met. It was a lovely blue and white Cyprus morning and little waves slopped gently against the sea front. He enquired about the safety of our men and said a few words about the supreme sacrifice that his fellow countrymen had made in the age-old struggle between Greek and Turk. He was completely convinced that Turkey would be moving to avenge her children within a few days.

Over the next two weeks tension rose and for a time it seemed certain that the Turks would invade. Every effort was made to avert this, the ultimate disaster. In the end American diplomatic pressure on Greece and Turkey had the desired effect. The Turkish price was high. Grivas was to be removed from his command and from Cyprus, and with him were to go all the Greek troops with their tanks and their guns, other than those allowed under the 1959 Zürich and London agreements. The Turks probably reckoned that the Greek Cypriots without the Greeks would be unable to hold up a future Turkish invasion even for the few days which would be needed to mobilize world opinion against Turkey. It was reasonable to assume that this factor would condition Greek Cypriot leaders of the future against further reckless gambles, and against overvaluing their moral position as the majority community in relation to the armed strength of Turkey. In the event, the arrangements reached after the battle of Kophinou gave Cyprus more than six years of complete peace which only ended when a further Greek gamble threw the whole island into turmoil once more.

From my point of view the gradual easing of tension enabled me to revert to the sort of life which I had hoped to lead on arrival in Cyprus. But although I entered wholeheartedly into the low-level negotiating and into the social life of the United Nations Force, I was determined never again to be a pawn in a game between under-cover men of power. I was equally determined to prevent having my freedom of action inhibited by the leaders of either side. Accordingly we set to work at once to find out who wielded the power. Using the dodges which I had picked up over the years, I soon discovered where the real power lay and although continuing to pay my respects to local community spokesmen, I also saw to it that when-ever possible these people received the sort of instructions which suited us. Many years after leaving Cyprus I heard that this had not gone down well with the Turkish leader in Larnaca who described me to a senior British visitor as 'that rather difficult man'.

I made one other resolution after the battle of Kophinou. Al-though soldiers operating under my command in a peace-keeping situation might not always be liked, I was determined that they should at least be respected and, if necessary, feared. For things to be otherwise is unfair on the soldiers and is inconsistent with the achievement of the aim.

Part V

Studying Experience

Chapter 23

※

Framework

As Secretary of State for Defence, Denis Healey became known as an innovator and one of his ideas was to establish Defence Fellowships. Each year six or eight middle-aged officers were selected from the three services and sent off to a university to study some aspect of defence in the widest sense. Having failed to read the relevant Defence Council Instruction, I knew nothing of this until told to volunteer for a Defence Fellowship at the end of my tour of duty as a battalion commander. After filling in a few forms, I duly appeared in front of a distinguished board of senior officers and civil servants. Somewhat to my surprise I was selected to carry out an examination into the steps which should be taken in order to make the army ready to deal with subversion, insurrection and peace-keeping operations during the second half of the 1970s. My study was to last for one year and in October 1969 I duly took up residence at University College, Oxford, thanks to the kindness of the Master and Fellows. My work was to be supervised by Professor Norman Gibbs, Chichele Professor of the History of War.

It might be supposed that any person capable of handling an infantry battalion would have little trouble in preparing such a straightforward report, but that is not how it appeared to me at the time. One major problem was that the second half of the 1970s was still six years away and it was difficult to know what sort of counter-insurgency and peace-keeping operations would be likely to confront the army so far ahead. Another problem was to relate the experience which I had gained in Kenya, Malaya, Muscat and Cyprus to the business of preparing the army for future eventualities. On reflection, preparation in this context seemed to mean education and training on the one hand, and organization on the other, but before breaking the subject down in this way it would obviously be necessary to isolate the essentials of countering insurgency and of peace-keeping.

There has never been much doubt that the main characteristic which distinguishes campaigns of insurgency from other forms of war is that they are primarily concerned with the struggle for men's minds, since only by succeeding in such a struggle with a large enough number of people can the rule of law be undermined and constitutional institutions overthrown. Violence may play a greater or lesser part in the campaign, but it should be used very largely in support of ideas. In a conventional war the reverse is more usually the case and propaganda is normally deployed in support of armed might.

Although the ultimate aim of an insurgent organization is to overthrow a government, or force it to do something it does not want to do, it will first have to get the backing of a proportion of the population, if it is to stay in being and to fight: insurgents are bound to rely to a considerable extent on the people for money, shelter, food and information. Insurgents therefore need to build up a programme in which violence is carefully balanced by political, psychological and economic measures, if it is to be effective, and the population as a whole, rather than the government, is likely to be the target, especially in the early stages of the struggle. Often insurgents do things which seem pointless or even damaging to their own cause when viewed in the context of harming the government, but in fact the actions in question may be solely concerned with achieving support from the population by coercion or persuasion. In this connection there is little doubt that terrorism is a potent form of persuasion; it is sometimes described as armed propaganda.

The particular form which an insurgent campaign takes is likely to depend on the surroundings. If a country contains mountains or large forested regions, it may be possible for insurgents to build up the sort of revolutionary army which can ultimately take on the forces of the government in battle. If, on the other hand, there is inadequate cover in the countryside, but large areas of urban development, a campaign relying mainly on political and economic attrition brought about by propaganda, sabotage and a low level of violence is likely to be more effective. Cities are particularly well suited to this form of struggle because they provide a large reservoir of people who can be manipulated into producing propaganda in the form of riots or marches, and because journalists and television teams are quickly on the scene to report it. Furthermore there is a heavy concentration of targets for sabotage around a city and plenty of prominent people such as politicians, diplomats and judges to murder. Where a country combines large areas of cover together with cities, revolutionary armies can be built up in the countryside whilst the cities can be used as a supply and recruiting base for the insurgent movement, for making propaganda, and for diverting government forces away from the country at critical moments in order to guard against sabotage or demonstrations.

The first thing that must be apparent when contemplating the sort of action which a government facing insurgency should take, is that there can be no such thing as a purely military solution because insurgency is not primarily a military activity. At the same time there is no such thing as a wholly political solution either, short of surrender, because the very fact that a state of insurgency exists implies that violence is involved which will have to be countered to some extent at least by the use of legal force. Political measures alone might have prevented the insurgency from occurring in the first place, but once it has taken hold, politics and force, backed up by economic measures will have to be harnessed together for the purpose of restoring peaceful conditions.

And this brings me to a most important point. It is fatally easy to underestimate the ability of a small number of armed men to exact support from exposed sections of the population by threats. There is always a temptation to delay using the forces of the law against subversive elements because of the danger that it will drive uncommitted people into supporting them. But neither government pronouncements, nor the natural loyalty of a people, will avail if terrorists are allowed to build up their organization unchecked. Over and over again in Kenya, Malaya, Cyprus and in many other countries it has been seen that members of the public cannot stand up to terrorism unprotected. Anyone who has looked on the miserable heaps of human wreckage left behind by execution squads knows why this is so. Certainly the use of force against terrorists must be carefully worked out in conjunction with measures designed to mitigate any unfavourable impact which it may have on people's attitudes, but it cannot be avoided altogether and a certain risk of polarization may have to be accepted in order that people should feel that something is being done to protect them.

It can be seen therefore that an effective counter-insurgency campaign should consist of a mixture of political and economic measures combined with the operations of the forces of the law. It can also be seen that the relative importance of the various different sorts of measures will have to be tailored to the situation, in the same way as insurgents tailor their campaign to the surroundings. In practice, if the insurgency represents anything more than a very minor disturbance, it is probably fair to say that the sum of the political and economic measures necessary to combat it will involve the whole business of government in one form or another. In other words, the overall plan of campaign should not be regarded as an operational matter, but primarily as a major function of government, and the form which the plan takes will result from consideration of the insurgents, aims, strengths, weaknesses and the opportunities which present themselves to both sides in relation to such factors as terrain and urban development.

But although these are the factors which determine the sort of struggle which will be waged, and although these are the considerations which journalists and other commentators naturally concentrate on describing, there is little point in examining them closely except in the context of a particular campaign. What it is both desirable and possible to do, is to identify certain areas in which decisions have to be made in order that an adequate framework can be set up. To my mind there are four such areas and they can be likened to the top, the bottom and the two sides of a frame. If the frame is well constructed, as was the case in Kenya and also ultimately in Malaya, the campaign can be expected to work.

The first requirement for a workable campaign is good co-ordinating machinery. It is no good having an overall plan composed of various measures unless they can be co-ordinated in such a way that measures of one kind do not cut across measures of another kind. To take a much over-simplified example, it might be felt that unemployment in certain areas is contributing to the support which the insurgents are getting, and that a good plan of economic development should be instituted to try and rectify the situation. But unless properly co-ordinated with other measures, this project might do more harm than good, since the money required might only be available at the expense of a more important project – say the enlargement of the police. To undertake both projects might overstrain the economy and produce conditions which would play into the insurgents' hands. Furthermore even if co-ordination at the top is correctly achieved, the results could still be disastrous for a different reason, if a similar degree of co-ordination is not realized at the lower levels. To continue with the example, even if in national terms the economic development programme does not cut across other measures, the resultant new building in a particular region, if not properly co-ordinated, might lead to a population shift and thereby to a security situation which was beyond the power of available forces to control. In short, co-ordination of measures across the board is not only necessary at the national level, but must be repeated at lower levels as well, right down to the bottom.

This is an easy principle to enunciate, but a difficult one to put into practice, particularly in a complex democratic society. Despite the reams of paper which have been written on the subject, it seldom happens that arrangements which have worked in one place will fit another place because patterns of civil administration seldom reproduce themselves sufficiently exactly. In particular the very simple system which used to operate in our Colonies, where a Provincial or District Commissioner wielded authority over a wide range of activities, is not likely to be met with again, so that the methods of co-ordinating political, economic and security measures which were so effective in Kenya and Malaya would be quite impracticable in the modern world. On the other hand, it is usually possible to devise a workable system without too much trouble. The difficulty lies in getting it accepted because of the price which has to be paid in political, economic, and personal terms. A political price has to be paid for example, whenever a locally-elected body has to give up some of its authority to the central government or to a civilian or military representative of it. The price is economic whenever boundaries change or new offices are set up with all that this implies in terms of accommodation and communications. The price is personal when one man has his little bit of power or freedom curtailed to fit in with other people. In the early days of an insurgency campaign those in authority usually hope that the situation will not become sufficiently serious to warrant payments of this kind. Later on, they may feel that the end is in sight and delay paying up for that reason. It is never easy to get the price paid.

The second requirement of a workable campaign is just as important as setting up co-ordinating machinery and is even more difficult to produce. It concerns the business of establishing the sort of political atmosphere within which the government measures can be introduced with the maximum likelihood of success. Almost always at the outset of an insurgency the government will be at a disadvantage because the insurgents will have expended a lot of time and effort on whipping up hostile opinion in order to get the trouble started. Although the government may have been trying to influence public opinion in the opposite direction, it is usual for some time to elapse before waverers start coming down on the government's side and longer still before enemy supporters start to change sides. Furthermore the struggle once joined can go one way and then the other, and must be kept up until the end, which is merely another way of repeating that insurgency is largely a battle for men's minds. In order to show why it is so difficult to get this part of the campaign going well, it is necessary to look at the sort of things which can be done, at the same time highlighting the difficulties and dangers involved in doing them. At this point it is worth noticing that the propaganda battle has not only got to be won within the country in which the insurgency is taking place, but also in other places throughout the world where governments or individuals are in a position to give moral or material support to the enemy.

There are really two separate aspects to the business of developing a frame of mind which rejects unconstitutional activity. The first part of the problem is to devise a system which ensures that the effect it will have on people's opinion and attitudes is considered at all stages during the formulation and execution of policy. This depends primarily on making all those involved in devising and carrying out the government's campaign aware of the possible public attitudes to their ideas, statements and actions. It applies to people working out programmes of economic development and to soldiers on patrol. It applies to the highest and to the lowest in all sorts of different spheres of employment. Making people aware of their responsibilities in this field is an important function of direction and as such it can only be achieved if co-ordinating machinery exists. But more is needed than co-ordinating machinery and it would seem that special staff advisers are required at every level to ensure on the one hand that policy-making groups are briefed on the consequences of their plans and on the other that ways of educating public opinion are considered and implemented.

The second part of the problem could perhaps be described as the mechanics of the business and involves the provision of people to monitor the enemy's propaganda and prepare and disseminate material required for countering it and putting across the government's point of view. It can be achieved either by direct action, as for example by the provision of leaflets, or the setting-up of an official wireless or television network, or by trying to inform and influence the existing news media.

Neither the working out of the sort of organization required, nor the provision of men and equipment is likely to prove particularly difficult. So far as men are concerned, they can be drawn from the army, the police, the civil service or direct from civilian life, subject to availability and time needed for training: equipment likewise is easy enough to get. The real difficulty lies in the political price which a democratic country pays in order to influence the way in which its people think. An information service, such as the one described here, represents the erosion of a basic freedom and its very existence in the hands of the government could in the long term prove a greater danger than the insurgents themselves, since it could be misused. So important is this consideration, that it may even be necessary to conduct the campaign within a framework which is knowingly left weak in this respect. If so, there should be no doubt in anyone's mind about the serious consequences of opting out of the propaganda war. In practice of course it might be possible to compromise and provide a limited propaganda capability at a low risk to the country's freedom of thought, but it is an extremely delicate matter.

The third part of the framework is intelligence. Clearly an adequate supply of the right sort of information is needed at the top to enable the government to work out a sensible policy for countering the insurgents. Information of a slightly different kind is also necessary at every level for the successful conduct of operations. Establishing an effective intelligence organization is therefore a matter of the first importance.

The problem about establishing the sort of organization needed, is that in normal times the requirement can best be met by a small, highly centralized and highly secure system which produces a relatively small amount of precise top-level information, whereas once an insurgent organization builds up, the operational requirement is for a mass of lower level information which must of necessity be less reliable. At the same time the government continues to require the sort of information which it has always had. Somehow therefore the

intelligence organization must enlarge itself rapidly, must de-
centralize in order to give security force commanders at every level
access to it, and must change its methods of working so as to produce
the different sort of information that operational forces need.

There are many ways in which an intelligence organization can
set about adapting itself to the needs of the moment and as with co-
ordinating machinery the exact system can only be related to the
circumstances of a particular campaign. It is none the less probable
that a reorganization on the required scale will only be achieved at
a considerable price. The most common difficulty derives from the
fact that the head of the government in a democratic country is
normally responsible for the conduct of the intelligence organization
and can best keep control of it if it is highly centralized. Expansion,
decentralization and contact with the outside world in the form of
junior military commanders all bring in their train the possibility of
the odd indiscretion. At the very least, if direct access is afforded to
army officers it will inevitably increase the power of the military
which may be politically unwelcome in itself, quite apart from any
question of abuse. The problem will be greatly accentuated if part
or all of the military contribution comes from an ally or is provided
by a higher echelon of government than the one responsible for
handling the insurgency and the intelligence organization. It is surprising how often this happens. For example, in most of our colonial
Emergencies the bulk of the armed forces were controlled by Whitehall, although the responsibility for handling the insurgency and for
the conduct of the intelligence service remained with colonial
Government. A very similar situation prevailed in Northern Ireland
until March 1972 and in countries with a federal constitution the
same sort of problem could easily arise.

A major difficulty to reinforcing and decentralizing the intelligence service comes from the speed at which it has to be done, if it
is to keep up with the rate of expansion of the insurgents' organization. The actual business of finding and training the right people is
hard enough, but the security risk involved in bringing a large number of outsiders into such a sensitive sphere of activity at short notice
is even harder. Intelligence services are always worried about their
security and although this is sometimes used as an excuse for not
taking action which is unpopular for one reason or another, it is none
the less necessary to realize that the danger does exist. However, in
all insurgency situations an effective intelligence organization has to

be established, and established quickly. Somehow the government has to ensure that essential risks are accepted and that the necessary action is taken.

The fourth part of the framework concerns the law. No country which relies on the law of the land to regulate the lives of its citizens can afford to see that law flouted by its own government, even in an insurgency situation. In other words everything done by a government and its agents in combating insurgency must be legal. But this does not mean that the government must work within exactly the same set of laws during an insurgency as existed beforehand, because it is a function of government to make new laws when necessary. It does not even mean that the law must be administered in exactly the same way during an uprising as it was in more peaceful times, because once again a government has the power to modify the way in which the law is administered if necessary, for the wellbeing of the people, although the exercise of such power is usually – and rightly – subject to considerable constitutional restraint. It is therefore perfectly normal for governments not only to introduce Emergency Regulations as an insurgency progresses, but also to counter advantages which the insurgents may derive from, for example, the intimidation of juries and witnesses, by altering the way in which the law is administered. Ways by which the legal system can be amended range from changing rules governing the giving of evidence to dispensing with juries altogether, or even to introducing some form of internment without proper trial. It is a dangerous path to tread, and one that is justified only by the peril in which constitutional government and democracy are placed by insurgency.

In practice the constant interplay of action by insurgents trying to take advantage of loopholes in the law with counter-action by the government trying to block up the loopholes, constitutes one of the most intricate and important parts of an insurgency campaign. The difficulty, from the government's point of view, is that the loopholes themselves were probably built into the system to safeguard individual freedom so that blocking them up not only provides opportunities for enemy propaganda, but also genuinely endangers the liberty of the people. There is a parallel here to the countering of enemy propaganda by the setting up of an effective government information service. The extent and way in which the government should intervene in legal matters can only be discussed in the context of particular circumstances, but it must be accepted that this is an intensely political matter and one in which military commanders cannot expect to have anything like the last word. On the other hand it is their duty to ensure that they are not required to undertake operations which are incompatible with existing law, and a government which takes insufficient notice of this duty would be failing in its own constitutional duty as well as playing into the hands of the insurgents.

Before leaving the subject of the law there is one specific matter to which allusion must be made because it is fundamental to the whole business of dealing with insurgency. This concerns the way in which members of the insurgent organization should be treated on capture. In this connection four separate and sometimes contradictory requirements have to be met and it is important that the law should take account of them. The first requirement is that the captured insurgent should be prevented from doing further damage to the government's cause. The second is that he should be given every encouragement to change sides. The third is that maximum advantage should be taken of his ability to help the government, either through giving information, or in other ways. The fourth is that his treatment should be such as to influence others to return to their proper allegiance.

The key to the whole business lies in persuading the prisoner to change sides and all of his treatment, including his interrogation, should be carried out with this in mind. There must certainly be no brutality and the best results are usually achieved by holding prisoners in well-segregated compounds in small camps close to where they have been operating. This enables interrogation to be carried out by people in close touch with the operational situation, and it avoids the control which hard-core prisoners are likely to exercise over their fellows in large prisoner-of-war-type camps. This system is however expensive in terms of manpower and facilities and is likely to attract every sort of inhibiting propaganda assault from the insurgents who well realize the danger which it poses to their cause.

To summarize this chapter I would just say that in my opinion the first requirement for the successful conduct of a counter-insurgency campaign is for the government to set up a sound framework within which it can take place. This should consist of co-ordinating machinery at every level for the direction of the campaign, arrangements for ensuring that the insurgents do not win the war for the minds of the people, an intelligence organization suited to the circumstances, and a legal system adequate to the needs of the moment. I have no doubt that a system can be devised in each of these four spheres which will be capable of achieving the aim, but I am equally sure that such systems can only be implemented with great difficulty on most occasions, and it may even happen that sometimes the best system can only be obtained by the payment of too high a price. It would then be safer for the government to accept a less good one and endure a prolongation of the troubles. This is naturally a political decision and providing that it is made by the government in the full knowledge of the likely consequences then it is up to all concerned to accept it.

Of course my analogy of a picture-frame with its top, bottom and sides is artificial and would be misleading if carried too far. In particular it is worth noticing that the sort of decisions needed for establishing the framework are similar in kind to those needed for running the campaign as a whole. Indeed that is precisely what they are and in practical terms the framework evolves as the campaign progresses. This is true because decisions regarding the setting up of one part of the frame are often dependent on the existence of other parts of it. For example, it would not be sensible to make a radical alteration to the legal system unless an effective information service existed to keep enemy counter-propaganda in check, but such an information service could itself only work after a system of coordinated direction had been established at every level, which in turn might only be possible if the law was amended to permit it. There is therefore a chicken and egg aspect to building the frame which has little to do with carpentry. The evolving nature of the framework is also due to the fact that it must change to take account of changing circumstances. It cannot be set up and left alone thereafter.

So much for the framework. In the next chapter I discuss the essentials of carrying out operations against insurgents, but before doing so would like once more to stress the importance of the background against which they take place. Anyone who has previously been involved in such operations can quickly sense whether an effective framework exists. As crisis succeeds crisis, it is easy to tell which way the tide is flowing and it is reassuring to know that one is not swimming against it.

Chapter 24

*

Operations

Interlocking political and economic restraints encountered by those trying to establish a sensible counter-insurgency framework usually give rise to intense frustration and to a series of confusing compromises. But those who turn with relief towards the subject of Security Force operations expecting to find easily-defined problems and clear-cut solutions will be disappointed. Political and economic restraints relentlessly weave their way through the fabric of operations as well. In this chapter I will try to outline the part that operations play in a counter-insurgency campaign and show how closely they are bound up with other aspects of the government's plan.

At this point it may be convenient to group operations under one of two headings. Firstly there are defensive operations, which are those designed to prevent insurgents from disrupting the government's programme. Secondly there are offensive operations, which are those designed to root out the insurgents themselves. Before discussing each in turn it is worth noticing how important it is to strike a balance between them. If too little emphasis is placed on defensive measures in order to concentrate resources on the offensive, the insurgents are offered an opportunity to achieve easy successes, which they can use to embarrass the government and thereby undermine its support. If, on the other hand, too little emphasis is placed on offensive operations, the insurgent organization gets bigger and bigger and an ever-increasing proportion of the country's resources has to be devoted to the Security Forces for defensive countermeasures, so that eventually the insurgents achieve their aim by making it appear that the price of further resistance is too high.

It is perhaps worth highlighting the ways in which political considerations affect the achievement of a good balance between defensive and offensive operations. There is almost always political pressure on Security Force commanders to devote more resources towards defensive operations because of the short-term difficulties which the government faces after every spectacular insurgent success. Furthermore, if the operational commander is insensitive to this political pressure, he stands to find himself suddenly confronted by an unnecessarily large number of specific political demands for defensive measures designed to restore confidence among the population. Those demands might easily be big enough to disrupt the offensive plan altogether and thereby upset the balance in the opposite direction. Undoubtedly the insurgent leadership will do all in its power to ensure that the balance of the Security Force's plan is upset, both by planning their own operations with this in mind, and by the use of propaganda designed to inhibit offensive action on the part of the government's forces.

It is particularly important to understand the extent to which insurgents use propaganda when defending themselves against government offensive action. Anyone at home or abroad who can be persuaded to write, or broadcast or otherwise influence public opinion will be pressed into service. The aim is usually to try and get debilitating restraints imposed on the Security Forces, and a particularly effective line is to say that offensive Security Force action is driving uncommitted people into supporting the insurgents. Like all good propaganda this line is likely to contain at least an element of truth. What the insurgent propagandist naturally fails to point out, and what the writer or broadcaster often does not understand, is that the offensive action may be the lesser of two evils, in that failure to take it will result in a far greater increase of support for the insurgents as their organization grows unchecked and their power to coerce and persuade correspondingly increases. Of course the right level of offensive action depends on prevailing circumstances. The point which has to be understood is that a good balance between offensive and defensive action is difficult to achieve because of all the pressures which operate against it.

As already stated, the purpose of defensive operations is to prevent the insurgents from disrupting the government's programme and a number of different activities can be grouped under this heading. But although such a wide variety of operations can be described as defensive, and although many of them are far from being passive, there is one characteristic which is common to most of them: they are very expensive in manpower with all that this implies in economic terms. To understand why this is the case it is necessary to look briefly at some of the various types of operation which come under this heading.

Guarding and protection are the bread and butter of defensive operations. In any counter-insurgency situation there is bound to be a heavy commitment for the establishing of static guards on such things as military and police bases, power stations, broadcasting installations, docks, factories and commercial centres. In certain circumstances it may also be necessary to guard prominent people like judges and politicians. It is likely that there will be a requirement to protect exposed places where civilians are living, such as isolated villages or parts of cities which are particularly vulnerable to the enemy. It is often necessary to protect crops and stock in the countryside and shopping areas in the towns. Protection can sometimes be carried out satisfactorily by mobile patrols which is much less wasteful in manpower than the mounting of a guard.

A further extension of the business of protecting relates to the task of ensuring that legal assemblies, demonstrations and processions take place peacefully. Although such operations are of relatively short duration, they are immensely expensive in terms of manpower because they involve the gathering together of large numbers of people. It is fatally easy for violence to erupt under such circumstances and if there are too few members of the Security Forces available to control it, they will have to use undesirably severe measures or let the situation get out of hand.

Another form of defensive operation concerns the dispersal of illegal assemblies and riots. This is a subject for study in itself and involves a whole range of minor tactics and an understanding of the complete armoury of anti-riot gear and weapons. Perhaps the most important thing to realize is that riots are a symptom, rather than a disease in themselves. Some riots result from high spirits whilst others evolve spontaneously from legal gatherings. Some come about because factions of a divided community collide, whereas others represent deliberately engineered confrontations with the Security Forces to cause a diversion, to polarize feeling, or to make propaganda. Obviously different tactics should be used by the Security Forces in each case. For example, the aim when factions clash is to part them and get the contestants home as quickly as possible. The aim when insurgents deliberately activate a riot is to arrest a number of rioters and get them punished, so as to dissuade people from giving similar help to the insurgents in the future. Although it may seem odd to classify such an energetic pursuit as the handling of riots as a defensive operation, it is none the less correct to do so. Insurgents engineer riots to promote their cause and disrupt the government's programme; the purpose of controlling them is therefore preventative. Furthermore few opportunities exist for capturing insurgents themselves during riots as they seldom take a direct part.

One final group of defensive operations deserving mention covers activities of the Security Forces designed to prevent the insurgents from gaining an influence over the population. Such activities may amount to little more than keeping close contact with the civilian population day by day, but it can be extended to the provision of a link between the people and the civil authorities where this has broken down. A more ambitious scheme for aiding the civil community, known as a hearts and minds campaign, or a community relations programme can also be included. Occasionally government forces have gone even further and organized a complete set of committees amongst the civilian community, parallel to the network normally set up by the insurgents, with each committee chaired or attended by a representative of the army or police. This system for influencing people's opinions and attitudes can be most effective under certain conditions, providing the requisite legal backing is available.

This brief outline of defensive operations shows why so many men can get sucked in so quickly. An insurgent organization only has to stay in existence to the extent necessary for posing a relatively minor threat for the manpower bill to become almost unbearable. As indicated earlier, the main counter to the insurgents must come from offensive operations designed to destroy their organization and thereby re move the threat. But this may take years to become fully effective. Meanwhile two important palliatives can help to bridge the gap. The first is to make every possible use of technical developments to save men. A large number of gadgets now exist for carrying out all sorts of tasks: these range from surveillance devices, to information storage and sorting equipment and anti-riot gear. The second is to raise auxiliary forces from amongst the population wherever possible who can carry out the less skilled functions, particularly those related to guarding. There may be great risks involved in arming such people, especially when they are drawn from a heavily penetrated community, but the risks are usually worth taking. It may even happen that the process of involving a man whose loyalty is in doubt will bring him down on the right side of the fence and give a lead to others in the neighbourhood.

It is now time to look at offensive operations. The purpose of offensive operations is to identify and neutralize members of an insurgent organization by apprehending them under conditions which enable them to be held in custody. Normally the problem resolves itself into one of providing adequate resources at the right place and of obtaining the requisite information.

A large part of this book has already been devoted to describing how this process can be carried out and at this point it is only necessary to summarize in the broadest outline. Suffice it to say, that for many years the question of providing the required information was regarded as being primarily the responsibility of the intelligence organization. The basic idea was that from time to time the intelligence organization would produce the sort of information which would enable units of the Security Forces to make contact with insurgents and for the rest of the time these units would occupy themselves with their defensive tasks or by conducting hit-or-miss offensive action such as systematic patrolling in likely areas. By the very nature of things this system cannot work effectively because from the start of the campaign the insurgent organization is always likely to expand faster than the intelligence organization, with the result that insufficient pinpoint information will be available for the Security Forces to fulfil their commitment.

A more practical system, and the one which I tried to apply in Malaya, is to make the tactical commander, rather than the intelligence organization, responsible for getting the pinpoint or contact information which he needs. This can be done by what is best described as a chain reaction of analysis alternating with action designed to get information. In other words a company or battalion commander starts by analysing all the information which he can get from records, the intelligence organization, the outgoing company commander, and discussion with anyone who can help, and then gets further information by using his own men. He adds this to what he had before, and to any further information which he may get from outside sources, and then sends out his men to get further information designed to confirm his ideas and extend them. The system is designed to narrow down the probability of success to points in time and space of sufficient exactitude for available troops to exploit.

A number of conditions have to be fulfilled if this system is to work well. In the first place it requires a high degree of understanding on the part of the troops and their commanders, including training in methods of storing large amounts of information at a low level in such a way that it can be found. It also requires the company commander to have access to an expanded and decentralized intelligence organization geared to collecting and passing on many scraps of unrelated bits of information. Finally the system only works if the tactical commander can be left in comparative peace from outside interference, and if he can be left in one place for a good long time. If he is constantly being obliged to divert extra resources to defensive tasks, or if he is suddenly moved while building up his chain reaction process the system falls down.

With all these conditions to meet it might be wondered whether the new system has any advantage to offer over the old one and in this respect it is only necessary to point out that at least it can be made to work, whereas the old one was bound to fail for the reasons discussed earlier. In passing, it might just be worth saying that the system often proves unpopular from a political point of view because it involves investing comparatively junior operational commanders with the power which comes from the accumulation of information, especially the sensitive information which they are likely to pick up by being in direct and constant touch with the intelligence organization. There is of course no reason why a company commander should misuse power any more than members of the intelligence organization, but it is none the less true that many people become nervous when they see this sort of power in the hands of relatively junior officers. Insurgent propaganda may then fan the flames of nervousness in order to inhibit what, from their point of view, is a very dangerous threat to their existence. This is not an argument for devolving control, but for ensuring that political control is always effective, and seen to be effective.

Before leaving the subject of the offensive it is necessary to mention special operations which are almost always valuable for identifying and apprehending members of an insurgent organization, although naturally the form of operation used has to be carefully tailored to the prevailing circumstances. In general, it is probably fair to say that successful special operations are usually those which base themselves on the chain reaction system for developing background information into contact information, but with the difference that the men employed are specially selected, trained and equipped to take advantage of some particular system. In Kenya, for example, we were using ex-Mau Mau gang members, posing as current gang members, to develop background information collected by normal intelligence methods.

Special Forces can be organized to develop information to the point where contact with the enemy can be made by normal military or police units or they can be organized to take action on their own information when it is fully developed. In either case it is worth making two points. The first one is that there is absolutely no need for special operations to be carried out in an illegal or immoral way and indeed there is every reason to ensure that they are not because they are just as much part of the government's programme as any of its other measures and the government must be prepared to take responsibility for them. The second point is that special operations must be organized and implemented under the auspices of the normal machine for directing the campaign and the advantages to be gained from them weighed against the psychological implications of their becoming known. Furthermore normal Security Force units should be informed as to the nature and purpose of special operations as far as is consistent with the requirements of security so that they come to regard Special Forces as helpful colleagues and not as wild, irresponsible people whose one purpose is to steal the credit from those who carry out more humdrum, but necessary, roles.

Chapter 25

------------------------- ❈ -------------------------

A Soldier's Lot

The report which I produced at the end of my year at Oxford was written on the assumption that insurgency should be handled in the way described in the last two chapters of this book. I made a number of recommendations regarding the steps which the army should take to make itself ready to conduct operations in conditions of insurgency and subversion in the second half of the 1970s, some of which have now become accepted, and some of which have not. My report was published in 1971 under the title of *Low Intensity Operations*.

In order to stress the importance of viewing operations as only one aspect of a total counter-insurgency campaign, and in order to highlight the relationship which should exist between those responsible for operations and those responsible for government as a whole, I have so far avoided differentiating between policemen, soldiers, and auxiliaries, preferring to lump them all together under the heading of Security Forces. As a conclusion to this book I should like to abandon this practice and look briefly at three or four of the main problems which confront soldiers, since that is where my own experience has lain over the years.

In this connection the first point to make is that all eyes turn to the soldier when violence erupts. Before this happens warnings given by the army and precautions recommended, are sometimes ignored or treated with disdain. It is of course human nature to avoid the unpleasant for as long as possible, and potential insurgents are sure to give the public every encouragement to stick their heads in the sand whilst their preparations are in progress. But when the fighting starts the soldier will not only be expected to know how to conduct operations, he may also have to advise on other government measures as well. We have seen that it is only by a close combination of civil and military measures that insurgency can be fought, so it is logical to expect soldiers whose business it is to know how to fight, to know also how to use civil measures in this way. Not only should army officers know about the subject, they must also be prepared to pass on their knowledge to politicians, civil servants, economists, members of local government and policemen, where necessary. The educational function of the army at these critical moments is most important. Amongst senior officers particularly, ignorance or excessive diffidence in passing such knowledge on can be disastrous.

Getting agreement to the establishment of a proper framework within which the campaign as a whole can progress must obviously come high on the list of tasks facing a military commander. Sometimes the commander himself will be in a position to suggest what should be done in a particular sphere, although more frequently he is likely to content himself with urging the adoption of practicable plans thought up by others. Manipulating the framework in this way is something which lasts throughout the insurgency because circumstances are continually changing. At the higher levels of command, army officers are bound to spend a lot of time thinking, planning, persuading and agitating in this field.

Obviously the straightforward handling of daily military functions is the most time-consuming part of the soldier's task. As always, the officer's first concern is to ensure that his men know what they have got to do and why: in modern parlance they must be properly motivated and this is of considerable importance if enemy propaganda is being directed at them. Then there are all the activities attendant upon the allocation of resources and the execution of the various aspects of offensive and defensive operations. Clear thinking and courage, perseverance and patience, energy and the know-how which comes from experience and study, are the qualities required for success.

At this point it may be worth stressing the importance of knowledge. Military commanders in counter-insurgency operations cannot do without a real understanding of this sort of war in the widest sense. Traditionally the British army has assumed that its officers are adequately trained in all current types of warfare, so that successful performance in one operational field has been regarded as an adequate reason for appointing a man to command in a different operational field. Unfortunately the level of understanding and training in the sphere of counter-insurgency has not always been good enough for the system to operate effectively. Of course this is not to suggest that someone with a lot of theoretical knowledge, but without the ability to achieve an aim in an operational setting, would be more successful. Far from it. There is no single thing more important than being able to size up the situation, as it exists, and make the best of it. Carefully worked out plans often have to be sacrificed to short-term pressures, and a commander's skill lies in being able to do this without jeopardizing his important objectives. Assessing pressures and taking decisions are the functions which distinguish the commander from the academic or critic, and proven ability in this direction is still the most important qualification for command. None the less knowledge is necessary and must be collected over the years.

The next point which I should like to cover concerns the difficulties which face soldiers in trying to retain their freedom to act. From the start insurgents, their supporters, and sympathizers, constantly try to limit the soldier's ability to carry out his functions and to force him bit by bit into a state of uselessness. Sometimes this is done by direct action and sometimes by propaganda, but all the time they are trying to dominate the situation at the soldier's expense. Sometimes the pressure may be very subtle, as when overtly neutral people try to play one level of command off against another. Sometimes the insurgents' game is obvious, but difficult to counter, because of the balance of force. But one thing is certain, and that is that soldiers must not let their influence be undermined. Although there may be no evil consequences for a time, it means that power has shifted. It is absolutely necessary for commanders constantly to assess this balance of influence and to extend the influence which they can exert over events, whilst resisting efforts to undermine their position and that of their subordinates. Soldiers must be strong or they risk losing control and jeopardizing the struggle against insurgency, possibly at a time when they least expect it.

The last point which I should like to discuss concerns right and wrong. In years gone by soldiers seldom thought it necessary to question the rightness of their cause or the moral validity of their orders. No doubt there were occasions when individuals became worried, but for the most part soldiers were able to carry out their tasks without excessive wear and tear on their consciences, despite the fact that international war and imperial policing was just as rough as anything which the army has experienced in the last twenty-five years. But now more thought is devoted to moral problems and soldiers, like other people, have become increasingly aware of them. The difficulty is to establish an absolute standard of right and wrong in an age when so many men have abandoned the established tenets of official religion in favour of a variety of atheistic or agnostic notions.

Fortunately in practical terms there are two yardsticks which a soldier can use to determine whether a particular line of conduct is right or not before he is forced up against the wall of pure moral judgement. The first of these is the law. If a particular course of action is illegal it must be avoided, even if it appears to be morally right: conversely it is possible for something to be legal and at the same time morally wrong. The other yardstick is expediency. A legal action which is wrong will often be found to be inexpedient, probably because of the adverse effect which it is likely to have on people's attitudes. There is no cynicism inherent in this observation, but merely recognition of the fact that sometimes the reactions of others are as likely to reflect right and wrong as the judgement of one person exercised on purely moral grounds. But eventually a soldier may believe that something he needs to do in order to achieve his aim, or something which he has been told to do by a superior, is wrong, despite the fact that it is both legal and expedient. In that case he has a difficult choice to make. Fortunately it does not happen very often.

On the other hand there is one hazard which constantly accosts soldiers. The modern preoccupation with moral problems affords excellent opportunities for enemy propaganda and most insurgents take full advantage of the situation. Any military unit which becomes too effective is likely to find itself labelled brutal and ill-disciplined. Any individual whose performance poses a particular threat will be described as immoral and a war criminal. Accusations based on such considerations must be recognized for what they are, and fought tenaciously. Men and units can be put out of action by propaganda just as effectively as by bullets and it is necessary to defend them even when there is risk in doing so. Failure to defend soldiers in this situation is little different to abandoning them in the face of conventional attack. Insurgency is a dangerous business and soldiers realize that they will be exposed from time to time. On these occasions they rightly expect to be supported and sustained.

It is fitting that this book should close with the reader's attention focused firmly on the dangers which confront soldiers involved in this sort of war, and in passing, it might be worth sparing a thought for the hardship and boredom which often goes with the life. Furthermore it does no harm to remember that it is the soldier at the bottom of the tree who is most exposed to danger, hardship and boredom alike. I think that it is a matter of opinion whether a soldier's lot is a happy one, but it is certainly not as simple and straightforward as some people imagine. My own view is that a soldier lives an odd sort of life at times.

Index